To

Mary Carole —

A faithful friend
on the spiritual
journey —

Love,
Marie

Discerning Vocations to the Apostolic Life,
the Contemplative Life, and the Eremitic Life

Discerning Vocations to the Apostolic Life, the Contemplative Life, and the Eremitic Life

Marie Theresa Coombs, Hermit

and

Francis Kelly Nemeck, OMI

CASCADE *Books* · Eugene, Oregon

DISCERNING VOCATIONS TO THE APOSTOLIC LIFE, THE CONTEMPLA-
TIVE LIFE, AND THE EREMITIC LIFE

Cascade Books
An Imprint of Wipf and Stock Publishers
199 W. 8th Ave., Suite 3
Eugene, OR 97401

www.wipfandstock.com

PAPERBACK ISBN: 978-1-5326-3421-5
HARDCOVER ISBN: 978-1-5326-3423-9
EBOOK ISBN: 978-1-5326-3422-2

Cataloguing-in-Publication data:

Names: Coombs, Marie Theresa, author. | Nemeck, Francis Kelly, author.

Title: Discerning vocations to the apostolic life, the contemplative life, and the
eremitic life / Marie Theresa Coombs and Francis Kelly Nemeck.

Description: Eugene, OR : Cascade Books, 2018 | Includes bibliographical refer-
ences.

Identifiers: ISBN 978-1-5326-3421-5 (paperback) | ISBN 978-1-5326-3423-9
(hardcover) | ISBN 978-1-5326-3422-2 (ebook)

Subjects: LCSH: Vocation, Ecclesiastical and religious | Contemplation | Ere-
mitic life |

Classification: BV660 .C64 2018 (print) | BV660 .C64 (ebook)

Manufactured in the U.S.A.   09/20/18

To
Christ Jesus,
now and forever,

with everlasting gratitude
for the gift of
Lebh Shomea House of Prayer,
"a dwelling place of God in the Spirit"
(Eph 2:22)

Contents

Acknowledgments | xiii
Abbreviations | xv
General Notes | xvii

Introduction | 1

Part One: Fundamental Notions

1   Three General Vocational Lifestyles | 9
    The Need to Discern God's Calling   10
    Interrelatedness of the General Lifestyles   12
    Lifestyle Synergism   13
    The Focus of Vocational Discernment   14

2   The Apostolic Lifestyle | 16
    The Apostolate   17
    The Apostolic Life   18
    Alternate Phrases: Activity, Active, and the Active Life   19
    The Unique Position of the Apostolic Life   20
    Influences upon the Formation of an Apostolic Life   21
    Related Distinctions   22

3   The Contemplative Lifestyle | 24
    Contemplation in Reference to the Contemplative Life   24
    The Contemplative Life as Understood in This Study   27
    Those Called to This Lifestyle   28
    Contemplative Life in Relation to Monastic Life   29
    A Contemplative Vocation within an Apostolic Institute   30
    Contemplative and Apostolic: Two Additional Paradoxes   31
    Being Contemplative and Being a Contemplative   31

4   The Eremitic Lifestyle | 33

      The Designation "the Eremitic Life"   34

      Expressions of the Eremitic Vocation   35

      Misconceptions about Hermit and Eremitic Life   36

      Two Similar, but Distinct Callings   37

                    Part Two: The Apostolic Life

5   Biblical Roots of the Concept *Apostolic* | 43

      Key Biblical Terms for Mission   43

      Insights from the Hebrew Scriptures   44

      New Testament Teachings   44

6   Historical Perspectives on the Concept *Apostolic* | 48

      Christian Antiquity   48

      Medieval Times   48

      The Sixteenth Century Onward   49

      The Seventeenth Century   50

      Contemporary Times: Vatican II and Beyond   50

7   Discernment of a Vocation to the Apostolic Life | 55

      An Inclination toward Service   57

      A Need to Use a Personal Charism   57

      A Corresponding Need within a Community   60

      Recognition of the Limits of Ministry   60

      Formation of an Apostolic Lifestyle around Ministry   61

      Explicit Christocentric Quality in Ministry   62

      Growth in the Contemplative Dimension of Apostolic Living   64

8   Apostolic Expressions of Christian Virtues | 67

      Love   68

      Community   69

      Faith   70

      Hope   70

      Receptivity and Obedience to God   71

      Prayerfulness   72

      Holistic Orientation   73

      Study   73

      Poverty   74

      Leisure   75

      Self-Sacrifice   76

9 Concluding Pastoral Observations on the Apostolic Life | 77

Part Three: The Contemplative Life

10 A Christocentric and Trinitarian Love | 83
    The Profound, Intimate, Loving Relationship with Jesus   84
    A Sense of the Indwelling Trinity   90

11 Communion with God in Daily Life | 92
    Contemplation   92
    A Distinctive Contemplative Orientation to Life   95
    Peaceful Acquiescence in Mystery   96

12 The Quest for Solitude | 99
    The Womb of Society   100
    The Process of Being Born into Solitude   101
    The Contemplative as a Marginal Person   103
    Questions for Discernment   104
    Three Situations for Discernment   106

13 Solitary Life in a Communal Setting | 109
    A Celibate Context   110
    The Context of Marriage   111

14 A Contemplative Vocation within an Apostolic Institute | 114
    The Initial Response of the Apostolic Community   114
    Leadership's Difficulty in Discernment   115
    Three Initiatives in the Discernment Process   116
    Possible Contemplative Living Situations   117
    Pastoral Recommendations   117
    A Final Recommendation   120

15 Contemplative Receptivity to God | 122
    An Integrating Prayer Life   123
    Solitary Prayer   125
    Silence and Solitude   126
    Simplicity of Heart   129
    Stability in Life   130

16 A Contemplative Stance in Activity | 134
    Leisure   135
    Study   136
    Manual Labor   137
    Ministry   138

17   Emotional Maturity in the Contemplative Life | 142
        Stress Management   142
        Certain Contraindicative Traits   144
        Holistic Growth   145

18   Love of Neighbor in the Contemplative Life | 147
        Love of Neighbor for a Celibate Contemplative   147
        Love of Neighbor for a Married Contemplative   155

19   Concluding Pastoral Observations on the Contemplative Life | 157
        Readiness to Enter the Contemplative Life   157
        Transition to the Contemplative Life   158
        Perseverance in the Contemplative Life   160
        Commitment in Faith   161
        Emancipation   162
        The Contemplative Vocation as Mystery   163

                    Part Four: The Eremitic Life

20   The Process of Being Born into Eremitic Solitude | 169
        Toward a More Accurate Use of Certain Terms   169
        Two Prerequisite Vocational Experiences   171
        Contexts for Living the Eremitic Life   173
        Movement into Eremitic Solitude: Four Phases of Transition   174

21   An Increasing Solitary Thrust in Life | 179
        The Yearning for More Solitude   179
        Eremitic Solitude   180
        Positive Signs   180
        Countersigns   181

22   Life in a Hermitage | 185
        Practical Pastoral Approaches   185
        Daily Life in a Hermitage   187

23   Eremitic Being-In-Love with God | 192
        Love of God   192
        Person-Centered Focus   194
        Acceptance of Silence and Solitude   195
        Ability to Live in the Present   197
        Carefreeness   198

24   Eremitic Love of People | 201

Basic Maturity in Human Development   201

Interaction with People   203

Intimacy with Loved Ones   205

25   Eremitic Love of the Natural World | 209

Earth as Sacred Grounding   210

Communion with Creation in and through God   210

Communion with God through Creation   212

Renewal within the Natural World   213

The Providential Role of the Natural World   215

One Family of God Sharing a Common Home   216

26   Participation in the Paschal Mystery | 218

Acceptance of the Cross   219

Self-Knowledge   222

Acedia   224

Insatiability   226

27   Concluding Pastoral Observations on the Eremitic Life | 228

The Transition to the Eremitic Life   228

Summary of the Principles of Discernment   229

Perseverance as Gift   230

Eremitic Rapport with Society   232

Final Commitment   234

A New Creation | 236

Select Bibliography | 239

Acknowledgments

WE ARE GRATEFUL FOR all those persons with whom we have shared contemplative-eremitic community at Lebh Shomea House of Prayer. We thank them for the friendship, the spirit of searching, and the wisdom that they brought to our lives. Their faith seeking understanding has been a most important source of enrichment for our theological reflection upon vocation and vocational discernment.

In particular, these Christian communities have inspired us with their contemplative spirit and have been wellsprings of insight into what it means to be called by God: Eremos Community (Austin, Texas); Qu'Appelle House of Prayer (Fort Qu'Appelle, Saskatchewan, Canada); and The Upper Room Home of Prayer (Ottawa, Ontario, Canada). We thank the many church groups from various regions of Texas who joined with us in fellowship at Lebh Shomea. We appreciate the breadth and depth of perspective that they contributed to our pondering of the mystery of vocation.

We gained insight also from vocational experiences shared with us by individuals with whom we listened and discerned in the context of spiritual direction, by persons completing independent studies at Lebh Shomea, and by students participating in group seminars or classes that we facilitated.

To the following persons, we express our heartfelt gratitude for the many ways in which they helped bring this book to completion: Rev. Dr. Kim Cape; Evelyn Gullatt; Denise Gutierrez; Walter Hanss; Bishop Janice Riggle Huie; Sheila Coombs Johnson; Jennifer Knight; Rev. Dr. Michael Marsh; Andrea Morein; Sr. Rosemary O'Toole, CSJ; Dr. Michael Rock; Jean Springer; Carmen Zabalegui; and Rev. Glenn Zimmer, OMI. We thank them for the talents and skills each one brought to the task, as well as for the comments, questions, and encouragement they offered us.

In a special way, we thank Dr. Rilda Baker for her thorough review of the text and for her insightful observations on the content. We are immensely grateful for her contributions to clarity of thought and style in our presentation.

To the team at Wipf and Stock who partnered with us to publish this book, we extend our deep appreciation for their graciousness and professionalism throughout the process.

Abbreviations

Ascent	St. John of the Cross, *The Ascent of Mount Carmel*. References are by book, chapter, and paragraph; for example, *Ascent*, II, 6, 1.
Called by God	Marie Theresa Coombs and Francis Kelly Nemeck, *Called by God: A Theology of Vocation and Lifelong Commitment*. 1992. Reprint: Eugene, OR: Wipf and Stock, 2001.
CCSL	*Corpus Christianorum, Series Latina*. 211 vols. Turnhout, Belgium: Brepols, 1953–2017.
Contemplation	Francis Kelly Nemeck and Marie Theresa Coombs, *Contemplation*. 1982. Reprint: Eugene, OR: Wipf and Stock, 2001.
Dark Night	St. John of the Cross, *The Dark Night*. References are by book, chapter, and paragraph; for example, *Dark Night*, 1, 9, 4.
Divine Milieu	Pierre Teilhard de Chardin, *The Divine Milieu*. The source for our translations is *Le Milieu divin: Essai de vie intérieure*. Paris: Éditions du Seuil, 1957. For the convenience of readers, we refer in footnotes to this published English translation: Pierre Teilhard de Chardin, *The Divine Milieu*. New York: Harper & Row, 1960.
DVMCS	Marie Theresa Coombs and Francis Kelly Nemeck, *Discerning Vocations to Marriage, Celibacy and Singlehood*. 1994. Reprint: Eugene, OR: Wipf and Stock, 2001.

Living Flame   St. John of the Cross, *The Living Flame of Love* (Redaction B). References are by stanza of the poem and paragraph of the commentary; for example, *Living Flame*, 2, 4.

O Blessed Night   Francis Kelly Nemeck and Marie Theresa Coombs, *O Blessed Night: Recovering from Addiction, Codependency and Attachment, based on the insights of St. John of the Cross and Pierre Teilhard de Chardin.* Staten Island: Alba House, 1991.

PG   *Patrologia Graeca.* 161 vols. Edited by J. P. Migne. 1857–1865.

PL   *Patrologia Latina.* 217 vols. Edited by J. P. Migne. 1878–1890.

SC   *Sources Chrétiennes.* A series of translations of patristic texts, founded by Henri de Lubac et al. Lyon: 1942. Current publisher: Paris: Éditions du Cerf.

Spiritual Canticle   St. John of the Cross, *The Spiritual Canticle*, 2nd redaction. References are by stanza and paragraph; for example, *Spiritual Canticle*, 6, 5.

Spiritual Direction   Francis Kelly Nemeck and Marie Theresa Coombs, *The Way of Spiritual Direction.* Collegeville, MN: Liturgical, 1985.

Spiritual Journey   Francis Kelly Nemeck and Marie Theresa Coombs, *The Spiritual Journey: Critical Thresholds and Stages of Adult Spiritual Genesis.* Collegeville, MN: Liturgical, 1990.

TDNT   *Theological Dictionary of the New Testament.* 10 vols. Edited by Gerhard Kittel and Gerhard Friedrich. Translated by Geoffrey W. Bromiley. Grand Rapids: Eerdmans, 1964–1976.

General Notes

1. When speaking of the deity, we retain the biblical names for the Trinity, namely, Father, Son, and Spirit or alternatively Creator, Word, and Spirit. We readily acknowledge the feminine/female dimensions of God and the legitimacy of speaking of God as Mother. We recognize in the scriptures also the numerous images of God drawn from human experience, moral virtues, and the natural world. Still, God transcends all names, metaphors, and images.

   Frequently, we refrain from gender designation in reference to the deity by repetition of the word "God." We avoid when possible the use of pronouns such as *he* or *she*, *him* or *her* in reference to God.

2. Translations for all references from Hebrew, Greek, Latin, French, and Spanish sources are our own. We incorporate gender inclusive language in our translations, when appropriate.

3. Our references to the writings of St. John of the Cross follow this critical edition: *Vida y obras de San Juan de la Cruz*. Madrid: Biblioteca de Autores Cristianos, 1973.

4. We employ the word "soul" in this study as synonymous with "person," stressing the inmost recesses of that individual. This usage differs from classical scholastic meaning of *anima* as found in the body-soul distinction. This mystical usage derives rather from the Hebrew *nephesh* (breath, person, soul) and the New Testament Greek word *psychē* (life, self, soul).

5. The concept "nature" has multivalent meanings. When we refer to nature, the natural world, or the world of nature, we intend the evolving processes of all life forms, together with the interrelationship of all living creatures as one community that is inclusive of Planet Earth and the cosmos as a whole. When we refer to "creation," we consider from a faith perspective the living world of nature in relation to God as its Creator.

6. *A Personal Note from Marie Theresa Coombs:* On September 11, 2014, Francis Kelly Nemeck, OMI, passed into eternal life. Prior to his death, he and I had completed a preliminary version of this book. We had discussed also plans to revise certain sections and to include additional material. One of Fr. Nemeck's last requests was that, as coauthor, I finish the project. To the best of my ability, I have sought to incorporate into this book his final ideas and suggestions.

Introduction

May the God of our Lord Jesus Christ,
the Father of glory, give you
a spirit of wisdom and perception of what is revealed,
that you may come to full experience of him.
May God enlighten the eyes of your heart
that you may know the hope of his calling.

(EPH 1:17–18)

GOD'S CALLING COINCIDES WITH a person's initial reception of existence. In loving a person into being, the "Father of glory" destines that individual to transformation in Christ Jesus. Thus, the "hope of his calling" does not consist primarily of some *thing* such as a reward, a place, or certain privileges. God in God's own self is the hope that a calling holds.

Consummate transformation in God constitutes the enduring dimension of a vocation. That full participation in God's own life and love abides eternally. This side of the resurrection a calling has also temporal dimensions. In the context of space and time, these three distinct yet closely related aspects of vocation are integral to God's calling:

- self-identity: *who* God calls a person to be and to become;
- lifestyle: *how* God calls an individual to become transformed in God;
- mission: *what* God sends forth a person to do.[1]

In *Called by God: A Theology of Vocation and Lifelong Commitment*, we presented an evolutionary and relational theology of divine calling and human response. That revitalized theology incorporates insights from

---

1. See *Called by God*, 2–4, and *DVMCS*, 1–4.

1

contemporary biblical research and developmental psychology. It highlights also the successive phases of vocational consciousness and commitment.

In *Discerning Vocations to Marriage, Celibacy and Singlehood,* we concentrated upon Christian vocational lifestyles: the *how* of a personal vocation. We discussed in detail three *basic* Christian modes of living, together with the salient principles that are indicative of possible callings to them.[2]

The focus of this book continues to be Christian vocational lifestyles. We take up now a third area related to the mystery of divine calling: three *general* Christian lifestyles that integrate with the basic lifestyles of marriage, celibacy, and singlehood. These general modes of living are the apostolic life, the contemplative life, and the eremitic life.

Throughout this earthly sojourn, God gifts a person with a sense of the vocational direction welling up from within his or her inmost self. "The God of our Lord Jesus Christ" nurtures the emergence of that awareness by granting "a spirit of wisdom and perception of what is revealed." The gifts of wisdom and perception enable a person to recognize the significance of feelings, thoughts, and longings, together with the effects of myriad external influences upon daily life. That enlightenment lays the groundwork for vocational discernment and commitment to God in the combination of lifestyles through which the Father of glory draws the person to full experience of Christ Jesus.

Some people tend spontaneously to identify the designations "the apostolic life, the contemplative life, and the eremitic life" with certain institutes or societies of consecrated life that exist, for example, in the Roman Catholic tradition. They think immediately of celibate monks, nuns, sisters, brothers, and priests. This study indeed pertains to persons who seek to live their vocational lifestyles with public profession of vows and official blessing of the church. However, we include within the parameters of our study a broader spectrum of spiritual seekers. The content has application to all persons—whether married, celibate, or single—whom God calls to apostolic, contemplative, or eremitic modes of living and who desire to respond wholeheartedly to God through those lifestyles.

Our goals in this work are the following:

- to highlight each person's innate contemplative thrust as a primary guide in discerning a vocation to a Christian lifestyle;

- to recognize the interrelatedness of the apostolic life, the contemplative life, and the eremitic life, together with their synergistic effects, within the Christian community and in the world at large;

2. On the concept "vocational lifestyles," see *Called by God,* 74–77, 82–84, and *DVMCS,* 10–16.

- to describe the core features of the apostolic, contemplative, and eremitic lifestyles;
- to present principles of discernment that provide indications of callings to each of those three lifestyles.

As in our previous two books on the mystery of divine calling and vocational discernment, we approach the present subject from an evolutionary and a relational perspective.

In the context of this study, the term *evolutionary* stresses several aspects of vocation:

- God's calling of a person to the apostolic life, the contemplative life, or the eremitic life itself evolves. That divine initiative unfolds in time and space. God forms the direction and the specifics of a calling in relation to a person's ongoing response. God incorporates into the evolution of a vocation all the "yeses, nos, and maybes" that come forth from a person. In that process, God leads some spiritual seekers from one lifestyle to another.
- A person's consciousness of a vocation to one of those lifestyles also matures.
- As God's calling and an individual's vocational awareness evolve over time, the person's readiness to respond and capacity for commitment increase.

Thus, God's calling of a person to a Christian lifestyle, that individual's awareness of the calling, and the commitment to Christ Jesus through the lifestyle are developmental. Rather than being a static or a clearly defined entity, each of the three general vocational lifestyles is constantly undergoing change, modification, and renewal.

The designation *relational* as characteristic of our approach denotes emphasis upon a person's encounter with God, oneself, people, and all creatures of the world.

With respect to God's creation, many Christians have understood the apostolic life primarily as assertive involvement in the world, the contemplative life as passive withdrawal from the world, and the eremitic life as ascetical flight from the world. A relational perspective toward vocation stresses something other than assertive involvement, passive withdrawal, or ascetical flight vis-à-vis the world. A relational perspective embraces these features:

- It accentuates God so loving the world as to become flesh in Jesus of Nazareth. It emphasizes the Spirit of God indwelling each human being and relating to the world from within creation. It bespeaks communion with God who remains closer and more present to a person than one could ever imagine, feel, think, or grasp.

- "Relational" highlights the intimate connection between a person's interior life and vocational lifestyle. God indwelling the individual sets in motion a calling to the apostolic, the contemplative, or the eremitic life. That vocational direction is integral to the person's identity as a child of God.

- "Relational" emphasizes the importance of presence: God's presence to a human being and that person's presence to God. Those general vocational lifestyles are not only contexts for human activities; above all they are modes of being and becoming. They are milieus in which each Christian not only bears lasting fruit in the reign of God by means of active endeavors, but also advances in the process of transformation in God.

- "Relational" draws attention within the context of a specific vocational lifestyle to a person's direct and immediate loving communion with God in contemplation. It designates also a person's interaction with God through significant persons, things, activities, and events, as well as through nonhuman creatures.

- "Relational" underscores the value of immersion in creation. The apostolic life, the contemplative life, and the eremitic life emphasize involvement with creation, but each lifestyle does so in a distinctive way. All three lifestyles promote human interrelatedness with the world, but each lifestyle summons forth a unique form of participation.

- These three general lifestyles stand in relation to each other and relate as a unity to Christ. All three work together in Christ for the glory of God.

The content of this book, as with our previous two works on Christian vocational lifestyles, has as its foundation our faith experience, our study and teaching of theology and related disciplines, and our practice of ministry. While our faith development has taken place primarily in the Roman Catholic tradition, we have worked with and been enriched by our sisters and brothers from other segments of the Christian family, from religious traditions other than Christianity, and by spiritual pilgrims unaffiliated with any religious institution.

For approximately forty years each of us lived a form of contemplative-eremitic life at Lebh Shomea House of Prayer, Sarita, Texas. We served there as members of a core community that oversaw the direction of the house of prayer. Prior to life at Lebh Shomea, each of us at different geographical locations engaged in the apostolic life. Furthermore, for over four decades at Lebh Shomea we practiced the ministry of spiritual direction and spiritual accompaniment. A special focus of that ministry was toward those persons who desired to foster the contemplative element of their lives and those persons who were seeking to discern their vocational lifestyles. During that time, we assisted also in the formation process of persons who were preparing to practice as spiritual directors.

Reflection in faith upon our life experiences and our contemplatively oriented ministry has led us to express herein something of what we have come to see. We believe that what we identify as the core of the Christian vocational experience, together with our accompanying suggestions for discernment, corresponds to the experience and the discernment of numerous persons throughout the ages. We hope that those persons who seek to plumb the depths of their calling to a Christian lifestyle, those who practice as spiritual directors, those in religious communities who engage in the ministry of spiritual formation, and those who teach in areas of adult Christian education will find the content of this book helpful in their efforts to discern vocational lifestyles and to behold deeply the mystery of God's calling.

Part One: Fundamental Notions

Part One: Fundamental Notions

CHAPTER 1

Three General Vocational Lifestyles

IN TWO PREVIOUS BOOKS on vocation, we spoke of marriage, celibacy, and singlehood as *basic* Christian lifestyles.[1] We referred to those Christian lifestyles as basic for these reasons:

- Those three modes of living form a basis upon which other vocational lifestyles rest.

- Usually, a person lives only one of those three lifestyles at a time.

- Each spiritually adult Christian is basically either married, celibate, or single.

In this book, we take up the apostolic life, the contemplative life, and the eremitic life. We qualify them as *general* Christian vocational lifestyles for the following reasons:

- In comparison to the basic lifestyles, the apostolic, contemplative, and eremitic lifestyles are extremely general modes of living. It is more difficult to describe what uniquely constitutes each of them and virtually impossible to pinpoint in many instances where one lifestyle leaves off and another begins.

- Each of those three lifestyles is lived in conjunction with and has as its foundation marriage, celibacy, or singlehood.

- Each maturing person experiences apostolic, contemplative, and eremitic leanings. Regardless of the vocational lifestyle—whether basic or general—all three orientations assert themselves to some degree in a person's life. Everyone has some mission or purpose in life, enjoys some intimacy with God, and needs some solitude. Nevertheless, one of those three propensities becomes so dominant within an individual that it gives rise to an all-embracing lifestyle.

1. *Called by God*, 73–81; *DVMCS*, 9–17.

9

The Need to Discern God's Calling

In our book, *Discerning Vocations to Marriage, Celibacy and Singlehood,* we compared marriage, celibacy, and singlehood to three peaks towering over a landscape.[2] Although most spiritual pilgrims struggle somewhere along the slopes or even still down in the valleys, those peaks represent clearly delineated points of reference.

As we turn our attention toward the general lifestyles, that landscape analogy needs some modification. We can no longer speak of peaks and valleys, since the contrasts among these general lifestyles are often quite subtle and less pronounced. We might, therefore, compare the apostolic, contemplative, and eremitic lifestyles to three areas of rolling hills or undulating plains that in certain locations almost imperceptibly blend into one another. So less defined are their contours that many sincere pilgrims may be unable at times to identify precisely which general Christian lifestyle they are living. In fact, that uncertainty could be indicative of movement forward in their vocational response.

Debates over the relationship of apostolate and contemplation, action and contemplation, or missionary and contemplative have arisen throughout the history of Christian spirituality. Much of that academic wrangling was not only irrelevant, but also misdirected. Pierre Teilhard de Chardin made some observations in 1924 upon the many disputes among spiritual authors over whether activity should precede contemplation or whether contemplation should be a preparation for activity. Teilhard judged those issues to be pseudo-problems. He confessed that such questions meant absolutely nothing to him. He professed his abiding communion with Christ Jesus to be the animating and integrating source of both his contemplation and his action. He summed up his experience in this manner: "First, foremost, and always, I am in *Christo Jesu,* and only then do I act, or do I suffer, or do I contemplate."[3]

Teilhard's insight resonates profoundly with our views on the preeminence of dwelling in Christ. Yet Teilhard was not addressing the subject at hand. He was not referring to the discernment of Christian vocational lifestyles. Rather, he was pondering the relationship of action and contemplation as two dynamic orientations within each person's life, irrespective of lifestyle.

We believe that not only *can* Christians differentiate, broadly speaking, the apostolic life, the contemplative life, and the eremitic life, but also

2. See *DVMCS,* 4.

3. Teilhard de Chardin, "My Universe," 75.

they *must* do so in order to assent more voluntarily to God's calling. Even if those three general lifestyles remain difficult to define in both theory and practice, it is important to identify their respective charisms and to discern their salient features.[4] That insight guides people as they seek awareness of their deepest vocational attraction and respond to God's calling with ever more deliberate self-commitment.

Both Christian churches and the civil laws of many western countries tend to highly institutionalize marriage. The Roman Catholic tradition institutionalizes celibacy within the contexts of clerical orders and various forms of consecrated life. Outside those ecclesial contexts celibacy remains wholly charismatic. Of course, even within an institutional context people thrive in a celibate lifestyle when they undertake it as a freely given calling from God and not merely as an obligation or a requirement for certain ministries. Neither churches nor societies institutionalize singlehood.

Beyond certain church-regulated frameworks, the term "institutionalization" has virtually no application to the apostolic, the contemplative, and the eremitic life. The varieties, overlappings, and flexibilities of those forms of life exceed the wildest imagination. Consider a few examples. The priest-paleontologist Pierre Teilhard de Chardin (1881–1955) led an extremely active life, yet he was a contemplative at heart. St. Teresa of Jesus (1515–82) was a contemplative's contemplative, yet she traveled more extensively and was more involved in business transactions than many of her most apostolic contemporaries. Peter of Morrone (1215–96) was living as an inconspicuous hermit when he was called to serve as Pope Celestine V.

In this work, we approach the three general vocational lifestyles from the stance of faith seeking understanding. We endeavor to describe the core features of vocations to the apostolic, the contemplative, and the eremitic life. We do not attempt to describe the fringes of these vocational lifestyles where one way of living blends imperceptibly into another. Nor do we think it necessary to be able to determine precisely where one lifestyle leaves off and another begins. We offer also an ensemble of principles of discernment for each of those three lifestyles.[5]

Each ensemble of principles for discernment contains signs that emanate from the existence within a person of a distinctive calling from God. Although each person and each vocation are unique, those facets of experience are observable in varying degrees among most people called to a specific lifestyle. The presence of those principles of discernment as an ensemble is indicative of a spiritual direction asserting itself from within a person.

4. On vocational discernment, see *DVMCS*, 18–33.
5. On principles of discernment, see *DVMCS*, 34–39.

The principles of discernment specific to each general lifestyle constitute explicit processes and practical procedures for vocational discernment.
As such, those principles are not at all mandates or rules to which those
persons discerning vocation must conform with ego-generated initiative or
at the command of a spiritual guide or a religious institution. The principles
are simply perceptible effects of God's interior calling, which a seeker can
see and use as a basis for enlightened vocational response.

Thus, the principles of discernment are primarily inductive by nature,
not deductive. Those signposts are recognizable by faith, and they invite
the searching pilgrim to a faith response. For those discerning, as well as
for their spiritual guides, a general overview of these principles or signs
does not suffice. Attention to the details of each one and application of
those details to the situation at hand enhance immensely the quality of
vocational discernment.

Interrelatedness of the General Lifestyles

The apostolic life, the contemplative life, and the eremitic life represent
three unique Christian vocational lifestyles. Nonetheless, they interrelate in
several ways.

First, every Christian life contains apostolic, contemplative, and solitary dimensions. Each person experiences a leaning toward an *apostolate* or
mission; that is, a work for God and for the good of creation. Each individual
has *a contemplative dimension*; that is, an innate longing to remain lovingly
receptive to God. Each person discovers *an eremitic aspect*; that is, a need
for some silence and solitude, which at the outset could be on a very minimal basis. While those apostolic, contemplative, and solitary inclinations
persist throughout a person's life, one of those propensities tends to prevail
over the course of time in terms of purpose and meaningfulness. The dominant attraction becomes eventually an irresistible spiritual direction that the
person embodies in a corresponding vocational lifestyle.

Second, a certain sequential movement from apostolic to contemplative
to eremitic occurs. As a person flourishes in a vocational lifestyle, the rhythms
of that way of life point with increasing intensity toward the next mode of living, but without necessarily taking on its core characteristics. Thus, a married,
celibate, or single person living an apostolic life becomes increasingly conscious of the specifically contemplative element of life.[6] By the same token, a
person living the contemplative life grows in the awareness of a more solitary
or eremitic thrust emanating from within that lifestyle.

6. See *Spiritual Journey*, 89–95, 99–124.

Third, for some people, the threefold sequence is such that one vocational way of life evolves into another. These persons come to a crossroads wherein one lifestyle gives way entirely to the next. Thus, a married, celibate, or single person called to the contemplative life passes first through an apostolic mode of living. In a similar manner, a celibate called to the eremitic life moves through appropriate forms of the apostolic life and the contemplative life. A calling from one general Christian lifestyle to another proceeds according to at least the rudiments of that sequence. Successful passage through the preceding lifestyle is ordinarily a precondition for entry into the next vocational mode of living. Dependent upon the specifics of God's calling, a person's transition from one lifestyle to another could occur in a non-institutional or an institutional context, with or without public ecclesial rituals to celebrate the passage.

Lifestyle Synergism

The apostolic, contemplative, and eremitic lifestyles retain their distinctive features and interrelate with each other. Moreover, all three lifestyles work together as an organic whole within the Christian community and for the world. By the power of the Spirit, all three function synergistically in the Body of Christ. In so doing, their overall transformative effect in building up the Mystical Body is greater than the sum of their three autonomous contributions.

Most Christians see readily the need for and the value of the apostolic life. Many of those people take a different view, however, when it comes to the contemplative life and the eremitic life. They consider those lifestyles to be foreign to their experience and difficult to comprehend. Similarly, some persons living the contemplative life or the eremitic life fail to appreciate the complementarity between their vocational lifestyles and the apostolic life of their sisters and brothers.

Attentiveness to the apostolic, contemplative, and solitary dimensions of one's life can become a window of insight not only into one's own dominant lifestyle attraction, but also into the core of the other two vocational lifestyles. Cherished personal values of service, loving receptivity to God, and solitude awaken appreciation of the apostolic life, the contemplative life, and the eremitic life as distinctive yet synergistic vocations. Thus, a person comes to see that all three lifestyles work together as a whole to contribute to the well-being of the Christian community and the fulfillment of its mission to the world.

The Spirit comes to each person in a unique way and bestows gifts for a good purpose. The one God works in all people and in all gifts (1 Cor 12:4–11). Consequently, the unity of Christians in a diversity of vocational lifestyles bears fruit in holiness.

The Focus of Vocational Discernment

God's calling to a general Christian vocational lifestyle, a person's consciousness of that calling, and the pursuit of that direction entail a lengthy process of development.

Initially, most people tend to approach the issue of vocational lifestyle from the perspective of conformity to the established Christian order. That approach occurs especially in the case of persons who from childhood were practicing members of a Christian community. As people advance in vocational awareness, they redefine their perspective in light of personal rapport with God, with significant people, and with the world around them. Eventually, maturing consciousness of God's calling opens to them the experience of vocation as an existential inability to become otherwise.[7] In other words, out of a sense of vocational awareness they are so impelled to choose a specific direction and so full of desire to proceed that way that they *have to* do so. They are so free to be true to their deepest self-identity and to God that they cannot *not* commit themselves to their calling. For them, taking that vocational path becomes a spiritual imperative.

In our discussion of the apostolic life, the contemplative life, and the eremitic life, we concentrate upon vocational awareness and response primarily as an existential inability to become otherwise and as a spiritual imperative. That phase of vocational consciousness is especially significant in view of discerning a person's readiness to make a long-range or a lifelong commitment to God through one of those lifestyles. Maturing vocational awareness brings with it the experience, knowledge, self-identity, and personal freedom necessary for wholehearted commitment to God through a specific Christian way of life.

We have addressed in two previous books the discernment of vocations to the basic lifestyles of marriage, celibacy, and singlehood. Therefore, in this book we refrain from in-depth discussion of that subject. We assume for the most part that those who are discerning their calling to a general vocational lifestyle have delved into the more fundamental question of basic vocational lifestyle. Many Christians undertake both discernments simultaneously in their actual life circumstances. Most of those persons

7. See *Called by God*, 115–22.

find that awareness of their basic calling and stability in living it for some time enhance readiness for long-range vocational commitment to God through a general lifestyle.

Virtually all Christians live some form of the apostolic life for many years before the emergence within them of a mature sense of calling to marriage, celibacy, or singlehood. In this case, their vocational consciousness and their commitment to God through the apostolic life continue to increase over time. Nonetheless, until people can situate their vocation to apostolic living in relation to their basic vocational lifestyle (marriage, celibacy, or singlehood), they lack some understanding necessary to their apostolic calling.

CHAPTER 2

The Apostolic Lifestyle

THE LOVE OF GOD is manifest in Jesus. He is the Word-Made-Flesh. Being chosen by Jesus and called to himself elicits within an individual a twofold imperative to listen to him with loving attentiveness and to go forth in his name: "Jesus called to himself those whom he chose . . . that they might be with him . . . and that he might send them forth" (Mark 3:13–14). Thus, both a contemplative thrust (being with him, listening to him) and an apostolic orientation (going forth) are integral to a person's identity as a child of God and as a brother or sister of Christ Jesus.

Those contemplative and apostolic inclinations coexist within each person throughout the spiritual journey. Along the way, the two inclinations are continuously interacting, maturing, and realigning. They develop in accordance with God's desire for a person, that individual's awareness of God's design, and the person's responsiveness to God's initiative.[1] Each maturing Christian is both contemplative and apostolic, in varying intensities and in innumerably unique ways.

Contemplative and apostolic aspects of identity are complementary energies within every person, irrespective of vocational lifestyle. Nonetheless, we can speak also of *an apostolic person* or of *a contemplative person*—someone in whom one quality appears to take precedence over the other. We can speak, furthermore, of *the apostolic life* and *the contemplative life*. The designations "the apostolic life" and "the contemplative life" have had widespread use throughout history. Yet those terms are not without ambiguity, even up to the present time.

In this chapter, we present fundamental notions relevant to the apostolic mode of living. We distinguish "apostolate" and "the apostolic life," although in practice the two concepts blend together. Apostolate is a vocational "what"—*what* a person does. It is the service, ministry, or constellation of ministries that a person undertakes out of a sense of having been sent forth

1. See *Spiritual Journey*, 41–52, 55–59, 89–95, 99–102.

by God to do so. The apostolic life is a vocational "how"—*how* God calls an individual to live in relation to a ministry or constellation of services.

The Apostolate

In the apostolic exhortation *Evangelization in the Modern World*, Pope Paul VI included among those domains with the potential to be apostolates the vast and complicated world of politics, society, and economics; the world of culture, of the sciences, and of the arts; the world of international life and of mass media. He included also as potential apostolates other spheres such as human love, the family, the education of children and adolescents, professional work, and human suffering. Paul VI urged followers of Jesus to exercise to the utmost their Christian charism by engaging appropriately in those fields of action. He taught that the involvement and contribution of Christians place those realms at the service of God's reign and of salvation in Christ Jesus. He implored Christians to involve themselves in those fields of action in a manner that respects the human content of their work and points simultaneously to an "often disregarded transcendent dimension" of their endeavors.[2]

Thus, depending upon a person's interior disposition, virtually any good work, career, or profession has the potential to be an apostolate. Farming, trucking, fishing, acting, homemaking, parenting, office work, manual labor, space exploration, environmentalism, patient suffering of long-term physical, mental, or emotional illness—just to cite a few examples—can be apostolates. They can be works that embody a person's response to a calling by Jesus to discipleship and mission.

What then converts a good work into a Christian service? What changes a specific profession from "a career" to a ministry? Where does a task like pumping gas or cleaning hotel rooms leave off as "a job" and turn into an apostolate? At what point does working for social justice or for the well-being of the environment go beyond a humanitarian service and become a ministry?

In each instance both the instrument of change and the precise turning point are hard to define, to judge, or to say exactly. Nonetheless, awareness within a person of the relatedness of Christ to the specific endeavor authenticates an activity as apostolate. The shift to understanding a work as an apostolate occurs when a person's motivation and effort become directed toward care for other people and for all creation not for their sake alone, but also *explicitly for the sake of Jesus and the good news of God's reign.* That

2. See Paul VI, *Evangelii Nuntiandi*, 70.

intent and that labor make visible "the often disregarded transcendent dimension" of human action and service.

Most Christian churches require specialized training for members preparing to practice apostolates of an official and public nature. At the completion of such formation programs, many churches have ceremonies of commissioning for members. Within their respective communities, those trained and commissioned people function under the supervision of designated ecclesial representatives such as the clergy.

Yet the majority of Christians do not desire to serve in official ecclesial positions or to go through commissioning rituals. Many laborers, artists, homemakers, tradespeople, and professionals come to a phase of vocational awareness wherein they experience as apostolate the work in which they are already engaged. What they viewed previously as a secular undertaking, or even simply as something necessary for the provision of their basic human needs, then becomes for them a ministry. These people go forth conscientiously each day. They do the work by which they earn their daily bread and provide for their loved ones. They approach their endeavors with the intent of making the world a better place for the sake of Christ and the gospel. These persons adjust the circumstances of their lives in ways that enhance the quality of their Christian service.

Instead of discerning an invitation to take on an attitude of apostolate toward their immediate work, some people perceive the Spirit prompting them to a change of direction. For example, when the initial experience of intimate friendship with Christ occurs during a person's adult years, that life-changing encounter could hold a calling to a new occupation. Futhermore, several times over a lifetime, most committed Christians experience callings to move on from one ministry to another for the sake of Jesus and the gospel.

The Apostolic Life

The lifestyle that animates, nurtures, and supports an infinite variety of Christian apostolates, services, or ministries we term "the apostolic life." An apostolic life is a way of life calibrated toward a ministry, with that work as the principal catalyst shaping the lifestyle.

The apostolic life is an all-embracive and all-penetrating lifestyle that converges upon service for the sake of Jesus to humankind or to another segment of creation. The apostolic life is *all-embracive* in that all dimensions of a person's life stand in relationship to the apostolate, for example, friendships, recreational activities, spirituality, intellectual pursuits, family, and community. The apostolic life is *all-penetrating* in that, while each of those components of human life has its distinct meaning and purpose, the apostolate nonetheless exerts a profound influence upon each separate dimension and upon all of them as a whole. Thus, the apostolic life offers a supportive grounding for service, a creative foundation for ministry, and a nurturing base for good works.

The apostolic life sustains a person's loving presence and dedicated service to a portion of God's creation. In counterpoint to the apostolic lifestyle is the contemplative life. Contemplation itself remains the prime ministry in the contemplative life.[3] Those persons called to the contemplative life discern the scope of their other ministerial practices in light of that core emphasis on contemplation as apostolate. By virtue of the universal call to holiness, God invites everyone—even the most active apostles—to contemplation in the sense of immediate and direct loving communion with God.[4] Only relatively few people, however, are called by God to make contemplation as a ministry the focal point of their time and energy.

God calls some contemplatives to engage in certain apostolic works, but those ministries are not the raison d'être of their contemplative life. Thomas Merton is a contemporary example. Although his prodigious literary output entailed much activity, he remained not only a contemplative, but also in his last years a hermit.

It is then a question of accent with respect to the apostolic life and the contemplative life. What is the predominant thrust of a person's desire, ministry, and way of life? Is the person oriented primarily toward a service or toward contemplation? Is the individual inclined principally to work for God's creation and through creatures encounter God? Or is the inclination mainly to contemplate God and in God to encounter all creation? Apostles, contemplatives, and hermits are for God and for all God's creation. Each of the lifestyles associated with the three groups, nevertheless, expresses a distinctive mode of relationship to God and to creation.

Alternative Phrases: Activity, Active, and the Active Life

We have examined above the meaning of apostolate and the apostolic life. Some people use other designations for those entities: "activity" instead of "apostolate," "active" in place of "apostolic," "active life" for "apostolic life."

From one point of view, those alternative expressions are synonymous with their counterparts. From another perspective, activity is distinct from

3. See *Contemplation*, 141–46.
4. See *Contemplation*, 13–20; *Spiritual Journey*, 39–52, 89–95, 114–24, 223–26.

apostolate, being active is not equivalent to being apostolic, and active life differs from apostolic life. Everything that we do is activity in some sense. Yet, just as not every action on our part is inspired by God and directed to God, neither does every action qualify automatically as integral to our apostolate. In a similar manner, every apostolic lifestyle is an active life, but not every active life takes on the quality of an apostolic life. An apostolic life has a vital and explicit quality related to the risen Christ. Active life of itself can be devoid of christocentric meaning.[5]

Historically, many Christian writers have placed "the active life" in juxtaposition to "the contemplative life." Moreover, those teachers have proceeded from differing understandings of the two lifestyles and of the relationship between them. We highlight below four examples.

In the seventh century, St. Gregory the Great used the designations "active life" and "contemplative life" for two complementary aspects of each Christian's life: asceticism and prayer or good works and prayer.[6]

In the thirteenth century, St. Thomas Aquinas distinguished two general and all-embrace ways of living: the active and the contemplative.[7] He based that differentiation on the fundamental orientation of each lifestyle and on his understanding of contemplation.

In the fourteenth century, the author of *The Cloud of Unknowing* described a person's transition from discursive prayer to contemplation as a movement from the active life to the contemplative life.[8]

Since the close of the Middle Ages, use of the expressions "active life" and "contemplative life" has been extensive in ecclesial circles. As employed in that context, the phrases designate two distinctive lifestyles found in institutes and societies of consecrated life.

The Unique Position of the Apostolic Life

Of the three general vocational lifestyles under consideration in this book, Christians are most directly familiar with the apostolic life. All followers of Jesus have some experience of actually living an apostolic life. The majority of committed Christians remain engaged in an apostolic lifestyle for the

5. The concepts *christocentric, christifiied, christification, christic,* and *christogenesis* are central to the thought and writings of Pierre Teilhard de Chardin. See, for example, Teilhard, "The Christic," 80–102. Generally speaking, Teilhard is referring to the transformation of the evolving universe in the risen Christ.

6. See Gregory the Great, *Homilies on Ezekiel,* I, 3, 9–12; II, 2, 7–11; and *PL,* 76:809–11; 76:952–55.

7. See Aquinas, *Summa Theologiae,* 2a2ae, QQ. 179–82.

8. See *The Cloud of Unknowing,* 156–66.

greater portion of their lives. Participation in an apostolic life is a formative experience also for those persons who discern eventually a vocation to the contemplative life or to the eremitic life.

Even children, preteens, and adolescents who are being raised within a Christian environment and who have a personal rapport with Jesus practice the rudimentary elements of an apostolic life. As children and young people grow in their friendship with Jesus, they want spontaneously to share with other people their stories of his love at work in their lives. They seek to put Christian values into practice as they go about their daily activities. They try to help when needs arise within their families, friendships, and communities.

The Christian community seeks to nurture in children and youth those nascent beginnings of what will become with time and grace maturing expressions of the apostolic life. To that end parents and teachers provide children and youth with guidance as they seek to put their faith, hope, and love into action. Those efforts of children, preteens, and adolescents to express in kind deeds their friendship with Jesus constitute their first steps in the formation of a way of life centered upon service to other people and care for all creation for the sake of Christ and the gospel. Preparation for a full-fledged apostolic lifestyle proceeds in a developmental way throughout their childhood, adolescence, and early adulthood.

Influences upon the Formation of an Apostolic Life

The apostolic life can take on as many expressions as there are individual apostles or distinct apostolic groups. Numerous influences converge to shape an apostolic lifestyle.

Circumstances and events in a person's history affect the evolution of an apostolic lifestyle—for example, whether or not the individual was brought up from childhood in a Christian family that participated on a regular basis in the liturgical life and ministerial endeavors of the local church; whether a person has been from childhood nominally a Christian, but participated only minimally or even not at all in the Christian faith and practice; whether a person while not a professed Christian had always an inclination toward humanitarian service; whether a person's long-standing motivation of "making money in order to buy things" is now giving way to a need to give back something of substance to the world. Whatever the events of a person's history, God accepts those experiences as they are and uses them as catalysts in the awakening of vocational consciousness.

A person's vocation to a basic Christian lifestyle of marriage, celibacy, or singlehood also exerts profound influence upon the emergence of an apostolic lifestyle. For a married person, the mode of apostolic life will be grounded in married life with its spousal and familial commitments. For a celibate person, the calling to apostolic life will be anchored in the living of a celibate lifestyle, which ordinarily entails membership in an institute of consecrated life or affiliation in some manner with an alternate form of Christian community. For a single person, the calling to apostolic life will be rooted in the vocation to singlehood, and will respect the unique manner in which a single person relates to the world.

Moreover, each person experiences a continuing interplay between a calling to a basic way of life and a vocation to a general lifestyle. If a person is called to marriage and to the apostolic life, for example, each vocational mode of living will influence substantially the development of the other. The two lifestyles evolve together, as the person matures in the image and likeness of Christ.

The attitude of Christians toward their apostolate is still another influence upon their apostolic lifestyle. For example, some persons take the approach that *what* they do—preach, teach, or build, etc.—is "for now." They look at their specific service as having a provisional quality, as being of temporary importance, and as destined to give way eventually to a new work. When they move from one ministry to another, they adjust their apostolic lifestyle accordingly. In contrast, other people lean toward an apostolate that they hope will be "forever," metaphorically speaking. These people choose a form of ministry that entails the development and the long-term use of a specific talent or skill. They invest themselves and their resources extensively in preparation for practice in an area of specialization within a certain field of endeavor such as the arts, trades, science, medicine, teaching, or administration. Their chosen domain of service becomes for them their enduring apostolate, and that apostolate persists in shaping their apostolic lifestyle until their retirement years.

Related Distinctions

In the English language, often the articles "an" and "the" carry little significance for the meanings of words. However, a difference does exist between *an* apostolic life and *the* apostolic life. The phrase "an apostolic life" stresses a specific person's mode, style, or form of apostolic living. In this respect, there are as many expressions of apostolic living as there are individuals called to serve. The designation "the apostolic life" highlights certain commonalities observable in most, if not all, of those individual apostolic lifestyles. The word *the* in the phrase "the apostolic life" does not mean "the one and only." Rather, it indicates a general description based upon core features discernible among persons called to that vocational lifestyle. In the case of institutes or societies of consecrated life, a cluster of individual callings, each to "an" apostolic life, share a common charism and become a communal expression of "the" apostolic life.

Our subject in this book is *the* apostolic life. For many people, that phrase conjures up the image of a lifestyle lived only by celibates. They think of parish priests, missionary sisters, teaching brothers. However, the apostolic life, while lived by many celibates, is not exclusive to those called to the celibate mode of living. God calls the vast majority of married and single Christians, together with most of those who are celibate, to the apostolic life on a long-term or even a lifelong basis.

CHAPTER 3

The Contemplative Lifestyle

THE PHRASE "CONTEMPLATIVE THRUST" refers to each person's loving openness, dynamic receptivity, and heartfelt listening to God. The expression "apostolic orientation" alludes to each individual's propensity to go forth in service to God and creation. All people retain throughout their spiritual journey both a contemplative thrust and an apostolic orientation in their relationships with God, themselves, and creation. Both dimensions persist and evolve in each person throughout the spiritual journey.

While being contemplative and being apostolic remain qualities integral to human identity from inception to death, one of the two energies tends to dominate in shaping a person's lifestyle. Most people experience the apostolic attraction as the stronger influence in their approach to life. Those people engage in the apostolic life. Other persons find themselves drawn to a vocational lifestyle centered primarily upon the contemplative aspect of their identity. They experience themselves called by God to the contemplative life.

Contemplation in Reference to the Contemplative Life

Within the Christian tradition there exists a wide variety of suppositions, contexts, and usages for the word "contemplation" and its cognates.[1] We highlight below the meaning of contemplation and its relationship to the contemplative life as understood by four familiar Christian writers.

St. Thomas Aquinas (1225–74) described contemplation as the simple act of gazing upon Truth. As such, contemplation is a function of the intellect. Yet Thomas understood human desire to be the origin of contemplation, since it is love (charity) that impels a person to behold Truth. Thomas Aquinas identified the ultimate perfection of contemplation as the divine

---

1. For a brief history, see "Contemplation," *Dictionnaire de spiritualité*, mn 1643–2193.

truth being both seen and loved. According to Thomas, the acts of loving and gazing upon Truth awaken in a person delight in seeing God. That beatitude in turn enflames deeper love. The dynamic of loving, gazing, and delighting keeps repeating itself, as in a spiral movement. In this way, the person's contemplation of God takes on increasing breadth and depth. For Thomas, attentive listening to God fosters openness to contemplation. He emphasized the importance in listening of these three activities: calling upon the name of God, reading the bible, and engaging in meditation (*oratio, lectio, meditatio*).[2] In Thomas's view, we contemplate in order to share its fruits with other people: *contemplata aliis tradere*.[3] Thomas not only summarized in his teaching on contemplation the thought of his predecessors, St. Augustine, St. Gregory the Great, and Richard of St. Victor, but also he integrated a key element of the Dominican charism; that is, a person studies and prays lovingly and receptively the mysteries of God so as to evangelize more effectively. In the understanding of Thomas Aquinas, therefore, the contemplative life would be a lifestyle that favored contemplation as a preparation for the apostolate. Thomas's perspective on contemplation vis-à-vis the contemplative life contains insight into the contemplative experience in its broad sense. His understanding contains also a flavor distinctive to the charism of The Order of Preachers.

St. Ignatius of Loyola (1491–1556), the founder of the Jesuits, described contemplation in his *Spiritual Exercises* as gazing upon God's work or wisdom by means of the imagination.[4] That understanding of contemplation includes a method of prayer in which a person moves through a sequence of distinct acts. For example, when we contemplate a gospel scene in this Ignatian style, we imagine ourselves in the biblical setting. We let ourselves see, hear, and feel what might have taken place in the time of Jesus. Then we apply that insight to our present circumstances and give praise to God for our blessings. Ignatius designated also as contemplation a more simplified approach to God in prayer. In that sense, contemplation, though still basically discursive in nature, consists primarily of attentiveness to the presence of God in the gifts of God, in the divine indwelling, and in all creation. Ignatius designed *The Spiritual Exercises* primarily for beginners in the spiritual life. In relation to those persons who were maturing spiritually, his understanding of contemplation included probably a more wordless, imageless mode of loving communion with God. Ignatius did not

2. Aquinas, *Summa Theologiae*, 2a2ae, 180, 3.

3. See Aquinas, *Summa Theologiae*, 2a2ae, 188, 6 & 7.

4. See Ignatius of Loyola, *Spiritual Exercises*, Ganss, ed., 9–63, 113–214; Fleming, 20–143.

address the contemplative life as such. Rather, he promoted the practice of continuous communion with God in and through action. Ignatius believed that a person could encounter God by uniting human desire and activity with God's will and salvific activity. He encouraged people to find God in all things and to do all things for the greater glory of God. The Ignatian accent upon the contemplative dimension inherent to apostolic action influenced greatly the way in which many religious institutes have come to understand their charisms and their missions.[5]

St. John of the Cross (1542–91) was a Spanish Discalced Carmelite. John followed in the footsteps of spiritual writers such as St. Gregory of Nyssa, the Pseudo-Dionysius, the Rhino-Flemish mystics, and the author of *The Cloud of Unknowing*. He understood the core of contemplation as immediate and direct communion between a person and God. According to the sanjuanist understanding of contemplation, God indwelling a person exerts a transforming, enlightening, and purifying influence within that individual.[6] The human response to that divine indwelling and activity consists of sheer loving receptivity to God and wholehearted self-abandonment in faith, hope, and love to Christ Jesus, the Beloved. John viewed contemplation as both epitomizing and transcending all modes of discursive prayer. He taught that the person whom the Spirit has drawn into those contemplative depths of union with God does not need to proceed through a sequence of discursive acts or even to engage continually in the simplified use of an image, an affection, or a thought. For St. John of the Cross, the contemplative life not only favors contemplation, but also contemplation is the sole raison d'être of the contemplative life. All facets of a contemplative lifestyle converge upon and derive their purpose and meaning from contemplation in the sense of remaining loving one's Beloved.[7]

Thomas Merton (1915–68) lived for twenty-seven years as a Trappist monk at the Cistercian Abbey of Our Lady of Gethsemani in Kentucky. His view of contemplation vis-à-vis the contemplative life was similar to the understanding of St. John of the Cross.[8] Merton applied the sanjuanist teaching to the monastic life and to twentieth-century society. With respect to the monastic life, he lamented the fact that although many monasteries were designated canonically as "contemplative," the actual lifestyles of

5. See Gannon and Traub, *The Desert and the City*, 152–72.

6. See *Contemplation*, 36–43; *Spiritual Journey*, 75–95, 114–24, 201–26; *O Blessed Night*, 47–97.

7. In *Sum of Perfection*, line 4, John of the Cross describes contemplation as *Estarse amando al Amado*. See *Contemplation*, 22–23, 39–40.

8. See Merton, *Seeds of Contemplation*; *New Seeds of Contemplation*; *Contemplation in a World of Action*; *Contemplative Prayer*.

those communities were otherwise. After wrestling with that discrepancy for many years, Merton came reluctantly to this point of view: he acknowledged that perhaps a monastic community could be considered "contemplative," provided that most of its monks or nuns were contemplative in spirit, if not in their individual lifestyles. In reference to society, Merton spoke of "contemplation in a world of action." His use of that phrase is equivalent in most contexts to what we term the "contemplative thrust" in life[9] and to "being contemplative" in contradistinction to "being *a* contemplative." (We discuss that point later in this chapter.)

The Contemplative Life as Understood in this Study

Our understanding of "contemplation" and "the contemplative life" aligns closely with the perspectives of St. John of the Cross and Thomas Merton.

We consider contemplation as immediate and direct communion with God. Contemplation consists of God's transforming, enlightening, and purifying love operative within a person, together with that person's attentiveness in faith, hope, and love to the risen Christ. For one called by God to the contemplative life, contemplation is the reason for being and the animating energy of that mode of living. All facets of the person's contemplative life flow from and redound to contemplation of God. Contemplation itself draws all dimensions of that individual's life into an all-embracive and all-penetrating lifestyle centered upon communion with God and with all creation in God.

A calling to the contemplative life is not entirely a solitary vocation. A person with a contemplative vocation desires affiliation with a Christian community. Dependent upon the particulars of God's calling to each contemplative, the primary community could constitute any one of a number of possibilities or even a combination of several options. It could consist, for instance, of an informal faith-sharing group, a parish, or an ecclesial institute or society of consecrated life.

By the expression "the contemplative life" then, we are not indicating specifically God's gift of the contemplative thrust innate to being human, although that thrust remains a dimension of the lifestyle.[10] That calling to become increasingly contemplative in all dimensions of life—a vocation of each Christian, whatever the person's mode of living—is distinct from the question of the contemplative life as a unique lifestyle to which God calls some Christians. By the phrase "the contemplative life," neither are we

---

9. See *Contemplation*, 13–20; *Spiritual Journey*, 19–32, 39–52, 89–95, 99–124.

10. See *Spiritual Journey*, 89–95.

referring directly to the universal invitation to contemplation that is integral to the universal call to holiness, although that invitation is surely an aspect of the contemplative life.[11] Nor are we addressing explicitly the situation of people who in the apostolic life yearn for more silence and solitude than their responsibilities have thus far made possible. In the latter case, most of those people discern that their calling is to incorporate additional silence and solitude into their apostolic mode of living. A few of them do come to see eventually that their longings for an increase of aloneness and quietude represent the first stirrings of a vocation to a contemplative lifestyle.[12]

Similar to our distinction between *an* apostolic life and *the* apostolic life, we differentiate also the two phrases "*a* contemplative life" and "*the* contemplative life." The expression "*a* contemplative life" indicates an authentic mode, style, or form of contemplative living for a specific person or for a distinctive group. There are as many modalities and expressions of a contemplative life as there are individual contemplatives and contemplative communities. Even so, we can speak authentically of "*the* contemplative life." Again, the adjective "the" in that phrase does not mean "the one and only." Rather, the designation suggests the contemplative core discernible in those personal vocations and group traditions.

In this book, we focus on *the* contemplative life so as to explore its mystery and to formulate principles for the discernment of possible vocations to this Christian lifestyle.

Those Called to This Lifestyle

Many people assume that only persons with a calling to celibacy have a vocation to the contemplative life. However, not all people with a contemplative vocation are celibates.

Although extremely rare, God does seem to call certain married persons to lead a veritable contemplative life within the context of their marriages and family life. It could be a case of two spouses who experience a calling to live the contemplative life specifically as a couple. It might also be an instance of one spouse with a contemplative vocation and the other spouse with an apostolic calling. These people do not thereby experience a need to discontinue the conjugal aspects of their marriages or to relinquish parental responsibilities, if they have children.

God calls also to a contemplative lifestyle persons who up to a certain point have had a sense of vocation to the single life. In the cases that

11. See *Contemplation*, 13–20, 27–35.
12. See *Contemplation*, 97–109.

we have known, when the single persons became aware of a vocation to move from an apostolic lifestyle to a contemplative life, they experienced as well a calling to celibacy. Thus, it would appear that there are no single contemplatives. The intimacy between the person and Jesus characteristic of the contemplative life seems to entail a vocational change from single-hood to celibacy.

God is utterly free to call anyone, anytime, anywhere to a contemplative lifestyle. That unrestricted divine freedom suggests that the Spirit will lead people with a contemplative vocation to live in a variety of settings. Thus, contemplatives abide in homes with their spouses, in houses of prayer, and alone in their dwellings, as well as in monasteries, abbeys, or convents.

Contemplative Life in Relation to Monastic Life

Most people spontaneously associate the contemplative life with monastic or cloistered life. Yet identification of the contemplative life with monastic life is not entirely accurate.

Several "contemplative orders" exist in the church. Two of the most widely known are the Trappists and the Discalced Carmelites (especially the nuns). It is readily apparent to anyone familiar with the membership of those orders that not every Trappist or Carmelite lives a contemplative life. Many monks and nuns live in effect intensely apostolic lives, often with a pronounced ascetical bent, within the enclosure of their abbeys, monasteries, or convents. The lifestyle of those persons is primarily one of *doing* a multitude of things, for example, making vestments, manufacturing cheese, carrying out massive mail campaigns, or farming land.

That fact does not necessarily run counter to the monastic charism in general or to the charism of a specific institute or society of consecrated life. The presence of some persons who are clearly apostolic and other persons who are decidedly contemplative in their modes of living enriches life in some communities. A necessary condition for that outcome is respect within the community for the sacredness and the uniqueness of each member's vocation. Without that respect, conflicts between apostolically inclined members and contemplatively oriented members give rise to division within the community.

An analogous situation occurs in those monastic communities wherein membership includes both persons called to the contemplative life and one or more individuals called to the eremitic life. Moreover, it is possible to find all three lifestyles—apostolic, contemplative, and eremitic—complementing each other within the same community.

Some monastic communities pursue modes of living other than apostolic, contemplative, or eremitic. Many of those communities are little more than penitential bastions. Their focus is not contemplation, but asceticism. Silence, solitude, and contemplative prayer are not the prevailing values. Rather, rules, schedules, penances, and saying prayers receive priority. Other monastic communities become consumed with liturgical or para-liturgical matters. Those groups invest most of their time and energy in rigorous preparation for liturgical events, in the recitation or chanting of all the Liturgy of the Hours, and in the meticulous performance of liturgical rites. Ascetical or liturgical orientations within monastic life do not in themselves lack authenticity. Either emphasis might be what both God and a specific community truly desire. That focus could be integral to the group's contemplative charism. But let us neither assume nor pretend that lifestyles centered upon those practices are thereby automatically contemplative.

Thus, a distinction exists between the canonical designation of a group as a "contemplative order" and the actual experience of the contemplative life. Ideally, one entity would affirm the other. However, many are *called* contemplatives, but comparatively few persons truly are.

A Contemplative Vocation within an Apostolic Institute

On occasion, the following situation presents itself: a long-standing member of an apostolic institute discerns a calling to the contemplative life, together with a calling to live that lifestyle with continuing membership in the group.

The founding charism of each religious institute or society has a contemplative core. That is, the charism contains the mandate to bring to fruition in this world a unique manifestation of love of God and love for God. Consequently, the charism of an apostolic group contains within itself the possibility of the emergence of a contemplative vocation within a member. Both the leadership and the membership within apostolically oriented institutes and societies, therefore, can expect from time to time the emergence of such "a call within a call." Moreover, if an authentic contemplative vocation never emerges, a group would do well to examine the overall vibrancy of its spiritual life.

A decidedly apostolic religious institute or society would not admit for membership a candidate who is clearly seeking from the outset the contemplative life. Still, the Spirit is supremely free to guide as God wills the vocational development of each apostolic member. The emergence of a contemplative vocation in an experienced member can be a special gift from God to the entire apostolic community.

Contemplative and Apostolic: Two Additional Paradoxes

Two further paradoxes come to mind as we probe the distinctiveness of the contemplative life in relation to the apostolic life.

On the one hand, the invitation to contemplation is integral to the universal call to holiness.[13] At some point, God calls each person—whether married, celibate, or single; whether living an apostolic life or a contemplative life—to contemplative prayer.

On the other hand, the contemplative life itself has an apostolic dimension. Contemplation, the heart and soul of the contemplative life, is an authentic ministry within the church and to the world. As such, contemplation itself remains a vital spiritual service to other people and to all God's creation.[14] The designation of St. Thérèse of the Child Jesus, a Discalced Carmelite contemplative nun, as the patron saint of missionaries expresses something of that truth.

Being Contemplative and Being a Contemplative

A person can be *contemplative* (adjective) without necessarily also being *a contemplative* (noun).

Being contemplative—which is by far the more important of the two—designates the inner disposition of persons in whom God is intensely and directly active. Those persons have some awareness of that divine activity, and they voluntarily acquiesce to it. They let it be done in, through, and despite themselves. Being contemplative in this sense is compatible with virtually any Christian lifestyle. Being *a* contemplative, on the other hand, usually designates a person who lives the contemplative life as such.

In describing themselves, the members of some apostolic communities say, "We are contemplatives in action." With that assertion, they make no claim to be living the contemplative life as a distinctive lifestyle. Rather, they express the hope that they are lovingly receptive in their communal life, their prayer, their mission, and their ministry. These persons aspire to be contemplative without necessarily becoming contemplatives. Their lifestyle remains apostolic, while they grow in receptivity to God. In this context, the contemplative dimension of their lives pertains more properly to *who* they are and to *what* they are doing than to *how* they are becoming.

Who are they? They are contemplative in their basic identity as unique human beings and as beloved children of God.

13. See "Contemplation," 13–20; *Spiritual Journey,* 89–90.

14. See "Contemplation," 141–46.

What are they? They are nurses, teachers, associate pastors, ecologists, computer experts, laborers, etc., whose contemplative orientation animates their apostolic work and whose apostolic work is itself imbued with a contemplative spirit. They commune with God in their apostolic activity and they work with God in what they do.

How are they? They are "in action", and, therefore, not "contemplatives" in the sense of persons called to the contemplative life.

Whatever the modalities of a vocation, God calls each person to an increasingly receptive stance toward divine love, light, and life. Moreover, in Christ Jesus each person has to discern daily the balance of contemplation and apostolate appropriate to an evolving vocational lifestyle. "Each morning the Lord awakens me to listen, to listen like a disciple" (Isa 50:4).

CHAPTER 4

The Eremitic Lifestyle

JESUS COMMUNED WITH THE Father and he was sent forth by the Father. Christians participate in that communion and that missioning through the contemplative and the apostolic dimensions of their lives. A third aspect of Jesus's relationship with his Father has significance for Christian living; that is, Jesus's need for some physical solitude.

The four gospel accounts indicate that Jesus habitually sought out a solitary place in order to be alone with God; for example, "Jesus would always go off to desert places and pray" (Luke 5:16). The Scriptures identify specific instances of Jesus going off by himself to a solitary place. On one occasion Jesus spent the whole night alone in prayer to God (Luke 6:12). At another time, he was led by the Spirit to be alone in the desert that he might be tempted (Matt 4:1; Luke 4:1). Jesus underwent his agony alone in the garden on the Mount of Olives (Luke 22:39–46; Matt 26:36–46; Mark 14:32–42). In the desert of his heart, he was always alone in loving communion with the Father and the Spirit (John 14:7, 10–26).

Clearly, for Jesus some physical aloneness worked in unison with his prayer and his missionary endeavors. His contemplative, apostolic, and solitary inclinations were vital interacting facets of his unceasing loving attentiveness to God. Moreover, Jesus discerned on a daily basis what would be for him an appropriate balance of prayer, service, and solitude (Mark 1:16–39).

In addition to contemplative and apostolic inclinations, each Christian experiences a solitary leaning. Every person in relation to God needs some time to be alone, to be quiet, to be. Each one needs at times to go apart to a secluded place to think, to pray, to discern, to ponder. Moreover, following the example of Jesus, each person has to integrate that need for solitude with the contemplative and apostolic components of life.

Although contemplative, apostolic, and solitary orientations reside within each Christian, a person's vocational lifestyle accentuates at any given time one of those directions. Dependent upon God's calling, either the apostolic, the contemplative, or the solitary thrust of a person's life becomes the organizing energy for a corresponding vocational lifestyle.

Most people have an attraction toward a vocational lifestyle with ministry or service as the central feature; that is, the apostolic life. Some persons long for a lifestyle centered upon contemplation and inclusive of communal participation; that is, the contemplative life. For a few people, aloneness with God becomes the core value around which the Spirit draws them to shape their lives. Silence and solitude for the purpose of communion with God become for these persons the "treasure hidden in the field" in exchange for which they desire to give up all else (Matt 13:44). God calls these persons to the eremitic life.

The Designation "the Eremitic Life"

The word "eremitic" comes from the Greek *erēmos*. As an adjective, the Greek word means "alone" or "solitary." As a noun, the word designates a desert, a wilderness, or an uninhabited region.

In this study, we understand a vocation to the eremitic life to have these underpinnings:

- It is a free and gracious calling of a person by God to a contemplative life alone in the silence and solitude of a hermitage.

- Most aspirants to the eremitic life have the interior readiness to embark upon that lifestyle only after they have persevered for a suitable time first in an apostolic way of life and then in a contemplative mode of living.

- When an eremitic vocation exists, a person's intensity of aloneness, silence, and solitude reaches a critical threshold wherein that individual passes from the contemplative life and enters the eremitic life. Thus, a transition from one Christian vocational lifestyle to another occurs.

- The eremitic life is primarily a continuation of the contemplative life rather than a movement into an ascetical or penitential mode of living.

- While having continuity with the contemplative life, the eremitic life is a vocational lifestyle in its own right.

- The eremitic life witnesses in a radical way to the solitary, desert, and prayerful dimensions of the life of Jesus and of each human life.

Our approach to discernment of an eremitic vocation emphasizes a process wherein a person journeys through an apostolic life, through a contemplative life, and into an eremitic life. Some persons discerning a possible eremitic vocation have membership in an institute or society of consecrated life. Other persons are not members of a canonically recognized community. In either situation, it is the *process of vocational development* that remains the pivotal starting point and continuing focus of discernment.

In the case of a possible eremitic calling, principles of discernment and ecclesial requirements serve at their best when they nurture a person's emerging vocational consciousness and continuing response to God. Moreover, it is ordinarily the way of the Spirit to affirm the presence of an eremitic vocation through significant people, such as spiritual guides, church leaders, community members, and soul friends.

An eremitic calling impels a contemplative toward living alone in radical silence and solitude. Moved by the Spirit, a person becomes attracted to living a life "hidden with Christ in God" (Col 3:3). The person chooses the eremitic life for the sake of contemplating the risen Christ becoming all in all (Col 3:11). The contemplative's sense of vocation expresses itself in the actualization of an all-embracing and all-penetrating eremitic lifestyle.

We refer to a person whom God calls to the eremitic life as a hermit. A hermit's maturing vocational experience unfolds along these lines: I have encountered God's love for me, manifest in the risen Christ, in such a way that I have to remain for the rest of my life alone in silence and solitude loving God and loving all creation in God. Love renders me existentially unable to be other than a hermit. An eremitic mode of life is for me a personal and compelling consequence of God's unique love, as well as of my love for God, for people, and for all creation. My option for this direction does not arise out of disgruntlement, failure, or disappointment with society or with life. Rather, the élan of my immersion in and emergence through creation with Christ has brought me to this spiritual imperative.

Virtually all hermits live their eremitic life in conjunction with the basic Christian lifestyle of celibacy. An eremitic vocation evokes within a person a permanent commitment to God through that solitary mode of living.

Expressions of the Eremitic Vocation

Although each eremitic vocation is unique, several distinctive approaches to eremitic living are evident among those called to this lifestyle. In the Roman Catholic tradition, the Camaldolese and the Carthusians were founded explicitly as eremitic institutes. Other monastic traditions such as the Benedictines and the Carmelites view the eremitic life as a coming to fullness within some members of their institute's contemplative charism. The Roman Catholic 1983 *Code of Canon Law* (Canon 603), with certain stipulations, recognizes as living a consecrated life a hermit who is not a member of a canonically designated community.

Thus, some hermits express their commitment to God through the eremitic life within the context of a contemplative or an eremitic institute of consecrated life. Other hermits do not have membership in a specific religious institute, but make a commitment according to the stipulations of Canon 603 of the Roman Catholic Code of Canon Law. Still other hermits live their eremitic calling in a private way without affiliation with any religious institute and without official ecclesial recognition.

As in the case of the apostolic life and the contemplative life, we distinguish between *an* eremitic life and *the* eremitic life. The phrase "*an* eremitic life" stresses a hermit's personal mode, style, or expression of a solitary life. In that respect, there is no "typical" hermit and no exclusive way in which the eremitic life is to be lived. There are as many authentic eremitic modes of living as there are persons called by God to the eremitic life. Consequently, the adjective *the* in the designation "the eremitic life" does not mean "the one and only." Rather, it highlights certain features common to most, if not all, of those individual eremitic lifestyles.

In this book, we consider *the* eremitic life. We identify its core features, and apply that insight to the discernment of possible eremitic vocations.

Misconceptions about Hermit and Eremitic Life

Even within the Christian community, it is unusual for people to know well or even to have casual interaction with a hermit. Perhaps that absence of direct contact contributes to misconceptions that many people have about the eremitic life.

Those misconceptions are evident in popular understandings of the word "hermit." Some people apply the term in a generic way to anyone who lives alone for virtually any reason. In effect, that individual could be a fugitive from the law, a loner, a misfit, an extreme introvert, a single person who simply enjoys being alone, or an artist who needs seclusion for creative endeavors. For other people, the word "hermit" conjures up bizarre images; for instance, a rugged withdrawn eccentric who inhabits the woods, an ascetic bent on doing penance alone in the wilderness, or a person who by insisting on living alone has become too extreme in a spiritual quest. Of itself none of those understandings of the term "hermit" necessarily implies a personal consecration to God.

Some people consider any calling that entails an extended degree of solitude to be equivalent to an eremitic vocation. In reality, the two modes of living are fundamentally distinct. A significant vocational difference exists, for example, between a contemplative who is *inclined* toward more solitude within the framework of a contemplative lifestyle and a contemplative who is *actually* a hermit. (We expand on this difference later in this chapter.)

Many persons who genuinely value solitude believe that the mere fact of living in a hermitage for several months or even for a few years makes them hermits at least for a while. Other persons, when they go apart for a time of solitude, speak of taking a "hermit day" or a "hermit week," as if they become hermits for that interval. God does draw many people to spend a limited time in a hermitage or in a solitary place. That calling also differs from a vocation to the eremitic life.

Misconceptions about "hermit" and "the eremitic life" do not represent merely faulty images or harmless quibbling over words. Many of those attitudes result from an inadequate theology of the eremitic vocation, combined in some situations with a whimsical assessment of what God is trying to accomplish within a person. A shallow understanding of one's faith experience can be a substantial impediment to vocational awareness and response to God.

Two Similar, but Distinct Callings

It is often easier to say what an eremitic calling is *not* than exactly what it *is*. Two callings in particular have features similar to certain characteristics of an eremitic lifestyle, but those callings represent something other than an eremitic vocation. Those two callings pertain to a contemplative-eremitic life and to an extended time of more solitude than usually possible in daily life.

A Call to a Contemplative-Eremitic Life

The contemplative life and the eremitic life are two distinctive vocational modes of living. Yet we can speak also of a *contemplative-eremitic* lifestyle; that is, a way of life that remains decidedly contemplative but with a strong bent toward silence and solitude.

Solitude is integral to each contemplative vocation. So too is some form of communal affiliation. Because a contemplative vocation contains both solitary and communal aspects, the daily regimen of a healthy contemplative community makes provision for all members to have appropriate measures of both physical aloneness and participation in the common life.

However, a few contemplatives are called by God to a contemplative-eremitic lifestyle. In the context of the shared life of a contemplative community, they participate in the routines of the group, but with their propensity for solitude quite accentuated. They share in the common life, but secure more aloneness than most of their brothers or sisters. They remain contemplatives, and do not become hermits. They live the contemplative life, not the eremitic life. They seek out extensive solitude within the parameters of their contemplative lifestyles rather than embark upon the eremitic life itself.

A Call to an Extended Time of Solitude

God calls certain persons occasionally to more external solitude than the circumstances of their lives ordinarily permit. Those people could be married, celibate, or single. They could be living the apostolic life or the contemplative life. The interval of more aloneness could range from brief to prolonged.

These persons enter more intense solitude for a designated time, and then return with renewed fervor to their usual lifestyle and ministry. Examples abound. A parish priest makes a forty-day desert experience. A nurse from an apostolic community takes a sabbatical at a contemplative house of prayer. A grandmother makes a weekend retreat. A used-car salesman takes time off to go camping alone in the woods, communing with God in nature. A nun in a contemplative order moves for a year into a vacant cottage at the extremity of the cloister.

When a calling to an increase of solitude requires that a person integrate into the ordinary daily schedule designated times for aloneness with God, that vocational direction tends to continue indefinitely, perhaps even for the remainder of the person's life. Consider these examples: a middle-aged religious brother discovers a need to cut back his teaching involvements in order to spend more daily time alone with God. A wife and mother feels drawn to go apart from her family for a little while each day in order to pray alone. A religious sister who is a social worker experiences a calling to terminate a few ministerial activities for the purpose of having more time each day for solitude.

The above examples represent genuine callings to enhanced solitude. In each situation, including that of a contemplative-eremitic life, the person is not called to live completely apart from society. Whatever the amount of extended time necessary for solitude and even in the physical aloneness itself, the person retains substantial proximity to other people. The aloneness characteristic of the eremitic life exceeds immeasurably what befits those situations.

In this first section of our study we have presented certain fundamental notions that underlie our understanding of the apostolic life, the contemplative life, and the eremitic life. We move on now to an in-depth consideration of each of those general Christian vocational lifestyles.

Part Two: The Apostolic Life

CHAPTER 5

Biblical Roots of the Concept *Apostolic*

OF THE THREE LIFESTYLES under consideration in this book, the vast majority of Christians experience the apostolic life as their vocation. Certain general living situations are expressive of callings to the contemplative life and the eremitic life. With the exception of those lifestyles, virtually all other general living situations that people undertake with a sense of vocation constitute expressions of the apostolic life.

Throughout the centuries, other designations have been used for the apostolic life, for example, "active life," "ministerial life," "service-oriented life." We prefer the modifier "apostolic" because of its biblical nuances and rich history.

Thus, we proceed to ponder the biblical roots of the vocational lifestyle designated as "apostolic."

Key Biblical Terms for Mission

The word "apostolic" is a virtual transliteration of the New Testament Greek word *apostellō*, the meaning of which is influenced directly by the Hebrew word *shalach*.[1]

In Hebrew, *shalach* means to send forth. This word designates the activity of someone appointing a delegate to fulfill a special task. *Shalach* accentuates the initiator of the mission rather than the envoy. The role of the emissary is to embody the presence and the message of the sender.

The Greek *apostellō* is a compound word, composed of the preposition *apo* (from) and the verb *stellō* (to dispatch). *Apostellō* denotes to dispatch from, to send forth, to let go, to commission. Like the Hebrew *shalach*, the word *apostellō* emphasizes the identity and the will of the sender rather than the personhood and the work of the one sent forth. Again, the emissary's

1. See Rengstorf, "*Apostellō*," *TDNT*, I, 398–447; Hamman, "'Mission' in Holy Scripture," 3–30.

function is to witness in one's personhood, words, and works to the sender's identity, will, and message.

Insights from the Hebrew Scriptures

The Hebrew Scriptures, especially the prophetic literature, present a wealth of experiences in relation to mission. Isaiah, for example, responds to his inaugural vision: "Here I am, [Lord]. Send me" (Isa 6:9). With this instruction, God silences Jeremiah's hesitations about his mission to be prophet to the nations: "Go now to those to whom I send you. Say whatever I command you" (Jer 1:7). God is no less emphatic to Ezekiel: "Son of man, I am sending you to the Israelites. . . . I am sending you forth to proclaim, 'Thus says the Lord Yahweh'" (Ezek 2:3–4).

The above Hebrew texts, together with other similar biblical accounts of missioning, share in common these features:

- It is God who sends forth a person.

- The chosen one becomes aware of God's imperative to go forth. That person accepts the mission willingly and embarks upon it voluntarily.

- The mandate to go forth involves a task to fulfill. At the time of commissioning, the exact manner in which the envoy is to accomplish that mandate could be unclear. Nonetheless, the one being sent forth has a sense of urgency to act and a direction in which to proceed.

- In fulfilling the mission, the emissary is both witness and herald.

New Testament Teachings

The Hebrew notion of "being sent forth" underlies what is designated in the Christian tradition as apostle, apostolate, and the apostolic life. The personhood and the life of the one sent forth are intrinsically bound to the sender and the message. The one being sent forth is not only a spokesperson, but also the living embodiment of the message. The going forth is indeed in service to other people, but only after God's word has permeated every fiber of the messenger's life. The one sent forth is *an apostle*. The words and works of the one sent forth constitute *the apostolate*. A calling to an apostolate gives rise to an *apostolic lifestyle*.

The New Testament, especially the Johannine corpus, reveals the trinitarian aspects of God's activity of missioning. The Father in his love sends forth his Word Incarnate (John 6:29, 57; 17:8, 21), not to condemn the world, but to save it (John 3:16–17). The Father and the Son send the Holy Spirit (John 14:26; 15:26; 16:7) into human beings to sanctify and to divinize them.[2] As people undergo that transformation, they partake in the missioning activity of Father, Son, and Spirit.

In prayer with his Father, Jesus spoke of his own sending forth of his disciples as both a participation in and an extension of the Father's missioning of him: "As you, Father, have sent me forth into the world, so I send them forth" (John 17:18). Jesus included in that prayer not only those disciples with him at that time, but also all those of all times who would come to believe in him: "Father, may they all be one in us, as you are in me and as I am in you, so that the world may believe it was you who sent me" (John 17:21). A person's apostolate is, therefore, a prolongation of the Father sending forth Jesus and also an accomplishment of their work.

The synoptic gospel accounts express similar teaching on mission. In the Gospel according to Luke, Jesus commissioned twelve of his followers, and gave them the name "apostles" (Luke 6:13). On one occasion Jesus sent forth the seventy-two disciples ahead of him into those towns and places that he intended to visit (Luke 10:1–12). The interrelatedness of Jesus's mission from his Father and Jesus's missioning of his followers is evident in this proclamation: "Anyone who listens to you listens to me. Anyone who rejects you rejects me, and those who reject me reject the one who sent me" (Luke 10:16; Matt 10:40).

Jesus not only commissioned the twelve and the seventy-two, but also all his disciples until the end of time. The Gospel according to Matthew concludes with these instructions of Jesus to his disciples: "Go and make disciples of all nations, baptizing them in the name of the Father, the Son, and the Holy Spirit and teaching them to obey all that I have commanded. Behold, I am with you always, even to the end of time" (Matt 28:19–20).

The final mandate of Jesus in the Gospel according to Mark is similar: "Go into all the world, and proclaim the good news to all creation" (Mark 16:15).

St. Paul gave compelling witness in his writings to the apostolate as both a prolongation of the Father's sending forth of Jesus and a continuation of Jesus's mission and ministry. Paul experienced God sending him to the Gentiles. Paul expressed his desire to do all he could to make up in his own body all that Christ has still to undergo for the sake of his body, the church. It was the mission to proclaim Christ within us, our hope of glory, which impelled Paul to struggle wearily on with his work. He strained forward

---

2. The Greek verb *pempō* is used in these references, but with the same basic sense as *apostellō*.

toward the fulfillment of his mission, with the power of Christ urging him forward irresistibly (Col 1:24–29).

Paul does not use the verb *apostellō* as frequently as do the evangelists (three times as compared to one hundred and twenty-six). However, Paul does use the verb in two key texts. The first text refers to all followers of Jesus: "How then can they preach, if they are not sent forth?" (Rom 10:15). The second text denotes the nature of Paul's own mission: "Christ did not send me forth to baptize, but to evangelize" (1 Cor 1:17).

As one would expect, the Acts of the Apostles (literally, "the Doings of Those Sent Forth") is replete with examples of missioning in the primitive Church. Representatives of various Christian communities selected in the name of Jesus individuals for missions to specific geographical locales. For example, the apostles in Jerusalem "sent forth Peter and John" to Samaria (Acts 8:14). The members of the church at Antioch, having laid hands on Barnabas and Saul, "sent them on their way" (Acts 13:3). In other cases, a person experienced the missioning as directly from the risen Christ. Ananias was "sent forth" by Jesus to Saul (Act 9:17). Paul recalled the words of Jesus in directly commissioning him during their first encounter: "I am Jesus, whom you are persecuting. . . . I appoint you as my servant and witness. . . . I send you forth to open the eyes of [Jews and Gentiles] and to turn them from darkness to light" (Acts 26:15–18).

In his first recorded address to the Jews at Antioch in Pisidia, Paul declared: "This word of salvation has been sent forth to you" (Acts 13:26). In his final recorded address to the Jews in Rome, he proclaimed: "I want you to know, therefore, that God's salvation is being sent forth to all nations, and they will listen to it" (Acts 28:28).

A complement to the New Testament notion of being sent forth is the verb "to come" (Greek: *erchomai*).[3]

Jesus described his missioning from the Father also as a coming: "The works I do testify that the Father has sent me forth. . . . I have come in the name of my Father" (John 5: 36, 43); "I have come from God. I did not come on my own. I was sent by God" (John 8:42).

Elsewhere, Jesus related his coming to specific goals, for instance, to proclaim the gospel (Mark 1:38), to call sinners to a change of heart (Mark 2:17), to fulfill the law and the prophets (Matt 5:17), to set the earth ablaze (Luke 12:49), to give us life, and life to the full (John 10:10), to save the cosmos (John 12:47), to bear witness to the truth (John 18:37).

3. See Schneider, "*Erchomai*," *TDNT*, II, 666–84.

Jesus, coming from the Father, invited all people to draw near to him: "Come to me, all you who labor and are overburdened, and I will give you rest" (Matt 11:28).

In the Johannine corpus, the action of a person "coming" to Jesus denotes readiness for commitment to him and willingness to labor with him in advancing God's reign (John 1:39; 3:8; 6:35). Those who come to God are "those taught by God" (John 6:45).

A recurring theme throughout the New Testament writings is that of the second or final coming of Christ. The Book of Revelation provides a familiar example: "Yes, I am coming quickly. Amen, come, Lord Jesus" (Rev 22:20).

The verb "to come" highlights the contemplative dimension of having been sent forth by God. Those persons going forth do so with loving attentiveness and dynamic receptivity to the sender. They evoke within other people a stance of listening and beholding toward the sender.[4] That contemplative dimension harkens back to God's tender covenant of love revealed in the Hebrew Scriptures, as in these texts: "Come then, my love, my lovely one, come" (Song 2:10); "Come to the water all you who are thirsty. Though you have no money, come. . . . Come to me. Listen, and your soul shall live" (Isa 55:1, 3).

Based on the above biblical insights, the Christian concept of "apostolic" denotes above all a person's participation in the life and missions of the Trinity. That participation involves being a witness, doing a work, and living a corresponding way of life. In respect to being a witness, "apostolic" designates a sense of self-identity, a quality of character, and a personal commitment to God. With reference to work, "apostolic" means engaging in a career, a profession, a task, or a job for the sake of Jesus and the gospel. As a lifestyle, "apostolic" designates a mode of life that animates, fosters, and nourishes that apostolic endeavor.

4. See *Contemplation*, 40–43.

CHAPTER 6

Historical Perspectives on the Concept *Apostolic*

ANCHORED IN ITS RICH biblical background, the term "apostolic" has assumed over the centuries a variety of distinct, though interrelated meanings.[1] Even today all those nuances of understanding occur in a wide range of contexts. Usually, a particular meaning gains dominance when it corresponds to a concern of the Christian community or to a segment of that community. We outline now the primary understanding of "apostolic" in reference to each of five historical periods: Christian antiquity, medieval times, the sixteenth century, the seventeenth century, and the contemporary era.

Christian Antiquity

Until approximately the fifth century the designation "apostolic" was employed primarily in relation to the twelve apostles and to things originating with them; for example, their writings, teachings, traditions, and successors. In the West, the adjective tended to be reserved for reference to the Roman See and its occupant. "Apostolic" is found in the early Christian creeds as a mark of the true church, founded upon the apostles (Eph 2:20).

Hence, throughout the early centuries of Christianity the word "apostolic" was used principally in an official ecclesial context to refer to things pertaining to the original twelve apostles, to churches founded by the apostles, to churches aligned with the apostolic churches, and to the Apostolic See.

Medieval Times

During the Middle Ages, the word "apostolic" continued to be employed in the ecclesial sense of descent from the original twelve apostles. The concept

1. See Holstein, "The History of the Development of the Word 'Apostolic'," 31–49.

48

took on also a new accent. "Apostolic" came to designate a Christian way of life conformable to that which the apostles had instituted in the primitive Church (as portrayed, for instance, in Acts 2:42–47), or at least to the way of life ascribed by tradition to their institution. It became customary to use the expression *vita apostolica*, that is, apostolic life. Rather than denoting descent from the Twelve, the adjective thus emphasized resemblance to or imitation of the communal lifestyle that the Twelve had promoted.

Most Christians of medieval times believed that living a life modeled on that of the primitive apostolic community at Jerusalem could be done optimally only within a monastic or a canonical context. For most medieval Christians, monastic life was the apostolic life. They saw the monks and nuns with their common life, their poverty, and their cloister as probably the closest possible approximation of any group to the first apostolic community in Jerusalem.

During medieval times followers of *The Rule of St. Augustine* witnessed in a distinctive way the communal dimension of the apostolic life. *The Rule of St. Augustine* inspired in due course a renewal of apostolic life among the clergy. Around the thirteenth century, use of the expression "apostolic life" was extended to the mendicant orders. One such example was the Order of Preachers (the Dominicans), which in imitation of the apostles combined a life of itinerant preaching with prayer, study, poverty, and communal living.

The Sixteenth Century Onward

The geographical adventures of European explorers during the sixteenth century posed for Christians of that era the issue of what to do in relation to lands and peoples who did not yet know Christ. In response, church leaders began to send forth missionaries to preach the gospel to those peoples. The massive missionary movements spanning the next three centuries accentuated a new understanding of the word "apostolic." Its primary meaning for Europeans became that of going forth under the auspices of the church to spread the gospel in foreign lands.

Christians came to view that missionary activity in foreign lands above all as a participation in and an extension of the mission and ministry of the original Twelve—a mission and ministry grounded in that of Jesus himself. The new understanding of "apostolic" included also reference to the virtues required by persons in order to fulfill their missions. Furthermore, the word "apostolic" highlighted the zeal of those missionaries. People like Francis Xavier and Marie of the Incarnation were described as apostolic men and women. Groups such as the Franciscans, Dominicans, and Jesuits came to be seen as apostolic religious orders.

The Seventeenth Century

By the seventeenth century the notion of the apostolic life as a way of life consecrated to the apostolate was well established. Moreover, by that time the meaning of the term "apostolic" had extended beyond its reference to foreign missionary endeavors to encompass service in the home missions as well. Thus, priests and religious who worked in European parishes, hospitals, schools, orphanages, jails, and rural districts were seen as living apostolic lives.

Contemporary Times: Vatican II and Beyond

Throughout the twentieth century and into the twenty-first, the Christian experience and understanding of "apostolic" have taken on still another emphasis. Along with the accent upon the apostolic lifestyles of clergy members and religious communities, widespread recognition of the apostolic dimensions of the lives of Christian laity has gained prominence. Within the Roman Catholic tradition numerous ecclesial documents have reflected that expanded understanding.[2] To illustrate this inclusiveness of all Christians—whether married, single, or celibate—in relation to the apostolate and the apostolic life, we focus below on two of those documents: Decree on the Apostolate of Lay People (*Apostolicam Actuositatem*) and The Joy of the Gospel (*Evangelii Gaudium*).

Decree on the Apostolate of Lay People (1965)

The Second Vatican Ecumenical Council in its *Decree on the Apostolate of Lay People* described the church's foundational mission as that of spreading the reign of Christ over the entire earth for the glory of God. The goal of that labor is the participation of all people in God's gifts of redemption and salvation, together with the development through humankind of right relationship of all creation to Christ. Thus, Christians seek to spread the gospel

2. See, for example, from the Second Vatican Ecumenical Council: *Lumen Gentium, Ad Gentes, Presbyterorum Ordinis, Apostolicam Actuositatem*. See also: Paul VI, *Evangelii Nuntiandi*; John Paul II, *Christifideles Laici* and *Redemptoris Missio*; Francis, *Evangelii Gaudium*.

and to build up God's reign in this world through promotion of love, unity, justice, peace, and integrity of creation. Christians accomplish that apostolic work through a diversity of ministries but in a unity of mission.

The content of the decree on lay apostolate had its origins in the laity's increasing involvement in social action and in the desire of ecclesial leaders to affirm that pastoral practice. The decree expressed truths that continue to affect Christian apostolic praxis. The following are salient features of the decree's teaching:

- Every activity of the church as the Mystical Body of Christ, with the intent and the purpose of spreading the gospel and extending God's reign in our world, goes by the name of "apostolate."

- The vocation to be Christian entails by its nature a calling to the apostolate.

- Therefore, those people who exercise an apostolate extend beyond the categories of clergy and members of religious institutes to the inclusion of all laity.

- Christians who live in the midst of the world and of secular affairs share in the priestly, prophetic, and kingly dimensions of Christ. Thus, God calls them to make of their apostolates, through the vigor of their Christian spirit, a leaven within the world.

- The labor of lay men and women becomes leaven within the world when these people work directly for the evangelization and sanctification of humankind and when they go about their ordinary daily tasks in ways that bear clear witness to Christ and advance God's reign.

- The apostolate of a Christian is to be supported by a way of life lived in conjunction with the unique circumstances of that person's state in life; whether that is married life, family life, celibacy, singleness, or widowhood.

- Certain qualities and components integral to an apostolic lifestyle foster the development of a Christian's apostolate. Those qualities and components include the following:

  - nurturance of union with Christ through prayer;

  - experience of membership in the one family of God;

  - participation in the liturgy and reception of the sacraments;

  - engagement in activities that promote personal health;

  - collaboration in professional and social endeavors;

- attentiveness to the needs of marriage and family life;

- faithful fulfillment of one's duties and responsibilities at work;

- consciousness of the moral issues of times and cultures;

- development of a well-informed conscience, which prompts one to discern and to implement Christian values;

- attunement to the signs of the times;

- acceptance of the cross in daily living;

- a sense of community with other Christians engaged in a personal or a group apostolate;

- awareness of the specific gifts that the Spirit is prompting a person to use in service and ministry.

The Joy of the Gospel (2013)

On November 24, 2013, Pope Francis issued to all Christians everywhere—including clergy, members of religious institutes, and lay people—the exhortation entitled *The Joy of the Gospel*. In that address, Francis invited all followers of Jesus to embark upon a new phase of evangelization marked by joy.

Francis insisted in *The Joy of the Gospel* that renewed missionary outreach is "paradigmatic for all the Church's activity." That is, each aspect of church life—liturgy, catechesis, family life, celibate life, theology, pastoral practice, or exercise of ecclesial ministries, for instance—stands in relation to evangelization. Moreover, he asserted that the church must review and adapt each dimension in light of the new evangelization.

Francis spoke of his dream for a missionary option or impulse with the power of transforming all things. He expressed his hope that as a consequence of that transformative energy, the church's customs, ways of doing things, times and schedules, language and structures will become directed toward evangelization of today's world instead of toward the church's self-preservation. Francis identified his intent in composing *The Joy of the Gospel* as that of pointing out new paths in the church's pilgrimage for many years to come.

We highlight below certain pivotal points presented by Francis in his exhortation *The Joy of the Gospel*, which bear upon our exploration of the meaning of "apostolic" in the present era.

- The love of God made visible in the person of Jesus is the good news that Christians are sent forth to proclaim. It is God's love that gives joy to the church and to each Christian.

- Jesus himself, the risen Christ, is at the heart of the church's missionary activity. He is the first and greatest proclaimer of the good news. It is he who commissions his disciples to go forth and to proclaim the gospel to all creation.

- Personal encounter with Jesus, or at least an openness to encounter with him, is for Christians the source of their impulse to engage in the apostolate.

- The essential witness and message of a missionary is how one's encounter with Jesus has touched all aspects of one's personhood and life with salvation and transformation. Going forth to be that witness and to proclaim that message embraces all dimensions of the missionary's life. Indeed, that apostolic activity initiates a way of life. Thus, each Christian is to be a missionary disciple.

- The whole church evangelizes. The entire church is a "missionary disciple"—that is, simultaneously a disciple (one who listens to Jesus) and an apostle (one sent forth in his name to continue his work).

- Each "missionary disciple" goes forth in communion with the entire Christian community to minister within the church and to the world. A disciple approaches apostolate and apostolic life not as a lone individual, but always as a member of the Body of Christ.

- The proclamation of the gospel has a quality of eternal newness rooted in the God who reveals immense divine love in the crucified and risen Christ. The initiative in a person's going forth comes from God. Ultimately, it is God who also accomplishes the apostolic work. Each individual Christian and the church as one community are co-creators, co-workers, and collaborators with Christ in that endeavor.

- Christians as individuals and communities need to attract people to Christ by enriching friendship and the "art of accompaniment."[3] The imposition upon people of more heavy burdens and obligations is counter to the new spirit of evangelization.

- This new evangelization calls for a process of conversion within each Christian and a continuing conversion on the part of the church

3. Francis describes "the art of accompaniment" in pars. 169–73 of *Evangelii Gaudium*.

itself—in its structures (including papacy, nationality, diocese, parish, base communities), in its customs, and in its values.

- The church's implementation of the new evangelization requires many forms of preparation for missionary disciples, for example, spiritual formation, pastoral training, development of the gifts of the Spirit, and growth in the wisdom that comes from experience.

- The mission of evangelization embraces for the entire church and for each Christian, however, not only gifts and skills, but also human limits, faults and failings. God works with both human strengths and weaknesses, turning all things to good.

- The new evangelization reaches out toward inclusion of all people, especially those who are poor. Indeed, the mission involves care and compassion for the entirety of God's creation. The Christian community seeks to bring to all the world good news that will activate peace and justice for all creatures.

Historically, we find ourselves at a point in time wherein to be a Christian is to be what Pope Francis terms a "missionary disciple" and wherein all Christians as community are a "missionary disciple." By virtue of being a follower of Jesus and a member of the family of God, a Christian is one who has a vocation to be an apostle, to undertake an apostolate, and to live an apostolic life (unless or until at some point a calling to the contemplative life or to the eremitic life emerges).

CHAPTER 7

Discernment of a Vocation to the Apostolic Life

WE HAVE PONDERED THE biblical roots of the concept "apostolic." We have noted also nuances of meaning in the historical usage of the term. Having situated a calling to the apostolate within the flow of that rich faith experience, we focus now upon the actual process of vocational discernment.

The three designations "apostle," "apostolate," and "apostolic life" describe something of the *who*, *what*, and *how*[1] of an apostolic vocation.

The word "apostle" refers to the *who* of a vocation. An apostle is a person entrusted by God with a mission. God sends forth each apostle as a unique individual to proclaim the good news of Christ Jesus.

The term "apostolate" indicates the service, ministry, or work to which God sends an apostle. Thus, apostolate highlights a vocational "what"—*what* ministry, or over a period of time *what* series of ministries, a person undertakes in building up the Body of Christ.

The phrase "the apostolic life" designates an all-embrace and all-penetrating lifestyle—a vocational *how*. It is a habitual mode of Christian living that supports the values, the virtues, and the activities of a married, celibate, or single person who engages in an apostolate.

Each follower of Jesus experiences on either a temporary or permanent basis a calling to be an apostle, to have an apostolate, and to live an apostolic life. All Christians begin their commitment to Jesus with an apostolic vocation. For most people that apostolic calling sets the course for their continuing spiritual journey. For a minority of Christians that vocation prevails until it gives way to a calling to the contemplative life or the eremitic life. Unless strong indications of a vocation to the contemplative or the eremitic life exist within a person, discernment of vocation to a general Christian lifestyle begins with the recognition of a calling to the apostolic life. The objective of discernment is then the person's growth in attentiveness and response to that evolving apostolic calling.

1. See *Called by God*, 1–3; *DVMCS*, 1–4.

As we take up discernment in relation to apostolic living, we elect not to discuss *specific* apostolic lifestyles. Their sheer number exceeds the scope of this work. Even within any one category of the apostolic life many variations exist.

Take, for instance, apostolic religious institutes or societies. Although all these groups live the apostolic life, they represent nonetheless a wide range of specific missionary undertakings. Moreover, each group that forms around an identifiable apostolic outreach integrates explicit acknowledgment of its unique communal spirit and mission into the formation of its membership. In addition to looking for indications of a calling to the apostolic life, formation personnel seek to discern in prospective members signs specific to the charism of their institute or society. Oblate Missionaries follow their plan for initiates to their lifestyle, while Maryknoll Missionaries have their guidelines for screening candidates.

Another example of variations within a specific category pertains to persons called to the apostolic life who are not members of religious institutes or societies. A homemaker and mother of three, who serves as a counselor in a drug rehabilitation center, would have complexities to discern in relation to her apostolic vocation that would differ from those of a single person working as a Peace Corps volunteer in Latin America.

Discussion of apostolic lifestyles specific to a distinctive group is beyond the scope of this study for yet another reason. That is, the structures and mores of each context for apostolic living are in constant flux. As times, cultures, and needs evolve, so also do apostles' way of living in relation to them. For example, the pastoral contexts and cultural settings for Jesuit missionaries in the twenty-first century differ considerably from those of Jesuit missionaries in the nineteenth century. Moreover, people take for granted today certain apostolic lifestyles that were inconceivable in the Middle Ages. By the same token many future forms of apostolic life have not yet even entered the human imagination.

A vocation to an apostolic life indeed has characteristics and nuances unique to each person and to each group. Yet, in this chapter, we opt to concentrate on the features or qualities common to most expressions of the apostolic life. We discuss seven principles of discernment that apply whether the person discerning vocation is married, celibate, or single. Those principles of discernment are both signs and conditions, which when present together indicate a person's maturing vocational consciousness, response, and commitment in living an apostolic life. These are the seven principles:

- an inclination toward service for the sake of Jesus and the gospel;

- a longing to use a personal charism;

- a community's need for that service;
- the apostle's recognition of the limits of a calling to ministry;
- development of an apostolic lifestyle centered around a ministry;
- communion with the risen Christ as the source, the sustaining impetus, and the goal of an apostle's identity, ministry, and lifestyle;
- continuing growth in the contemplative aspect of apostolic living.

An Inclination toward Service

A person's experience of a longing to serve provides a starting point for discernment of an apostolic vocation. That attraction impels a person toward a sustained form of apostolic involvement with the world.

An inclination toward self-giving service could have as its purpose the direct good of other people, such as in raising a family, teaching, preaching, or nursing. The desire to minister could be also indirectly for the benefit of people. For example, certain forms of medical research, computer programming, or administration entail little or no immediate interaction with people. Yet achievements in those areas contribute immensely to the well-being of humankind.

Many Christians in our time feel a longing to serve segments of creation other than human beings. To that end some of these people collaborate in works that promote the welfare of creatures such as cats, dogs, birds, bees, butterflies, elephants, whales, and dolphins. Other persons desire to labor for the protection of endangered species who inhabit the land, sea, and sky. Still others want to engage in responsible stewardship of the earth's natural resources and in reduction of air, soil, noise, and water pollution.

Does the person then feel a desire to minister? Toward what kind of service does that yearning guide the apostle? How mature is that inclination for service? Are there indications that the person's desire to minister in a specific way can withstand the test of time?

A Need to Use a Personal Charism

A charism is an ability or talent that God bestows freely upon a person for the benefit of humankind or for the good of another segment of creation. A charism contributes also to the spiritual genesis of the one who receives it.

A person's awareness of a need to use a charism constitutes a further sign of a maturing commitment to God through an apostolic life. A professor desires to teach. A lawyer likes to practice law. A surgeon wishes to operate. A carpenter wants to build. A mother or father longs to nurture. The need to use a special gift or talent varies in intensity from person to person. Even within any one person the acuteness of that need ebbs and flows. Moreover, a specific talent or skill can take on various expressions over the course of time.

St. Paul offers several lists of charisms. The letter to the Romans identifies these works: prophecy, administration, teaching, preaching, almsgiving, works of mercy (Rom 12:6–8). The letter to the Ephesians (Eph 4:11) includes also among those people with charisms apostles, evangelists, and pastors. The first letter to the Corinthians (1 Cor 12–13) mentions still other charismatic works: preaching with wisdom, preaching with instruction, the gift of faith, the grace to heal, the power of miracles, discernment of spirits, the gift of tongues, and the interpretation of tongues.

According to St. Paul, those various gifts originate from the same Spirit, and all are directed toward the one Lord (1 Cor 12:4–5). Paul observes elsewhere that in the exercise of the diverse charisms Christians work together to promote God's reign: "The saints together make a unity in the work of service, building up the Body of Christ" (Eph 4:12).

A person who feels a need to use a specific charism in service of creation has a responsibility to test the authenticity of that leaning (1 John 4:1). Instruments in that discernment process include prayer, study, experiences in ministry, and self-evaluation in those pastoral situations, coupled with appraisal by co-ministers, spiritual guides, and recipients of the service.

Some apostles have gifts that remain unused in a direct way. God calls some people to sacrifice certain gifts—either temporarily or permanently—for the purpose of developing other gifts. For example, a person with a vocation to a celibate life may have the qualities necessary to make an excellent spouse and parent. The potential for happiness in marriage and parenthood exists, but the person sacrifices that possibility in view of the calling to celibacy. To sacrifice a talent in that way for God is to use it eminently (as in Isa 49:2–4).[2] The existence of a charism then is not automatically a sign that God wills a person to use that gift in the usually expected way.

Nonetheless, God seems to intend that Christians use most charisms in a straightforward and observable manner. The Spirit engenders within the recipient of a charism a desire and a need to use that talent according to the divine purpose. The indwelling Spirit impels the recipient to move forward freely in that direction. The Spirit guides the person also to create a mode of apostolic life supportive of the exercise of the charism. For

2. See *DVMCS*, 143–45.

example, a nurse quits a secure position at a large city hospital. He perceives the Spirit moving him to work full-time with a nonprofit organization that provides on-site medical services for people living on the streets. Whether he is married, celibate, or single, his identity, ministry, and lifestyle will undergo transformation as he pursues that apostolic direction.

A person's sense of urgency to exercise a charism, together with perseverance in practice, indicates readiness for maturing commitment to God through the apostolic life. That urgency is an energy pressing up from within the person's inmost being. It differs completely from impatience or impetuosity. Some apostles experience the sense of urgency as a spiritual imperative: "I cannot *not* do this work. I *have to* freely do this." That intensity of apostolic desire and activity is ordinarily a strong indication that God desires the use of a specific charism. Furthermore, such heartfelt zeal implies that the exercise of the charism will contribute to the recipient's own spiritual genesis. Ministerial practice will be for the apostle a matrix of deepening communion with the risen Christ.

Needing to exercise a specific charism is not the same as liking or enjoying a certain ministry. Ordinarily, enthusiasm and gusto do accompany the need to serve, but on occasion what God wants is the very activity that an apostle finds most distasteful. For example, a shy person may find excruciating any service that requires constant interaction with people. Nonetheless, that bitter medicine may be exactly what is necessary for personal growth. The prophet Jeremiah is a case in point (Jer 1:4–10; 20:7–18).

If an apostle remains long enough in a ministry, the first fervor inevitably fades and the initial sense of meaningfulness wanes. Enthusiasm and gusto give way to emptiness and aridity. The apostle struggles at times with feelings of monotony and boredom. In itself, that reversal does not mean that the time has come to find a new apostolate. On the contrary, God could be calling the person to continue the same service, but with a more qualitative stance of faith, hope, and love. The apostle's perseverance then flows primarily from a sense of mission, conviction, and responsibility rather than from emotional surge or tangible satisfaction. Eventually, a renewed sense of purpose will emerge. A subtle joy and peace will prevail. Involvement in ministry then becomes for the apostle a way of decreasing so that Christ can further increase within him or her and within all creation (John 3:30).[3]

---

3. See *Spiritual Journey*, 41, 45–52, 99–113.

A Corresponding Need within a Community

Another dynamic integral to an apostolic vocation is the convergence of personal charism and communal need. Not only does the apostle feel an urgency to exercise a specific charism, but also a segment of creation experiences a corresponding need for the service. God's providence brings together the one sent forth and a community requiring assistance. That convergence of charism and need elicits the apostle's commitment to the community and the community's receptivity to the apostle.

Most people have the capacity to do many things well. Which specific gifts, talents, and skills do they choose to develop? That determination comes about in large part through their encounter with the needs of the world around them. Frequently, it is in perceiving a want within a community that a person becomes aware of an ability and a readiness to minister to that group.

An event in the life of Jesus offers an example. He and his disciples had set off by boat for a solitary place in order to rest awhile. When they reached the location, they discovered there a large crowd waiting for them. Seeing the people's need, Jesus changed his plans and attended to them. "He had compassion on them, because they were like sheep without a shepherd. So he began to teach them many things" (Mark 6:34).

Recognition of the Limits of Ministry

God sets limits to each apostolate. An apostolate entails a specific service, not a nebulous enterprise. It comprises a mission with distinct goals, not a vague mandate without a valued purpose. An apostolate is for the good of a designated segment of creation and is not meant to save the whole of creation all at once. It occurs for a designated duration of time and at a specific location, not just anywhere anytime.

A person's ability to recognize the limits of an apostolic calling and to stay within those boundaries is a further sign of a maturing apostolic vocation. God does not expect one apostle to address all the staggering needs of this world, much less satisfy all people. Jesus himself did not cure every ill at once or create a perfect world over the course of his human life. Each apostle makes a uniquely valuable, yet limited contribution to the advancement of God's reign.

The poverty of spirit of both apostles and the people whom they serve constitutes yet another form of limitation upon effectiveness in ministry. Apostles have only so much time, so much physical, cognitive, and emotional energy, so much talent to expend in works of service. People are capable of listening to and of assimilating just so much. Moreover, numerous situations occur that require of apostles patient and tedious endurance. Countless circumstances exist in which they exercise no obvious influence whatsoever. Having reached their limits, apostles can only entrust to God what is beyond their ability to improve or to change.

Most apostles possess many abilities and talents beyond those necessary for their ministry. In certain situations, a decision to use those additional gifts can be to the detriment of the ministry. For example, a dedicated social worker has good home-repair skills. She takes it upon herself to assist some impoverished clients in fixing the plumbing or the roofing of their homes. Although she has good intentions, she quickly finds herself spread too thin and completely exhausted. Consequently, she cannot keep up to her primary responsibilities as a social worker.

Recognition of limits to ministry is essential for fruitful service to a segment of God's creation. Apostles have to respect the limits of their apostolate or the quality of their service will diminish. Should apostles become engaged in too many endeavors at once, their service tends to deteriorate into sheer busyness. The quality of their ministerial activity becomes superficial, scattered, and impersonal. They find themselves on the road to burnout.

Formation of an Apostolic Lifestyle around Ministry

Involvement in an apostolate requires of a person substantial self-investment and altruism. Service to a segment of God's creation consumes enormous time and energy. Even at a day's end, memories of people and events encountered in ministry tend to filter through an apostle's thoughts, feelings, and prayer.

An apostolate is not separate from the rest of a person's life. To the contrary, it forms a center around which an apostolic life takes shape. Like a magnet with its field of attraction, a ministry draws into its sphere of influence all areas of an apostle's life. Involvement in ministry affects, for example, the apostle's community or family life, leisure, relaxation, solitary and communal prayer, study, and personal relationships. The Spirit guides a person in shaping all aspects of life into an all-embracing and all-penetrating apostolic lifestyle supportive of the apostolate.

An apostolic mode of living exists in a constant state of flux. It is the responsibility of an apostle to work toward keeping in balance all dimensions of an apostolic life, even as that balance is continuously shifting.[4] Each facet of an apostolic life has a vocational life of its own, so to speak. Each facet is in itself a vibrant unfolding reality, whether that be, for instance, personal relationships or participation in recreational activities. Each aspect presents new challenges and unforeseen nuances from day to day. However, an apostolic vocation requires that all these components individually and collectively be kept in right relationship to the apostolate. It takes continual discernment, adaptability, and creativity for an apostle to establish that balance. Striving for that equilibrium situates the apostle at a point of optimal readiness for communion with and witness to the risen Christ.

At least to external appearances, imbalance does prevail occasionally. The genuine demands of ministry could cause an apostle to give insufficient time and attention to other priorities such as solitary prayer or intimacy with a loved one. If the exigencies of an apostolate are truly from God, the situation will be temporary. If the overload of work continues indefinitely, a review of the complexities of the ministry will help the apostle to discern what is from God and what is not. Areas may exist wherein the apostle must say "no" in order to live a deeper "yes."

Explicit Christocentric Quality in Ministry

The ministry of persons who have a maturing sense of vocation to the apostolic life takes on a unique christic quality. For them the person of Jesus, together with the Father and the Spirit, is the origin, the sustaining force, and the goal of all their apostolic works and apostolic living.[5] Christ becoming all in all is the mystery that pervades their entire lives. That christic accent is essentially what distinguishes a ministry from a job, an apostolate from a career, a mission from a profession. "For Christ" makes the difference.

Loving communion with God inspires a person to undertake apostolic activity. God's love manifest in Jesus awakens within the disciple an interior yearning to share with creation the good news of the risen Christ. The disciple's purposefulness, zeal, and joy in ministry and apostolic life flow from and redound to Christ Jesus. All suffering and pain endured for the apostolate and the apostolate life become integrated into transforming union with Christ crucified and risen.

Jesus came to do the will of the Father and to complete his work (John 4:34). Their union was such that the Father was actually completing his own work in and through Jesus: "The words I say to you I do not say from myself.

---

4. See *Contemplation*, 125–40.
5. See *Contemplation*, 133–40.

It is the Father abiding in me who is doing this work" (John 14:10). Furthermore, Jesus revealed that the apostolates of all his followers represent a continuation of and a participation in his own work: "As you, [Father], sent me forth into the world, so I have sent them forth" (John 17:18); "As the Father has sent me, so do I send you" (John 20:21).

Thus, the work of the Father continues through Jesus and through those persons whom Jesus sends forth. Apostles, then, possess some awareness of having been sent forth in their ministry to accomplish an aspect of the Father's intent. They perceive in some measure the Father radiating his compassionate love to creation through their service. In their union with Jesus, they experience the Father continuing his work through their apostolate.

Whatever awareness that apostles have of the fruits of their ministry, their insight is but a minuscule glimpse of the whole truth. God alone knows the full reach and total effectiveness of human apostolic endeavors. The gospel story of the boy who had only seven barley loaves and two fish illustrates how God can use a little to go a long way (John 6:1–15). The child offered to Jesus the loaves and fish to help feed the hungry people. Jesus took those gifts, gave thanks, and from that meager resource distributed enough food to feed the crowd. So bountiful was the food that after the meal leftovers filled many baskets. By the grace of God, the child's small offerings brought sustenance to numerous people. Similarly, God uses the small ordinary works of apostles to produce a superabundance of good for creation.

From a christocentric perspective, this experience lies at the heart of an apostolic vocation: I do not bring Christ to people as if he were not already within them. To be sent to them means that through me Jesus intensifies their awareness of him already present and operative within them and their world. Through my presence and my actions, Christ brings himself forth more fully where he already abides, even if he is as yet unrecognized. Moreover, in my ministering I also receive Christ in and through those persons to whom I am sent.

Thus, ministers are ministered to by their ministry and by the people they serve. Those apostles whose ministry is directed toward care for the environment or care for creatures of the land, the sea, and the sky share also in that christic experience. As apostles minister to creation, the risen Christ ministers to apostles through the segment of creation that they serve.

Growth in the Contemplative Dimension of Apostolic Living

Maturing vocational consciousness and commitment to God through the apostolic life become discernible also in this sign and condition: as a person lives the apostolic life, a contemplative orientation to all aspects of life flourishes.

But how does a person's contemplative thrust relate to being an apostle, having an apostolate, and living an apostolic life?

Contemplative Thrust in Being an Apostle

By virtue of having been created as a child of God, each person has a fundamental openness to God and an inherent orientation toward fullness of life in the risen Christ. That openness to God and that spiritual direction constitute a contemplative thrust innate to each human being.

A contemplative thrust denotes also a person's deliberate stance of attentive listening, loving surrender, and vibrant receptivity toward God. It bespeaks voluntary cooperation with God's initiative throughout life. A contemplative thrust inclines a person toward ever-increasing transformation in God, until in death that individual is "filled with the utter fullness of God" (Eph 3:19).

That contemplative thrust remains alive, active, and developing in each apostle.

Contemplative Thrust in an Apostolate

A contemplative thrust has bearing upon a person's apostolate in these three ways:

First, attentive listening to God is the milieu in which the apostle discerns a calling to a specific ministry. Without a listening heart that is able to discern, a person tends to opt for what is nothing more than ego-generated activity. Even after discernment affirms a calling to a particular apostolate, it is essential that a person's attitude of listening like a disciple persist each day.

Second, apostolic work itself has an innate contemplative dimension. A person's activity of providing a service is a mode of contemplative communion with God and with all in God. It is an expression of communion because God is sending forth the apostle to accomplish the work out of love and for the good of creation. The Father and Jesus go on working, and so does an apostle in union with them and in the continuation of their mission.

Apostolate, understood as a mode of contemplative communion, does not imply that apostles must be every moment thinking of God, talking to God, or feeling God's presence, as they merely go through the motions of their work. On the contrary, the contemplative dimension of an apostolate demands of people unwavering focus upon what they are doing. Apostles commune with God by immersing themselves wholeheartedly in the task at hand, by focusing all their energies upon the work to be accomplished, by putting their mind, heart, and soul creatively to the endeavor. They do so for the sake of Christ and the gospel.

Third, not only is an apostle's good intention and active labor important, but also the qualitative completion of a mission contributes in a contemplative way to the building up of the Body of Christ. The fruitful outcome of an apostle's effort and labor serves to advance God's reign in this world and in the world to come.

Pierre Teilhard de Chardin spoke eloquently of the contemplative fruitfulness of work itself:

> Any increase that I bring upon myself or upon things is trans-
> lated into some increase in my power to love and into some
> progress in Christ's blessed hold upon the universe. . . . Through
> our work, we complete in ourselves the subject of divine union.
> And through it again, we somehow make grow in stature the
> divine term of the One with whom we are united, Our Lord
> Jesus Christ.[6]

Contemplative Thrust within an Apostolic Lifestyle

The contemplative thrust within an apostle and within the apostolate extends also to the apostolic life. As an apostle matures spiritually, an apostolic lifestyle becomes increasingly for that individual a mode of contemplative communion with God. An apostle lives and moves and exists in God. All that the person is becoming and all that person does unfold in union with the risen Christ.

Because the work reflects the divine will and because the lifestyle accords with God's design, an apostle grows in self-surrender to God through an apostolic vocation. A maturing contemplative orientation in being an apostle, in having an apostolate, and in living an apostolic life could be described in this manner:

6. *Divine Milieu*, 32.

In Christ Jesus:
I am. I am becoming.
I think. I act. I do. I love. I feel. I eat. I sleep.
I pray. I play. I relate.
I encounter all creation anew each day.
In Christ Jesus:
My apostolic identity, work, and lifestyle
constitute a revelation of love,
a countenance of love,
a fruit of love, a profession of love.
In Christ Jesus:
My vocation to be an apostle,
to have an apostolate,
and to live an apostolic lifestyle
is love incarnate, love enfleshed,
love present
here and now.

CHAPTER 8

Apostolic Expressions of Christian Virtues

IN THE PREVIOUS CHAPTER, we considered principles for discernment of an apostolic vocation. The concomitant presence of those signs and conditions, together with continued growth in each of those areas, gives indication of a person's maturing vocational awareness and commitment to God through an apostolic mode of living.

We take up now another area of significance in the apostolic life: the practice of Christian virtues. We refer to "virtues" in the broad sense of attitudes, qualities, or values that promote the development of a person's self-identity, ministry, and lifestyle for the sake of Jesus and the gospel. Exercise of the virtues is integral to each Christian lifestyle. Yet the modalities of a specific virtue vary according to the nature of the vocational lifestyle in which it is practiced. Take chastity, for example. Marital chastity differs radically in expression and content from celibate chastity. Chastity as practiced in the single life is distinct from the forms of chastity appropriate to marriage and celibacy.

In this chapter, we consider Christian virtues in their apostolic expression. By the phrase "apostolic expression" we mean, for example, the way in which an apostle practices faith through action or exercises hope in the midst of turmoil. We do not intend to offer a comprehensive description of all virtues in their apostolic expressions. We limit ourselves to the following selection: love, community, faith, hope, receptivity and obedience to God, prayerfulness, a holistic orientation to life, study, poverty, leisure, and self-sacrifice. Furthermore, we highlight only a few prominent features of the apostolic expression of each of those virtues.

When apostles review their practice of the virtues, they gain insight into the quality of their apostolic orientation to life. Moreover, their reflection upon a virtue or series of virtues can be a tool for examination of conscience in relation to God and creation.

Love

Love the Lord your God with your whole heart,
with your whole soul,
with all your mind,
and with all your strength. . . .
And love your neighbor as yourself.

(MARK 12:30–31)

With those words, Jesus made love of God and love of neighbor inseparable for his disciples. On that occasion, he identified self-love as the model for love of neighbor: "Love your neighbor as yourself." Elsewhere, he beckoned his disciples beyond self-love as the norm for love of neighbor to that of loving one's neighbor with his own love: "Love one another as I have loved you" (John 15:12).

Astonishingly, Jesus revealed also that his love for his disciples is the same love with which the Father loves the Son: "As the Father has loved me, so I have loved you" (John 15:9).

The New Testament uses the Greek word *agapē* and its cognates to designate God's love for humankind, together with a human being's love for God, self, neighbor, and all creation. *Agapē* is the core of all spiritual development and all maturation in the apostolic life.[1] *Agapē* is also the soul of the apostolate. The Spirit pours forth God's love into the hearts of those persons called to the apostolic life. The Spirit enables apostles to grow in the ability to love with God's own love. When apostles love as Christ loves—that is, as the Father loves the Son and as Jesus loves with the Father's love—there is but "one Christ loving himself."[2]

Love of neighbor receives special emphasis in apostolic living. Involvement on a sustained basis with numerous people is a daily occurrence for apostles. Constant availability to people requires of apostles compassion, kindness, hospitality, affability, tolerance, forgiveness, and patience. Apostles give their time, their words, and their works. Above all, they give of themselves in love to their neighbor. They listen to and empathize with those whom they serve. They laugh with them in their joy and mourn with them in their sorrow. They remain poor with those who are powerless and stand firm with those who are strong. That availability and adaptability

---

1. See *Spiritual Journey,* 191–98.
2. Augustine, "Commentary on 1 John 5:1–3." *PL,* 35:2055.

recall St. Paul's concept of an apostle becoming "all things to all people" (1 Cor 9:22).

Community

Father, may they be one in us
as you are in me and as I am in you. . . .
With me in them and you in me,
may they be completely one.

(JOHN 17:21–23)

Ultimately, community refers to interrelatedness in Christ Jesus as members of the one family of God (Matt 18:20; Acts 1:14, 4:32). Community includes not only human beings, but also every living creature. All creation is one in the risen Christ. Even so, we highlight in this context the community of humankind.

An apostolic vocation is by nature community oriented. The first experience of community for most people consists of membership in a family unit and participation in family life. As persons move through childhood, adolescence, and young adulthood, their experience of community expands beyond the family circle to membership in a variety of groups with diverse purposes. Many opportunities present themselves throughout those early experiences of community for parents and educators to instill Christian values in young people and to guide them as they attempt to put those values into practice. That Christian formation invites children and adolescents to a mode of living that embodies increasingly the rudiments of an apostolic life.

The communal dimension of the apostolic life gives rise to apostolic communities. Various modalities of community are possible in adult apostolic living. Expressions of community include, for example, institutes and societies of consecrated life, groups that offer specialized services, and associations of spiritual formation personnel or spiritual directors. Local parishes and churches are themselves apostolic communities. Whatever their specific nature, apostolic communities comprise dynamic hubs in and through which apostles accomplish their mission. When based upon gospel values, those communities are centers wherein members share life with each other and pray together. Those communities extend hospitality, care, and compassion not only to their own members, but also to all persons who seek out their friendship and assistance.

Apostles are drawn to form bonds of community with other people. Socialization, togetherness, and camaraderie are routine aspects of their vocational lifestyle. However, community living is not necessarily what is sometimes termed "the common life," wherein everyone lives together under the same roof and engages together in the same daily routine. Indeed, community living challenges its members frequently to uncommon valor, commitment, and perseverance.

Faith

The life I live now I live in faith, faith in the Son of God,
who loved me and gave himself up for me.

(GAL 2:20)

All Christian pilgrims—married, celibate, or single; apostles, contemplatives, or hermits—journey in dark faith.[3]

In the apostolic life, faith in Jesus sustains the weary and sometimes anxious wayfarer through the constant surprises and ever-changing circumstances characteristic of most ministries.

For an apostle to become too settled, too organized, or too institutionalized militates against evolving faith in Jesus. The apostolic life requires creative experimentation. An apostle risks constant flux, not only welcoming it in faith but also working resourcefully with chaos and instability. Faith inspires an apostle to leave nothing undared and nothing untried for the sake of Christ and the gospel.

Hope

Love hopes all.

(1 COR 13:6)

Hope frees the human heart so that it can yearn for God in God's own self.[4]

---

3. See *O Blessed Night*, 89–97; 147–53; *Spiritual Journey*, 173–80.
4. See *Spiritual Journey*, 181–90.

The virtue of hope helps apostles prioritize the constantly changing elements of both their ministry and their mode of living. Hope sustains perseverance in times of trial and suffering. Hope keeps God in place—central to all that apostles are supposedly doing for God. Hope maintains their activities, ambitions, and energies in proper relation to the risen Christ and to the varied dimensions of his calling.

Receptivity and Obedience to God

The one who comes to me,

and listens to my words,

and acts on them . . .

is like a person who built a house on rock.

(LUKE 6:47–48)

Apostles come to Jesus and listen to him. They also obey him by acting upon his words. Loving receptivity to Jesus and active collaboration with him are simultaneously operative in an apostolic lifestyle. Those two components work together, thereby enabling apostles to be effective instruments of the Spirit.

Apostles both let God's will *be done* and they *do* God's will. Yet, apostles tend to set their minds and hearts principally upon doing the divine will.[5] They have a passionate desire to implement the will of the One who has sent them forth. They witness in a singular way to the missionary aspect of Jesus's life (John 4:34).

Discernment is essential to obedience. Discernment pertains more to doing God's will than to letting it be done. If Jesus desires a person to do something specific for him, he has first to indicate to that individual what to do and, if need be, how to do it. Often, discernment requires of an apostle endless listening, long meetings, lengthy discussions, and prolonged service on many committees. Those painstaking activities are integral to discernment in the apostolic life.

5. See *Called by God*, 13–18.

Prayerfulness

Remain in my love.

(JOHN 15:9)

Communion with God animates apostles, their apostolates, and their apostolic life. A variety of prayer forms sustains apostolic living.

Apostles engage in solitary, personal, and private prayer (whether discursive or contemplative).[6] Many apostles set aside an extended time, such as an hour daily, to be alone with God. That practice follows the example of Jesus, who "would always go off to some place where he could be alone and pray" (Luke 5:16). Most apostles participate on a regular basis also in communal or familial prayer, liturgical worship, and devotional prayer.

The Eucharist as a way of prayer holds immense significance for many people who live an apostolic life, especially those people who participate in Christian traditions wherein liturgical celebration of the sacraments is central to the faith experience. The Eucharist is the sacrament par excellence of the emerging contemplative element in each apostle's life.[7] Many apostles like to pray as members of a small group in the presence of the Blessed Sacrament—either in silence, in words, or with both forms of prayer interspersed. Other apostles prefer for their extended time of prayer to be physically alone in a solitary chapel before a tabernacle containing the Eucharist.

Mass nurtures perseverance in the apostolic life. It provides daily bread in many respects. At Mass, God's living word nourishes apostles. There they celebrate with a Christian community solidarity with pilgrims of all times and places. They re-present in the Celebration of the Eucharist the Passover of Jesus. They unite their daily passover with that of the risen Christ. They celebrate in sacramental form their abiding communion with the indwelling Father, Son, and Spirit. These apostles make participation at Mass a priority, even when they do not feel like celebrating it or appear not to have time for it.

A great temptation in the apostolic life is to make all prayer time a perfunctory exercise or to procrastinate solitary prayer until one feels better disposed. In some circumstances, an apostle reduces solitary prayer to snatches here and there, or even abandons it entirely. An apostle finds excuses on occasion also to cut back on communal, liturgical, and devotional forms of prayer, or even to avoid those ways of prayer altogether.

---

6. See *Contemplation*, 126–31.

7. See *Spiritual Journey*, 125–31; *Divine Milieu*, 99–107.

Holistic Orientation

Be renewed in the spirit of your mind,
and put on the new person, created like God
in righteousness and in holiness of the truth.

(EPH 4:23–24)

People with a holistic orientation to life behold something of the interrelationship of all things. They concern themselves primarily with wholes and with complete systems, rather than with individual components of an entity. For example, they see a human being as a living organism who is more than the sum of all the separate dimensions of personhood. They perceive the interconnectedness and the interdependence of the physical, spiritual, mental, volitional, emotional, sexual, psychological, and social aspects of human existence. They view a human being as a participant in a network of inclusive relationships with the surrounding world.

In living an apostolic life, a person grows in the image and likeness of God. The Spirit initiates and sustains within a person a constant expansion of personhood and renewal of outlook toward life. In so doing, God invites a person to a holistic outlook toward not only human existence but also all creation. Thus, apostles hold in esteem the integrity of creation. Interconnectedness, interdependence, and inclusivity become fundamental to all their relationships. Responsible enjoyment of creatures and care for creation as a whole are for them cherished values. Each creature is from God and according to its nature directed to God. Even the smallest creature witnesses something of God's love. Consequently, apostles grow in the conviction that any abuse or selfish use of creatures is counter to God's purpose.

Apostles who have a holistic orientation to life recognize that any good work can take on a quality of mission and ministry. They seek to do all for the glory of God (1 Cor 10:31). They learn to see as God sees. They are among the pure of heart who see God in all things (Matt 5:8). They work for justice and they promote peace (Matt 5:6, 9).

Study

The knowledge that I have is imperfect.
But then I shall know as fully as I am known.

(1 COR 13:12)

Each pilgrim's faith seeks some understanding.

Apostles are called by God to be of service to the faith of other people. Therefore, thorough study, persistent rethinking of the mysteries of salvation, and conscientious acceptance of intellectual challenge are essential undertakings for apostles.[8] It takes deliberate intent to set aside blocks of time for continuing study. It takes self-discipline for faith to persevere in seeking understanding. When apostles neglect sustained in-depth study, they drift easily into mediocrity, complacency, prejudice, and a know-it-all attitude.

Adaptation of the gospel to specific cultures, of worship to local customs, and of theologies to pastoral issues pertains to the essence of mission. But how can apostles accomplish that task if they do not reflect profoundly upon their faith, upon the culture and subcultures in which they are immersed, and upon the pastoral situations of those whom they serve?

Poverty

You know the grace of our Lord Jesus Christ,
that though he was rich, for your sake he became poor,
so that through his poverty you might become rich.

(2 COR 8:9)

Apostles become truly rich by becoming poor as Jesus was poor. His poverty holds the riches of Christian life.

The virtue of poverty pertains to an apostle's relationship to material things. For practical purposes, we distinguish three concepts related to poverty in the apostolic life: *simplicity* (having what is actually useful for oneself and one's mission); *frugality* (having merely what is necessary); *austerity* (having only the bare essentials).

Jesus gave explicit instructions to his apostles on how to go forth on their mission: "Take nothing for the journey: neither staff, nor sack, nor bread, nor money, not even a spare tunic" (Luke 9:3). Translated into contemporary expression, that text might read like this: Don't be dependent on your wheels, your trusty TV, PC, RV, smart phones, or video devices. You don't need expensive luggage full of fine clothing, jewelry, and cosmetics. I am all you need. And all I need is you in your poverty of spirit, gentleness, and grief (Matt 5: 3–5), in your hunger and thirst for holiness, justice, and peace (Matt 5:6–7, 9–10). You don't need gimmicks or tricks, flash

---

8. See *Contemplation*, 131–33.

or pomp. Be single-hearted. Be frugal. Be content with the essentials. Be yourself, with me in you.

Leisure

Come to me,
all you who labor and are overburdened,
and I will give you rest.

(MATT 11:28)

In common parlance, the word "leisure" refers to the freedom provided by a reduction in work or by a cessation of activities. Leisure is distinct from idleness. Leisure denotes restful well-being in a peace-filled space. Leisure offers people the opportunity to tap into creative energies that ferment within and around them. Idleness implies dissipation, shiftlessness, and laziness. The virtue of leisure bears fruit in holiness. There is a time-honored Latin phrase: "*In otio, deificari*" [In leisure, one is deified].[9]

Leisure animates every facet of an apostolic life. Leisure becomes evident in manifold ways: in presence to oneself, to people, to nonhuman creation, and to God; in attentiveness of mind and heart to whatever task is at hand; in the appropriate balance of all the diverse aspects of daily life—just to cite a few examples.

An apostle's failure to recognize the limits of a God-given mission, together with subsequent overextension in ministry, tends to destroy the spirit of leisure. Every apostle is called to make a real but comparatively small contribution to building up the Body of Christ. Whether as individuals or as a group, apostles are not saviors of the world. The demands that exist are virtually limitless. There is no end in sight to what needs to be done. Nevertheless, what God wants any one person to accomplish is limited to a definite time frame: a twenty-four-hour day and a brief lifespan.

Leisure is a virtue that invigorates all ministerial activity. Yet leisure in the apostolic life requires also intervals of freedom from ministry. Time apart from work not only makes good common sense, but also is necessary for nurturance of familial relationships and friendships, for personal health and well-being, for solitary prayer, for study, and for perseverance in apostolic living.

9. Augustine, *Letter X. PL*, 33:71.

Self-Sacrifice

Anyone who loses one's life
for my sake
will find it.

(MATT 10:39)

To sacrifice means to do something that apart from love one would never dream of doing or to abstain from something that except for love one would never imagine foregoing.

Apostles pour themselves out in loving service to God and creation. That self-giving entails self-sacrifice. The wholehearted engagement of apostles in the mission entrusted to them itself imposes a formidable asceticism. Their determination to do their best consistently requires fidelity to high standards of self-discipline, good intent, honest labor, and fruitful outcome. Every effort or success costs something in terms of their personal talents, time, and energy. To choose one direction means to give up the opportunity to pursue another attraction. The process of bringing about the fulfillment of a mission exerts a deeply purifying effect upon any narcissism and egotism within an apostle. In turn, that purification facilitates the apostle's advancement in transforming union with Christ Jesus.[10] To lose one's life for the sake of Jesus is to find transformed life.

The "so am I and more" of St. Paul (2 Cor 11:22–29) is the constant refrain of each missionary. In other words, the steadfast promise of each missionary is this:

Because I am about the Father's business,

I will strive to do my utmost in the work

that he sends me forth to accomplish.

I will persevere in the mission, despite the hardships involved.

I will be true to the end, even if in pragmatic terms I fail.

10. See *Divine Milieu*, 17–43 (especially 37–43).

CHAPTER 9

Concluding Pastoral Observations on the Apostolic Life

EACH CHRISTIAN HAS APOSTOLIC, contemplative, and eremitic inclinations. All three orientations persist in a person throughout life. Yet, dependent upon God's calling of a person, one of those thrusts becomes the catalyst for the formation of a vocational lifestyle. In that respect, all Christians live initially an apostolic life, and most of them continue that mode of living for the remainder of their lives. However, the contemplative orientation comes to dominate in some Christians, and emphasis on apostolic involvement then gives way to communion with God and creation by means of a contemplative life. A few of those with a contemplative vocation find the eremitic thrust becoming the most pronounced influence. These contemplatives make a transition to an eremitic lifestyle.

The concept "apostolic" has rich biblical roots and many points of reference throughout history. Drawing upon those sources, we understand the word "apostolic" and its cognates this way:

- An *apostle* is a person whom God sends forth to fulfill a mission. "Apostle" pertains to self-identity. It bespeaks an aspect of *who* God calls a person to be and to become.

- An *apostolate* is the ministry or service to which God sends an apostle. "Apostolate" relates to *what* God sends an apostle forth to do.

- *The apostolic life* is a Christian vocational lifestyle that enables and supports an apostle's service to a segment of creation for the sake of Jesus and the gospel. "Apostolic life" refers to *how* an apostle is to live in relation to an apostolate.

In accord with their vocation, apostles direct their energies toward these goals:

- They seek to awaken in people an increasing awareness of the risen Christ present within all creation and to call forth in people a heightened attentiveness to the Spirit's transforming activity within them and all around them.

- They desire to receive Christ already present wherever they are sent.

Thus, apostles minister to a segment of creation, and in turn the risen Jesus ministers to them through that community.

Becoming an apostle, doing apostolic work, and living an apostolic life entail a lengthy process of development. The presence of an apostolic vocation tends to produce within a person the following discernible effects:

- an inclination toward service for the sake of Jesus and the gospel;

- the reception and development of a charism, which the apostle needs to use for personal growth and for the good of creation;

- the recognition of a corresponding need within a community, plus its welcoming of the apostle's assistance;

- awareness of the scope of a mission and perseverance in staying within the parameters of a calling to ministerial activity;

- development of an apostolic way of life, with service as the nucleus;

- an explicit christocentric orientation in ministry;

- growth in the contemplative dimension of being an apostle, engaging in an apostolate, and living an apostolic lifestyle.

That ensemble of signs and conditions indicates maturing vocational consciousness within a person, together with advancing capacity for long-term commitment to God through the apostolic life.

Additional affirmation of an apostolic vocation comes to the fore in a person's habitual way of practicing Christian virtues. Those virtues include, but are not limited to, the following: love, community, faith, hope, receptivity and obedience to God, prayerfulness, a holistic orientation to life, study, poverty, leisure, and self-sacrifice. As an apostle practices the virtues, each virtue takes on an expression specific to the experience of an apostolic mode of living.

In the case of a person who seeks membership in an apostolically oriented institute or society of consecrated life, all the above signs and conditions apply. Moreover, in that situation additional principles of discernment related to the unique charism of the community of interest require attention. Each apostolic religious institute or society has its own understanding of the nature of its charism, together with a knowledge of the signs and conditions that indicate a neophyte's compatibility with the group's charism. For the most part that area is beyond the scope of this study. We leave that dimension of vocational discernment to the wisdom and expertise of formation personnel in those communities.

The presence of the above signs and conditions of a call to the apostolic life, together with growth in the apostolic practice of Christian virtues, does not give *proof* that a person is maturing in vocational awareness, response, and commitment to God. Of all the factors involved in a person's decision for long-term or lifelong commitment to God through the apostolic life, the ultimate determining factor in a discernment process is faith—faith motivated by love, faith seeking understanding and attentive to signs, but dark risk-filled faith nonetheless.

Closure on any discernment process marks not only a completion, but also a new beginning. With a maturing sense of vocational consciousness and commitment to God through the apostolic life, apostles continue forward on their journey, always eager to fulfill the mandate of Jesus: "Go into all the world, and proclaim the good news to all creation" (Mark 16:15).

Part Three: The Contemplative Life

CHAPTER 10

A Christocentric and Trinitarian Love

IN THIS SECTION OF our work, we take up the discernment of vocations to the contemplative life. By the phrase *the contemplative life*, we refer to a vocational mode of living dedicated to the contemplation of God. We understand *contemplation* basically as a person's wordless and imageless communion in faith, hope, and love with God and with all creation in God. Contemplation in that sense is the vitalizing energy, the reason for being, and the organizing principle of a contemplative lifestyle. *A contemplative* is a person called by God to a contemplative mode of living that flows from and redounds to contemplation of the Risen Jesus.

Within Christianity, there are long-standing contemplative traditions, some of which go back over a thousand years. Contemporary expressions of the contemplative life, as found in urban centers, rural areas, and out-of-the-way places, contribute to the richness of that history. Our study focuses on the core features of a vocation to the contemplative life, irrespective of the specific tradition or milieu in which it is lived. Each contemplative group will have additional signs and conditions unique to its specific charism.

Most people aspiring to the contemplative life are already consecrated celibates in their hearts, if not formally so by professed vow. Certain single persons experience a calling to the contemplative life. In each such case that we have encountered in our ministry, the single person was moving already toward a celibate consecration. Although rare, a married person could experience a vocation to live the contemplative life, even as that individual continues to be a fully committed spouse and parent (if there are children).

The principles of vocational discernment that we present for the contemplative life are observable in people from diverse backgrounds who are called by God to this lifestyle: married, celibate, or single persons; clergy, religious, or laity; monks or nuns. The signs and conditions indicative of a contemplative vocation manifest themselves in contemplatives who live alone, in a community, or in a family, whether in a city, on a prairie, on a mountain top, at the water's edge, or in a desert.

We explored in earlier works various dimensions of the contemplative orientation innate to each human being, including God's calling of every person to contemplation by virtue of the universal call to holiness.[1] Some of the content in this section on the contemplative life has relevance for any person whom God has awakened to a realization of that contemplative thrust, whatever the individual's vocational lifestyle or combination of lifestyles. In this section though, we relate that content specifically to a calling to the contemplative life. When features of a principle of discernment differ significantly from group to group—for example, married persons in contradistinction to celibates—we indicate that fact.

We organize the content of this section into two areas. First, we identify principles to guide a person in discernment prior to entering the contemplative life (chapters 10 to 14). Second, we describe principles that authenticate perseverance as a person actually lives the contemplative life (chapters 15 to 18). These two areas have points of overlap. Nonetheless, this division remains helpful in relating the principles of discernment to a person's evolving contemplative experience. We conclude this section on the contemplative life with a summary of our pastoral observations (chapter 19).

The love of God manifest in Christ Jesus is the heart and soul of any contemplative vocation. Being-in-love with God impels a contemplative to enter upon the contemplative life and to persevere in it.

In this chapter, we consider two principles of discernment that emphasize the christocentric and trinitarian aspects of an aspiring contemplative's being-in-love with God:

- The aspirant experiences a profound, intimate, and loving relationship with Jesus.

- The aspirant has a sense of the indwelling Trinity.

The Profound, Intimate, Loving Relationship with Jesus

A first principle in discerning a possible call to embark upon a contemplative life is the presence within a person of a profound, intimate, loving relationship with Jesus as the eternally begotten Son of the Father and Co-Spirator of the Holy Spirit. By virtue of the universal call to holiness,

1. See *Contemplation*, 97–109; *O Blessed Night*, 94–97; *Spiritual Journey*, 89–95, 114–24.

all people are called to that quality of contemplative relationship with God, at least in death.[2] Obviously, not all people receive a vocation to the contemplative life.

Relational

The eternal Word-Made-Flesh is the sole reason for being of the Christian contemplative life. Jesus, the risen Christ, becomes increasingly the center of a contemplative's identity, the wellspring of all affections and desires, the focus of all thoughts and occupations. That depth of relationship with Jesus permeates every aspect of a contemplative's mode of becoming, including prayer, lifestyle, personal interactions, and activities. "Christ becoming all in all" (Col 3:11) is the mantra of the Christian contemplative.

Most aspiring contemplatives do not start off with full-fledged single-ness of heart toward Christ Jesus. Nevertheless, they must at least desire it and be growing into it before it is prudent for them to embark upon a contemplative lifestyle.

That singleness of heart does not imply that the Incarnate Word eradicates a person's other loves and substitutes himself in their place. To the contrary, in Christ all the contemplative's special affections remain present. In God each of those loves gradually reaches maturity. When Jesus called his disciples to love God with their whole heart (Matt 22:37), he was speaking par excellence of the contemplative thrust within each person. He was referring to the human heart not as devoid of natural loves and attractions, but as full of them. Thus, contemplatives do not divest themselves of their affections in order to substitute God in their place. Contemplatives are in love with Christ with their whole being and with all their other loves. Contemplatives retain in Jesus all their affections, with their maturities and immaturities, with their joys and pains. They let the Spirit purify those affections and transform them in Jesus's own love.[3]

Therefore, the following questions need to be explored thoroughly in discerning a person's readiness to begin living a contemplative lifestyle:

What is the aspirant really seeking? Is the person fixated on the contemplative life as an end in itself? Or is the aspirant's yearning directed toward relationship with Jesus, together with the Father and the Spirit? Does the aspirant relate to Jesus as the One with whom he or she is in love? Does the aspirant relate to the contemplative life as the ambiance in which to live out that communion?

2. See *Contemplation*, 13–20.
3. See *O Blessed Night*, 171–77.

Does the aspirant bring to that loving communion all personal desires and loves so that they can reach their fulfillment in God? Or is the aspirant looking for an impersonal, abstract deity with the power to eradicate rather than fulfill human desires and loves?

Profound

Experience of Jesus has to be profound if an aspirant is to thrive in the contemplative life. Encounter with the risen Christ needs to be immediate, direct, and interior. Contemplatives cannot induce this direct communion. They receive it. It comes at God's initiative and remains God's free gift to them. The immediacy of the encounter does not completely exclude communion with God by means of thoughts, symbols, images, gestures, or feelings. Nonetheless, those means no longer hold primary importance, and over time they become less and less significant.

Through profound interpersonal encounter with God, contemplatives come face to face with what is deepest, most mysterious, and most ineffable in Jesus: his humanity, his divinity, his interrelatedness with the Father and the Spirit. Contemplatives come to discover also their own inner depths and the uniqueness of their identity in God.

What then is the nature of an aspirant's encounter with Christ Jesus? Is it generally profound or mostly superficial? Is the communion with him immediate and direct, at least at times? Or is encounter with Jesus primarily through the mediation of images, feelings, and thoughts? Does the aspirant know Jesus firsthand or principally through the witness, teachings, and writings of other Christians?

Experience of Christ in a mediated manner is typical of the early stages of spiritual genesis.[4] Moreover, the instrumentality of both people and nonhuman creation in relation to God endures throughout each person's spiritual journey. Mediated encounter with Jesus, however, does not suffice to sustain a person in the contemplative life.

Intimate and Loving

This profound relationship with Christ Jesus is also intimate and loving to the point of familiarity. Contemplative familiarity evokes the closeness of soul friends and the communion of lovers. The contemplative and Jesus are not only friends loving one another, but they are also in love with each

---

4. See *Spiritual Journey*, 75–88.

other. Theirs is a relationship of lover and Beloved (*amada y Amado*),[5] of bride and Groom (*esposa y Esposo*).[6]

The distinction between the "Jesus of history" and the "Christ of faith" adds a nuance to this note of intimacy. The contemplative experience of Jesus Christ does not neglect the faith dimensions of the incarnation and resurrection—that "Jesus is Lord" (1 Cor 12:3). Rather, it brings into focus the human, the down-to-earth, the historical personage of the eternal Word to the point of familiar intimacy. To the contemplative, Jesus is real though wholly intangible. He is human though utterly mysterious, fully immanent, and entirely transcendent at the same time. A contemplative experiences Jesus as intimately personal—my Beloved—and also as the universal Christ, the cosmic Christ. The contemplative confesses to this paradox: From one perspective, I interrelate with Jesus so deeply, intimately, and lovingly that my whole being surrenders to him. From another perspective, I do not "know" him at all.

Does the aspiring contemplative then experience being loved by Christ Jesus and being-in-love with him? Does there exist between the aspirant and Jesus a mutual interchange of intimacy and tenderness? We cannot even begin to speak of a possible contemplative vocation apart from that depth of familiarity.

The aspiring contemplative does not have to be always feeling or thinking about this intimacy. The activity of loving transpires usually with utmost subtleness in the midst of unimaginable interior darkness, aridity, and emptiness. Intervals occur wherein, because of intense struggle and confusion, a contemplative loses all perception of loving and being loved. Even as that happens, intimacy continues, but on a level deeper than human awareness can penetrate. The presence of anxiety about not loving God rightly itself indicates that the person does indeed love. Only sincere love can elicit the desire to love more and the concern over not loving enough.[7]

---

5. See St. John of the Cross, poem *En una noche oscura* (In a Dark Night), stanza 5: *amada en el Amado transformada* (lover transformed in the Beloved). John consistently refers to the human person in the feminine because *alma* (soul) is feminine in Spanish. We chose the word "Beloved" rather than "Lover" in reference to Jesus, because "beloved" bespeaks his identity as revealed at his baptism (Mark 1:11) and transfiguration (Mark 9:8).

6. St. John of the Cross composed the poem *El cántico espiritual (Spiritual Canticle)* as a dialogue between the soul and the Bridegroom.

7. See *Contemplation*, 65–68; *Spiritual Journey*, 104–8.

Mutual Indwelling in Love

An intimate loving relationship between a contemplative and Jesus assumes the quality of mutual indwelling: I remain in him as he remains in me. I make my home in his love. I remain loving my Beloved with the same love with which he loves me.[8] That mutual indwelling in love has depths so profound that a person becomes Christ by participation in him: "I live now, no longer I, but Christ lives in me" (Gal 2:20).

Mutual indwelling in love is the matrix in which a contemplative journeys in the Spirit with Jesus to the Father.[9] Should people attempt to attain oneness with the risen Christ without being in love, union tends to elude them.

Some eastern philosophies seem to conceive of oneness with the divine as a return to a common base by means of suppression, negation, and withdrawal.[10] They seek union with the deity by retreating from the effort toward individuation and personalization that christogenesis requires.[11] Thus, emphasis upon absorption of self into the divinity replaces attention to maximum differentiation of the person and God as the individual is transformed in God. Such approaches could lead one to go to great lengths in prayer, for example, to produce by sheer willpower a mental, emotional, and psychological void or blank state. Motivation for that feat is often a belief that absence of all distraction or sensory awareness equals the presence of God.[12]

In the Christian faith tradition, to lose one's life is to find it. To die to self is to become one's true self. To become now "no longer I, but Christ living in me" is to reach the pinnacle of self-identity and individuation through transforming union with God.

The Eucharist

A profound, intimate, loving relationship with Christ Jesus evokes a reverence and an appreciation for the Eucharist within many aspirants to the contemplative life—especially participants in Christian faith traditions that emphasize liturgical celebration of the sacraments.[13] We include in refer-

---

8. See John 15:4, 9; *Contemplation*, 21–26, 39–40.

9. See *Spiritual Direction*, 20–23; *O Blessed Night*, 57–68; 171–77.

10. See *O Blessed Night*, 123–26.

11. *Christogenesis* refers to the transformation of the person in Christ by love.

12. See *Contemplation*, 36–37.

13. See *Spiritual Journey*, 125–31.

ence to the Eucharist: Mass (Celebration of the Eucharist), the reception of Communion, and the reservation of the Blessed Sacrament.

Mass is the symbol par excellence of the paschal mystery of Jesus. His incarnation, life, passion, death, and resurrection become sacramentally present and operative in space and time during the Celebration of the Eucharist. Reception of Holy Communion at Mass enacts the welcoming of the Trinity present within the deepest recesses of each person, within the gathered assembly, and within all creation. Reservation of the Eucharist in a tabernacle signifies the accompaniment of the Risen Jesus with the communicant, the Christian community, and all creation on the daily journey to God the Creator.

Yet true contemplatives exercise freedom of spirit. They do not feel compelled to pray before the Blessed Sacrament when their inner prompting is to pray outdoors or in the privacy of their rooms. They do not feel guilty when they choose to spend time in solitude rather than to attend several Masses. The triune God is really present within each person's inmost being. Christ inhabits and indwells each soul. The Eucharist is a privileged witness to that presence, not a replacement for it. The Eucharist is the symbol of the divine indwelling, not a substitute for it.

Jesus, God, Trinity

A person not accustomed to the contemplative perspective may find confusing the constant switching back and forth among divine names such as "Jesus," "Christ," "God," and "Trinity". From the viewpoint of Christian contemplative practice, that interchange is spontaneous. Most classical writers in the western mystical tradition give evidence of this interchange of divine names. There is even a certain biblical counterpart to this practice. For example, Jesus affirms: "The Father and I are one" (John 10:30). St. Paul uses often the designation "God" where we might otherwise say "Father" (Rom 8:14–17; 1 Cor 1:9; Phil 2:6–11).

God is Father, Son, and Spirit. Each member of the Trinity is God. The Father is in the Son and in the Spirit, while the Son and the Spirit remain in the Father. Jesus is in the Father and in the Spirit. The Father and the Spirit abide in him. The Spirit is the Spirit of the Father and the Son, and the Spirit dwells in them. When we call upon the Son, we call upon the Father and the Spirit. When Jesus died for us, God died for us. Father, Son, and Spirit have redeemed us and are transforming us in God. To be christified means to be deified. To be transformed in the likeness of Christ (2 Cor 3:18) is to become divinized. Contemplatives experience intuitively and personally the interrelatedness, the harmony, and the unity of the Trinity.

A Sense of the Indwelling Trinity

The word "sense" in this context does not refer to a feeling or to anything specifically sensate. On the contrary, it denotes a delicate and intuitive appreciation, as in the expression "sense of mystery" or "sense of faith." It is a presentiment that impresses itself from within a person or an awareness that wells up out of a person's inner depths. Its source is a loving Presence, Someone intimate and compelling.

God as Trinity

The Trinity dwells within each person. God—Father, Son, and Spirit— makes a home within every human being. God abides within us, transforming, enlightening, and purifying us so that we can receive fullness of life (John 15:4–5).

God is the Almighty, the "I AM," the Transcendent One. But God is also the Loving Creator, the Word-Made-Flesh, and the Breath of Love who dwell within each one of us. God is more intimate to us than we are to ourselves.

Who is God? God is Father, Son, and Spirit. Who is the Father? The Father is *Abba*: intimate, loving, personal. Who is the Son? He is the Christ: Jesus, our Beloved, our Brother, and our Savior. Who is the Spirit? The Spirit is the Paraclete: the Advocate, the Comforter, the vivifying Breath of Love.

What are Father, Son, and Spirit? Each is God. Therefore, each is Love (1 John 4:8, 16), each is Light (1 John 1:5), each is Spirit (John 4:24). Father, Son, and Spirit abide within us. They indwell us. Love, Light, and Spirit live in us.[14]

Faith, Hope, Love

The Father generates the Son from all eternity. The Father generates the Son also in time, in space, in each person, and in all creation.

That generative activity of God constitutes the gifts of faith and hope within us. What we experience as faith and hope is an aspect of the eternal inner life of the Trinity reproducing itself within us in time and space. Our faith in God is the Father generating his Son in time within us, thereby

14. On participation in the community of the Trinity, see *DVMCS*, 148–54.

enabling us to commit ourselves to the fullness of God—at first gradually and piecemeal, until finally without reserve. Our hope in God is the Father generating the Son in time within us, thereby enabling us to strain forward unto the fullness of God—at first tentatively and with many hesitations, until finally with our entire being.

The Father and the Son intimately loving one another from all eternity spirate the Holy Spirit. The Father and the Son spirate the Spirit also in time, in space, in each person, and in all creation. That energetic flow of divine life is basically what the New Testament calls *agapē*: love. Our personal love for God, for fellow human beings, and indeed for the entirety of creation is the eternal inner life of the Trinity reproducing itself within us in time and space, thereby enabling us to love with God's own love. Commingled with our love in its initial form are aspects of narcissism and immaturity. Over a lifetime, God transforms and purifies our love so that it cannot rest until it rests in the fullness of God.[15]

Witness to the Inner Life of the Trinity

A Christian contemplative communes directly and consciously—though "dimly and in part" (1 Cor 13:12)—with the Trinity. A true contemplative knows, experiences, and beholds the Trinity in all aspects of the divine indwelling—not only God as God, but especially God as Abba, Beloved, and Lover. An authentic contemplative hopes in God the Loving Parent, believes in the Son, loves in the Spirit experientially, intuitively, and irresistibly. There exists a faithful communing of Father, Son, and Spirit with and within the contemplative.

The Father and the Son knowing each other in a contemplative constitutes the contemplative's faith. The Father and the Spirit longing in the contemplative to recapitulate all creation in Christ is the contemplative's hope. The Father and the Son spirating the Holy Spirit in a contemplative begets the contemplative's love. The Eucharist is the sacrament of the indwelling Trinity because it is the sacrament par excellence of communion with God in faith, hope, and love. The contemplative life witnesses in a special way to the inner life of the Trinity, just as the apostolic life witnesses in a unique way to the missions of the Trinity to creation.

Does the aspirant to the contemplative life then experience God as Father, Son, and Spirit? Does the person have a sense of the indwelling Trinity as Loving Parent, Word-Made-Flesh, and Breath of Love? Is the aspirant one who is growing in faith, hope, and love?

15. See *Spiritual Journey*, 173–98.

CHAPTER 11

Communion with God in Daily Life

BEING-IN-LOVE WITH GOD IS the core of Christian contemplative life. In that respect, the presence of a profound, intimate, loving relationship with the Risen Jesus and the existence of a sense of the indwelling Trinity constitute two principles for discerning the authenticity of a person's desire to enter the contemplative life.

Furthermore, being-in-love with God is inclusive of all dimensions of a person's life. Being-in-love with Christ Jesus alters radically a person's way of praying, working, recreating, and relating. Communion with the indwelling Trinity shapes the totality of life. Thus, aspirants to the contemplative life and their spiritual guides need to consider three additional principles of discernment that can indicate readiness to embark upon a contemplative lifestyle:

- The Spirit has led the aspirant to at least the beginning of the passage from discursive prayer to contemplation.

- The aspirant's overall contemplative orientation to life is sufficiently strong and vibrant.

- The aspirant has the ability to acquiesce in the unknown and to advance peacefully in Christ, who alone is the Way.

Contemplation

With a calling to the contemplative life, God bestows upon a person also the ability to be faithful in living that lifestyle. The crux of the vocational bequest is God's own self. The Spirit, lovingly operative within an aspiring contemplative, graces that person with God's direct and immediate presence. That grace is not only *from God,* but also *is God.* That gift constitutes the basis of contemplation.[1]

The Call to Contemplative Prayer

Loving intimacy with Jesus is not precisely the result of "saying prayers," no matter how sublime. Direct communion with the indwelling Trinity is not exactly the outcome of discursive modes of prayer—not even meditation, no matter how moving or insightful. Intimacy and communion are not the product of mind or imagination, of symbol or gesture. Rather, communion in love flows from the heart; indeed, from a listening heart (1 Kings 3:9).

Various forms of discursive prayer have an appropriate place in a person's spiritual genesis.[2] Nevertheless, discernment of the possibility of a vocation to the contemplative life requires a careful look at the contemplative quality of the aspirant's prayer.

Contemplation is integral to the universal call to holiness.[3] God invites all people to participation in the divine love, light, and life. Sooner or later, one way or another, the invitation to contemplation entails for human beings obedient surrender of themselves in faith, hope, and love to God. It is inconceivable, however, that God would call someone to enter the contemplative life without having begun to lead that person into at least the beginnings of contemplation.

How then does the aspiring contemplative pray? What characterizes the aspirant's communion with Jesus, the Father, and the Spirit? Is the person still engaged almost exclusively in meditation, or do there exist discernible signs of the inception of contemplation?

Four Signs of Contemplation during Solitary Prayer

It is especially in silent solitary prayer that contemplatives experience the indwelling Trinity. When concomitantly present, the following four signs and conditions indicate that during their solitary prayer aspirants to the contemplative life are being led by the Spirit beyond meditation and discursiveness into contemplation.[4]

1. See *O Blessed Night,* 79–86; *Contemplation,* 36–43, 141–46.

2. See *Contemplation,* 27–35, 44–52, 72–75, 110–15; *Spiritual Direction,* 193–96; *Spiritual Journey,* 39–52, 75–88, 227–31.

3. See *Contemplation,* 13–20; *Spiritual Direction,* 15–32; *Spiritual Journey,* 39–52.

4. See *Ascent,* II, 13, 1–8; *Night,* I, 10, 1–6; *Contemplation,* 53–59, 76–84; *Spiritual Journey,* 89–95, 114–24.

First, these persons find themselves unable to meditate as before. The kind of meaningfulness that they experienced previously in their prayer has now vanished. Fixing their attentiveness on a short biblical text, on the repetition of a simple phrase, or on a visual religious symbol does not give them the satisfaction to which they were previously accustomed. Moreover, these persons do not even desire to use such approaches in their solitary prayer.

Of itself, that inability to meditate can arise from laziness, interior dissipation, personal fault, or sin. Thus, there is need for a corroborating sign.

Second, not only are these persons disinclined to meditate on God or on what pertains to God, but also they experience during solitary prayer a disinclination to fix their attentiveness purposely on anything else. Yet, while they do not deliberately engage their emotional and cognitive processes, frequent distractions, tangents, and storms occur within them during prayer.[5]

Such trials cause these persons considerable distress and concern, and for good reason. Of themselves those symptoms too can originate in sources other than the Spirit, for example, in persoality disorder, psychosis, depression, or selfishness. Therefore, a further sign and condition is necessary to authenticate the previous two.

Third, while disinclined either to meditate or to focus intentionally on extraneous matters, these persons experience a strong inclination toward wordless, imageless presence to God. They find themselves becoming increasingly aware of a desire simply to remain loving their Beloved and to be loved by him. In their solitary prayer, they are drawn irresistibly toward abiding in silence and solitude, in interior quiet, rest, and repose, with peaceful loving attentiveness to God. They are content to remain lovingly present to Christ Jesus in darkness and aridity, without specific words, acts, feelings, or knowledge.

Fourth, these persons persevere in that form of prayer. Some people go through the motions of what appears to be contemplative prayer. Other strong-willed persons force themselves to remain for extended periods in external silence, while yet idling away the time by daydreaming or reading. God alone can initiate authentic contemplation in a person. Therefore, perseverance in contemplative prayer—day after day, month after month—can come only from God. Contemplation is usually too arid, too emotionally and intellectually unsatisfying, too *nada* to sustain for very long, if the initiative and the endurance do not originate from the Spirit.

The third and fourth conditions are the most compelling positive indications of authentic contemplation. They cause the changes described in the

5. See *Contemplation,* 85–96; *O Blessed Night,* 79–87.

first and the second signs. The frequent, immediate, and direct encounter in love with God, together with perseverance in that way of praying, produces both the inability to meditate as before and the disinclination to focus upon extraneous matters.

In discernment related to the above four signs and conditions, positive and negative motivations within aspiring contemplatives will surface. The key issue becomes then identification of the more dominant thrust. In order to affirm an aspirant's readiness to enter the contemplative life, the positive signs and conditions need to outweigh the deficiencies.

A Distinctive Contemplative Orientation to Life

When human beings come into existence, God gifts them with an innate contemplative thrust; that is, a basic loving receptivity to God. In the case of persons who have a contemplative vocation, passage through a certain critical threshold of maturation in that overall contemplative orientation is a prerequisite for entrance upon the contemplative life.

The following four signs and conditions are simultaneously present when aspiring contemplatives have undergone that basic development.[6]

First, in their involvement with creation, these persons come to an experience of an all-pervasive aridity. A marked diminishment in the kind of meaningfulness that they had previously experienced occurs in every aspect of their lives, for instance, community or family life, ministry or career, leisure activities, friendships. That all-encompassing dryness persists no matter how they try to elude it or to change it.

The cause of that aridity across the board is not dissatisfaction with life. Rather, the dryness that these persons experience is the logical outcome of their worthwhile effort and relative success in myriad endeavors. The aridity results from the awareness that no one or no thing except God in God's own self can fully satisfy the deepest longings of the human heart. That kind of aridity is the result of loving rightly. It is the consequence of beginning to pass through and beyond everyone and everything created to a loving, personal God who cannot be fully grasped in any perceptible way.[7] What primarily sustains persons immersed in this aridity and emptiness is a sense of vocation, conviction, and responsibility. They journey forward in dark faith, embraced in God who is mystery.[8]

---

6. See *Night*, I, 9, 1–9; *Contemplation*, 60–71; *Spiritual Journey*, 55–74, 89–95, 99–108.

7. See *O Blessed Night*, 57–68 and 171–77.

8. See *O Blessed Night*, 89–97 and 147–53; *Spiritual Journey*, 173–80.

Certain dysfunctions such as dissipation or boredom appear to have some similarity to the overall aridity. Those impairments originate, however, in causes other than a maturing contemplative orientation to life, for example, in lassitude, personality disorder, psychosis, or personal sin. A second sign and condition is therefore necessary.

Second, in reaction to the aridity and the loss of meaningfulness, these persons experience anxiety about possibly not being in God's service. They fear that they are now backsliding rather than advancing in union with Christ. Painful care and solicitude is a potential sign of interior progress because only sincere and searching persons are concerned about insincerity, infidelity, and sinfulness. What sustains people in this state of angst is a purified hope in God's love, mercy, and fidelity.

Since this solicitude could arise also from negative influences such as an anxiety disorder or a propensity toward excessive worry, an additional sign and condition presents itself.

Third, these persons are drawn to contemplation. In order to foster the interior solitude wherein they immediately and directly encounter God in love, they experience the need for an increase of exterior silence and solitude.

This sign and condition is the most significant of the three areas, since it is the root of the above symptoms and trials. The inception of contemplation causes within a person the all-pervasive aridity and loss of meaningfulness in relation to created realities, the anxiety about lack of fidelity to God, and the need for increased exterior silence and solitude.

Fourth, perseverance in bringing a deepening contemplative attitude to bear upon daily life offers further affirmation of readiness to embark upon the contemplative life. All Christians—irrespective of their vocational lifestyles—will experience at some point in their spiritual journey the above signs and conditions of deepening contemplative communion with God. For those called to the contemplative life, passage through that critical threshold of contemplative orientation to life is foundational to their future lifestyle.

Peaceful Acquiescence in Mystery

According to Thomas Merton, a person comes to know the meaning of contemplation through an intuitive and spontaneous preference for "the dark and unknown path of aridity" over every other way.[9] In the contemplative

---

9. Merton, *Contemplative Prayer*, 111.

life that path of aridity invites a person to acquiescence in the unknown and to peaceful advancement without seeing any way.[10]

At-Homeness with Mystery

To acquiesce means in common parlance to yield, to accept, or to comply with something or someone. In a spiritual sense, it signifies to be at home, to be comfortable, and to be at ease with mystery.

Contemplatives acquiesce in the unknown by letting God draw them consciously and voluntarily into ever deeper mystery. Acquiescence in that sense requires abandonment of themselves wholeheartedly to that which is deepest and most ineffable in God.

Acquiescence in the unknown entails also a willingness to let go certitude and to abide in faith. Fear is a usual human reaction to the unknown. A certain kind of fear is debilitating, paralyzing, and oppressive to human beings. Another kind of fear—in contrast, a healthy fear—keeps people from rushing in where angels would not tread. It makes people prudent and circumspect. But faith runs counter to all fear. Faith empowers contemplatives to risk, to dare, to advance where they cannot see the way. Faith holds a depth of hope that transcends even healthy fear. Faith contains a quality of love that drives out trepidation (1 John 4:18).

The gift of faith enables contemplatives to welcome and to be at home in the unknown, in the ineffable, in mystery. This "unknown" is a Person, not a thing. This unknown is Jesus, the risen Christ, beckoning ever so gently from within the depths of the darkest night: "Do not be afraid. I am" (John 6:20).[11]

The Peace of Christ

Contemplatives advance where they do not see the way. Jesus is the Way (John 14:6) who can no longer be seen with mortal eyes. How then do contemplatives embark upon this "Way"?

St. John of the Cross offers these words of wisdom:

10. Ibid, 118. The theme of contemplative acquiescence to mystery is found not only throughout the writings of St. John of the Cross and Thomas Merton, but it is also the leitmotif of the Pseudo-Dionysius (*The Divine Names* and *Mystical Theology*, PG, 3, 586–1064) and the author of *The Cloud of Unknowing*.

11. See *O Blessed Night*, 89–97; 133–37; 147–53.

To enter upon this way is to leave the road.

In other words, to pass on to the goal and to leave one's own way

is to enter upon that which has no way.

And that is God.

For the soul who attains this state

no longer has any ways or methods of its own.

Still less does the soul cling to such things, nor is it able to.

The soul contains within itself, though, all ways,

like one who possesses nothing yet has all.[12]

That advance into the Unknown—into Christ—is peaceful. It is permeated by "the peace which the world cannot give" (John 14:27), or understand, or adequately appreciate. That peace burns away (Luke 3:16, 12:49) immaturities and defense mechanisms. That peace cannot placidly tolerate sinfulness and egocentrism (Rom 7:24). That peace is unmistakable even in the midst of the most agonizing throes of the dark night.[13]

Therefore, these questions present themselves in the discernment of a possible vocation to the contemplative life: Has the aspiring contemplative yet begun to acquiesce to God as Mystery and to the Mystery of God? Is at-homeness with the Unknown and the Unknowable developing within the person? What resistances obstruct the aspirant's at-homeness with mystery? Is the aspirant making progress in letting go those resistances? Does the aspirant go forth peacefully without seeing the way? Is the aspirant content to have Christ be the only Way?

12. *Ascent*, II, 4, 5.

13. See *O Blessed Night*, 77–78.

CHAPTER 12

The Quest for Solitude

THE PRESENCE OF A love of God that has christocentric and trinitarian dimensions constitutes a first indication of an aspirant's readiness for the contemplative life. That love of God expresses itself in a profound, intimate, loving relationship with Jesus and in a sense of the indwelling Trinity.

The quality of an aspirant's communion with God in all aspects of daily life gives further indication of vocational readiness. That all-embracive intimacy with God becomes observable in the person's movement in solitary prayer from meditation to contemplation, in a continually deepening contemplative orientation toward all life, and in an increasing ability to acquiesce peacefully in mystery.

However, the presence within a person of those signs and conditions does not in itself warrant transition to the contemplative life. Those signs and conditions occur also in people who are called by God to other Christian lifestyles. Persons discerning a contemplative vocation need an additional indication of readiness before they embark upon a contemplative life.

When a genuine contemplative vocation exists, loving intimacy with God transforms not only an aspirant's way of praying and living, but also the mode of relating to creation. A calling to the contemplative life awakens in a person an intensifying need for more interior and exterior aloneness with God. With increasing frequency, the person goes apart from people and society for the purpose of solitary loving communion with God. Paradoxically, a new form of presence in God to all persons, creatures, and things accompanies that separation from people and absence from society.

This principle of discernment is then a further indication of readiness for transition to the contemplative life: the aspiring contemplative has a history of being born into increasing interior and exterior solitude.

Extensive aloneness is essential to any contemplative lifestyle. Yet, as Thomas Merton wisely observed, movement into silence and solitude is developmental. A person must be born out of the womb of society into solitude. Merton described that birthing process as occurring "carefully, patiently and after long delay."[1]

The Womb of Society

Broadly speaking, "society" denotes a body of people with a specified system for shared identity, personal interaction, value implementation, behavior, and commerce. A society could consist of a local, national, or global group. A society could be an ecclesial or a civic entity. It could consist of an association of people dedicated to a specific cause or interest.

Readiness for the contemplative life requires that aspirants have had sustained involvement with society over a prolonged time. The context for that preparation is the apostolic life (as described above in chapters 2, 5–9).

In the initial stages of spiritual genesis, society is as necessary for a person's spiritual growth as a mother's womb is for the development of a child. The womb of society is a milieu in which God nurtures and supports the person. It is the matrix of growth in every respect: emotional, cognitive, social, spiritual, physical, etc. It is also a shelter from and a protection against what a person cannot yet withstand. Despite the fact that the womb of society upholds and shelters an individual, it has a shadow side as well. It contains enticements and temptations that could lure a person toward dissipation and sinfulness.

Like a mother's womb, society holds the potential for care and neglect, for security and danger, for life and death. In the womb of society, a person can turn toward Jesus, turn away from him, surrender to him while still somewhat resisting him, or even remain mostly resistant to him while yet inexplicably attracted to him. Nonetheless, through God's providence, everything that happens to a person in the womb of society has the capacity to become an instrument for good (Rom 8:28).

Although a mother's body is essential for prenatal development, the time comes when for life to progress the child must be born out of her womb into the solitude of an existence physically separate from the mother. It is similar for a Christian in relation to society. For continuing spiritual growth, a Christian has to undergo at a certain point being born out of the womb of society into solitude. The individual has to become emancipated from the very source that has sustained life, while yet forming a new relationship to it. That spiritual birthing entails much travail, for it detaches a person gradually from all that is familiar and cherished. It thrusts an individual into increasing darkness and unknowing. The pain gives way to joy

---

1. Merton, "Notes for a Philosophy of Solitude," 204.

as the person's communion with God and with all creation in God increases immeasurably throughout the process. The solitude into which a person is born refers above all to solitude of heart, but it involves also a degree of external solitude appropriate to the person's vocation.

All Christians undergo this birthing into solitude in the course of their spiritual genesis. Those persons called to the contemplative life experience the travail in an especially intense manner.

The Process of Being Born into Solitude

Persons who have received from God a contemplative vocation enter the process of being born into solitude while they are still immersed in the womb of society.

In their involvement with the world, these people have positive experiences of loving, of being loved, of self-knowledge, and of success in their undertakings. Yet they discover that as meaningful as those experiences are, they cannot fully satisfy the deepest desire of the human heart. By means of the involvements that nurture their growth, society points these persons beyond itself to "something more." They come to see that God alone can fulfill their inmost yearning and longing. The womb of society thereby becomes for them a means by which the Spirit opens them more directly and immediately to the risen Jesus at the core of creation.[2]

Moreover, as these persons seek within the womb of society to develop a strong self and a better world for Christ, they inevitably experience hurt, opposition, and failure. That unavoidable suffering has a providential role in their process of being born into solitude. Confronted with their weaknesses, limitations, and sinfulness, they learn ever anew that God alone is their Savior. Through their endurance of the cross in Christian life, the Spirit guides them into that realm where they abide alone with Jesus. Even their successful endeavors as members of society entail some degree of suffering. The efforts of people to forge improvements, whether in themselves or in their world, demand significant self-denial and self-discipline. It costs time and energy, plus the foregoing of certain pleasures and comforts, to produce a work of value for God.

Those called to enter the contemplative life experience in the womb of society growth and diminishment, joy and pain, success and failure in their relationships and their activities. All those experiences have the potential to be sources of God's grace and catalysts for human growth. However, as

2. See O Blessed Night, 57–61, 168–77; Spiritual Journey, 55–61, 99–113.

Merton stated, the actual process by which people are born out of the womb of society into solitude unfolds "carefully, patiently and after long delay."[3]

Carefully

God awakens with the utmost sensitivity the desire for solitude within persons called to the contemplative life. God guides them with tender love throughout their spiritual journey. God is always full of care for their individuality, free will, and circumstances in life. Divine compassion sustains those with a contemplative vocation through untold dangers, as they advance into uncharted solitude. Divine purification may challenge the limits of their endurance, but God never demands of them more than they can bear.

Patiently

God does not needlessly accelerate the process of spiritualization. God lets time effect its own unique mode of transformation, enlightenment, and purification. God waits painstakingly for a human response to the divine initiative. Aspiring contemplatives in turn have to wait patiently upon God (Rom 8:25). They wait with persistent trust that in the fullness of time God's plan will attain completion (Phil 1:6).

After Long Delay

God's presence and wisdom overshadow the entire process of being born out of society into solitude. Personal discovery of a need for solitude is usually slow and gradual. By the time awareness of that desire emerges, most people find themselves already in solitude. Furthermore, God's manner of gifting contemplatively oriented people with solitude is not always according to human calculations and expectations. On many occasions, the "long delay" is from the perspective of human judgment, not from truth as God sees it.

Resistance to and rebellion against the Spirit's promptings do contribute to what people perceive as long delay. People move at times in directions that are completely alien to their self-identity and vocation. Even then God remains faithful: "The gifts and the calling of God are irrevocable" (Rom 11:29).

3. Merton, "Notes for a Philosophy of Solitude," 204.

The Spirit persists in seeking out those called to the contemplative life. The Advocate journeys with them and works for their good. The Breath of Love incorporates into the process all the delays caused by their human limitations and infidelities. The Spirit of God uses even their failures and defeats to draw these people ever deeper into the solitude of Christ.

The Contemplative as a Marginal Person

By virtue of the universal call to holiness, God invites all people to be born out of the womb of society into increasing interior solitude. For most persons, that invitation means becoming more solitary in the midst of society; that is, more conscious of belonging entirely to God as they go about their lives. It means also becoming more contemplative in the midst of apostolic living; that is, more dynamically receptive to God as they engage in their activities.

Thus, most Christians remain actively engaged in society, particularly in living an apostolic lifestyle, but with increasing freedom and detachment. Their spiritual liberation and loving relationship to creation are fruits of their communion with the indwelling Trinity. While the solitude of these persons is primarily interior, some physical aloneness becomes for them a necessity. The appropriate amount of exterior solitude varies from person to person and according to each one's vocational lifestyle.[4]

In the case of persons called to the contemplative life, they too grow into ever deeper solitude of heart as they participate in society. However, their ever burgeoning need for more exterior aloneness propels them, at a critical point in the birthing process, out of and beyond the apostolic life into the contemplative life. These persons develop a longing to live apart from society as it is usually understood and to terminate most of their involvements with society. By virtue of the interior and exterior solitude integral to their contemplative vocation, these persons are destined to live on the fringes of society—or to remain marginal, as some people would view the situation.[5] This apparent reversal in their lives is primarily a matter of divine choice and not of personal option, of divine initiative rather than of self-interested decision. It is a question of vocation.

Surely, no man or woman is an island. But being born *out of* society *into* solitude does mean that contemplatives pass beyond the fast lane, leave behind the market place, and are detached from the surface where "it's happening" in order to abide at the heart of the world where Christ

4. See *Contemplation*, 97–109.
5. See Merton, *The Asian Journal*, 305.

is happening. Contemplatives are "not of the world" (John 17:14). Nor are they above it or outside it. They remain very much "in the world" (John 17:15, 18), all the way to its heart. Contemplatives do not withdraw, retreat, or dissociate themselves from the world or society. Rather, contemplatives enter into the deepest recesses of both the world and society in order to commune directly at their source with their Source.

Becoming a contemplative entails growing up rather than remaining stagnant. It means going forward into solitude rather than regressing into isolation. It denotes being with society qualitatively rather than physically and spatially. It accentuates spiritual communion rather than social camaraderie.

Living on the fringes of society, contemplatives find themselves situated at the core of the world with God who is becoming all in all (1 Cor 15:28). From that vantage point, they have the opportunity to be more realistically in touch with the signs of the times than do many of the world's most frenzied doers. Contemplatives operate at the heart of matter. They are the animators par excellence of qualitative progress. While rejecting what is deceptive and illusory in the world, they behold the sacredness of God's creation. They have compassionate love for all people and all creatures. They understand the world's pursuits, attractions, and pain. They unite profoundly with the entirety of creation in one great act of giving birth (Rom 8:18–25).[6]

Questions for Discernment

A key consideration in the discernment of a possible vocation to the contemplative life is whether in fact an aspirant has been born out of the womb of society into not only solitude of heart but also extensive exterior solitude. The following four areas help to explore that issue:

A first area: In the course of apostolic living, has the person been able to integrate on a consistent basis available physical solitude with other facets of daily life? Does the person's quest for physical aloneness indicate an increasing need for more solitude? Is the person using all the readily available opportunities for solitude within the current circumstances of life?

Some people pursue the contemplative life when in reality they are still unable to integrate solitude and activity in the context of society. The grace to live a contemplative life presupposes that a person can be contemplative in the midst of action and happily solitary within society. The experience of having lived faithfully an integrated life for a prolonged

6. See *O Blessed Night*, 168–70.

period in an apostolic milieu provides a firm foundation for the solitude of a contemplative life.[7]

A second area: Does the person's history indicate overall movement toward deepening communion or toward isolation and withdrawal? Is the aspirant's desire for solitude the result of society pointing the person beyond itself to God? Or is rejection by society the origin of the person's propensity for aloneness?[8]

Spiritual directors have to be acutely sensitive to the latter possibility with people who consider themselves failures, who experience grave difficulties in working and interacting with other persons, or who give indication of psychological imbalance. Unresolved experiences of physical, mental, and/or emotional trauma—perhaps reaching far back into childhood—make it inadvisable for a person to enter upon a contemplative lifestyle.

Conversely, instead of society rejecting a person in some way, an individual could be attempting to reject society. That dynamic could be operative, for example, when an individual's surroundings offer love, affirmation, and multiple opportunities for growth, but the person severs connection to those life-giving sources. That behavior displays a preference for isolation and withdrawal over the solitude and challenge of the contemplative life. A loner does not a contemplative make.

A third area: What are the aspirant's attitudes and actions with regard to social justice and civic responsibility? Does the aspirant stay well-informed in matters related to justice, peace, and integrity of creation?

Abiding spiritually at the heart of the world with the risen Christ, contemplatives have a moral obligation to bring their wisdom to bear on the burning issues of their times. This responsibility pertains to the prophetic dimension of Christian contemplative life—that of being a voice in the wilderness for the voiceless, of preparing in the desert a way for the coming of Christ Jesus (John 1:23). Contemplatives exercise social justice and civic responsibility in many ways—for instance, by their presence, silence, and words or by their exercise of the right to vote in local and national elections. To be effective in dialogue concerning matters of justice and peace, contemplatives must educate themselves adequately with regard to those issues.

A fourth area: Does the aspirant experience a spiritual imperative to embark upon the contemplative life? Has the aspirant's history of being born out of the womb of society into solitude truly reached a critical threshold wherein he or she is existentially unable to do other than make a transition from the apostolic life to the contemplative life? Or is the aspirant's sense of

7. See *Contemplation,* 125–40.
8. See *Contemplation,* 98–99.

urgency to enter the contemplative life arising from impatience, impulsive-
ness, and lack of listening?

Signs of an aspirant's receptivity to God's timing throughout the process of being born into solitude include these qualities: self-acceptance, being "content with weakness" (2 Cor 12:10), gratitude for all God's blessings,
patience with failures and delays, peaceful acceptance of one's self-identity
and life history. People in too much of a hurry to enter the contemplative
life or to "reach perfection" lack the readiness and the freedom required for
contemplative living.

Three Situations for Discernment

Some persons tend to misread substantial difficulty or challenge in their apostolic lifestyles as a sign that they are being born out of the womb of society
into the solitude of the contemplative life. They misinterpret the presence of
a problematic issue as indicative of a calling to enter the contemplative life.

The following three situations exemplify something of that form of
vocational confusion: an inability to function in apostolic ministry, an experience of the apostolic life as being overly demanding, movement into the
retirement phase of human life.

An Inability to Function in Ministry

Some people living the apostolic life become unable to function even
minimally in their ministries. They find their usual daily routine so overwhelming that they become incapable of part-time, let alone full-time,
work. A few of those persons conclude that they are therefore called to the
contemplative life.

A person should not imagine that an inability to fulfill normal ministerial duties is a clear sign of a contemplative vocation. Nor should spiritual
guides immediately encourage that person in the desire for and the pursuit
of a contemplative lifestyle. An inability to function in ministry could result from any number of causes; just to mention a few, ministerial burnout,
a genuine need for a change to another ministry, a physical illness, or a
problem of psychological origin only now becoming evident. In the case of
a person who is a member of a religious institute, the underlying difficulty
could stem also from the existence of a vocation to a mode of living other
than the celibate life.

If people cannot function adequately in the apostolic life, neither will
they be able to do so in the contemplative life.

Escape from Demands of the Apostolic Life

Although some people remain functional in their apostolic lifestyles, they experience their way of life and their ministry to be extremely arduous and tiresome. They long for a less strenuous mode of living and a reduction in their workload. A few of those people interpret that experience to mean that they should leave the apostolic life and enter the contemplative life. Instead of trying to resolve their difficulties in apostolic living, they become fixated on the notion that they have a contemplative vocation. Should these persons embark on what they imagine is the contemplative life, the true cause of their impairment in the apostolic life will reassert itself in another form. They will find themselves again unhappy and discontented.

Each person has authentic physical, cognitive, emotional, and spiritual limitations. Some people are stretched far beyond their capacities and resources in ministry, and are genuinely called by God to a reduction of work. However, other people establish for themselves limitations that fall far short of their talents. These individuals settle for less than their capabilities and less than God desires of them. They shortchange not only their communities, but also themselves. Their pursuit of what they imagine to be the contemplative life seems powered by a wish to escape the usual demands of life. They appear to want a comfortable cocoon wherein someone will take care of them and ask little of them. Frequently, those persons use the excuse of poor health to excuse their diminished effort. They can produce just about any symptom they want in order to promote their cause or to get their way.

Semi-Retirement and Retirement

Christians who spend most of their lives engaged in the apostolic life begin inevitably to move toward semi-retirement and eventual full retirement. If a sense of vocation does not awaken them to that approaching direction, illness, loss of a loved one, or the aging process itself will do so in due course.

The elder years have the potential to be the most contemplative years of human life. Yet few people approaching retirement experience themselves as called by God to make a transition from the apostolic life to a veritable contemplative life. Most semi-retired and retired Christians seem called to live to the end of their days a transformed modality of their apostolic lifestyles.

A calling to semi-retirement or to full retirement is distinct from a vocation to the contemplative life. Many people who are approaching retirement from ministry experience attraction toward more freedom for solitary prayer, study, family events, travel, and recreational pursuits, together with a significant reduction in their work. That orientation bespeaks most often a calling to accentuate the contemplative component of their aging process and their apostolic vocation, not a vocation to the contemplative life itself. Competent spiritual directors can help those persons distinguish the grace to bring to fullness what has been always their calling from the need for a radical change from one Christian lifestyle (the apostolic life) to another way of living (the contemplative life).

Insight into what a contemplative vocation is *not* contributes immensely to an understanding of its true nature. A calling to the contemplative life is not the outcome of an inability to function in ministry. It is not a refuge from the demands of the apostolic life. It is not a calling to semi-retirement or to full retirement. Those situations stem from influences other than a vocation to a contemplative lifestyle. Discernment in those circumstances aims to bring to light the real issue and to help the seeker find the way forward on the spiritual journey.

CHAPTER 13

Solitary Life in a Communal Setting

AN ASPIRANT TO THE contemplative life manifests sufficient indication of a christocentric and trinitarian love of God, an increasing ability to commune with God in all aspects of life, and a history of having been born out of the womb of society into solitude. Given those positive signs, the next step in vocational discernment is for the person to live the contemplative life on a prolonged experimental basis in association with a community that is contemplative or at least welcoming of a contemplative member.

Each vocation to the contemplative life entails integration of solitude and community. On the one hand, a contemplative's being-in-love with God necessitates silence and solitude for the purpose of contemplation. On the other hand, a contemplative has an ardent desire to share life with other contemplatively inclined people.

A contemplative vocation is ordinarily inclusive of a calling to a religious sisterhood or a brotherhood in which members share a common life. In this case, the birthing into the solitude of the contemplative life occurs in such a way that the faith journeys of a number of pilgrims converge to bring them together as a community. The community element is so integral to a contemplative vocation that an aspirant drawn to live alone without membership in a religious sisterhood or brotherhood spontaneously seeks out association with a Christian community of some kind.

The communal emphasis in a life of solitude constitutes one factor that distinguishes the contemplative vocation from the eremitic calling. A hermit lives the contemplative life to the full, but in a solitary setting with maximum freedom from interactions, schedules, endeavors, and gatherings.

The communal dimension of a contemplative mode of living unfolds in relation to one of two vastly different basic Christian vocational lifestyles, namely, celibacy or marriage. Singlehood is also a basic Christian vocational lifestyle. Yet, with the emergence of a contemplative vocation, single persons tend to make a transition to celibacy. Theoretically, singlehood could give way to simultaneous callings to marriage and a contemplative life. In practice, that event is most unlikely to occur.

A Celibate Context

Aspiring contemplatives with a vocational commitment to celibacy have various options for communal affiliation during their period of living the contemplative life on an experimental basis. We identify below three familiar modes of association:

A first mode: The aspirant becomes an initiate in an established contemplative community. That "established contemplative community" could refer to a group that has ecclesial recognition as an institute or society of consecrated life. The designation "established contemplative community" could include also other stable forms of communal contemplative life that do not have official recognition in church law, such as contemplative houses of prayer.

An aspirant who opts to live in an established contemplative community could have the intent of eventual permanent membership in the group or of temporary membership with a view to gaining initial formation in contemplative living.

An established contemplative community provides an aspirant the opportunity to live with experienced contemplatives. Participation in the communal life of a contemplative group offers a challenging environment for practical testing of a possible vocation, together with the availability and the wisdom of persons proficient in the lifestyle.

A second mode: The aspirant commences living a contemplative life alone in a suitable residence and forms a loose-knit affiliation with a Christian community or combination of communities; for example, a nearby monastic group, a parish group, an ecumenical faith-sharing group, or a group dedicated to a specific mission such as Catholic Worker or L'Arche. In this case, the aspirant's primary community of affiliation could be dedicated to living the contemplative life or the apostolic life. The primary community would need to welcome and to value the aspirant's contemplative aspirations. Moreover, the presence of a few friends who are contemplatives and available for spiritual accompaniment in the immediate geographical area would be immensely beneficial to the aspirant.

A third mode: The aspirant is already a committed member of an apostolic institute or society of consecrated life, and seeks from those persons in leadership permission to live a contemplative life within that congregation. (We take up this situation in the next chapter.)

Whatever the mode of community affiliation, an aspirant would be wise to secure the assistance of a spiritual director who has experience and knowledge of the contemplative life, together with the gifts and skills necessary for discernment of a contemplative vocation.

Participation in community challenges contemplatives to love God and all creation with singleness of heart. The communal life serves as a catalyst in the Spirit's formation of each contemplative into the image and likeness of Christ. Consequently, these questions require attention in the discernment process:

Does the aspiring contemplative desire affiliation with a community that offers companionship, encouragement, and challenge? If not, what does the aspirant want as an alternative?

Does the aspirant feel an attraction to a specific contemplative community or contemplatively oriented group? Is that community receptive to the possibility of membership for the aspirant or to the aspirant having a loose-knit association with the group?

Is that community's charism such that it elicits in the common life a balance of solitude and togetherness, communal and private prayer, work and recreation that is compatible with the aspirant's spiritual needs?

A community's way of balancing the various facets of its common life has immense significance for an aspirant's discernment of a vocation to a specific contemplative institute. A person who needs extensive freedom and elbow room will not likely thrive in a tightly structured community. Nor will an aspirant with a pronounced leaning toward solitary prayer and physical aloneness ordinarily prosper in a group that accentuates prayer, work, and recreation in common.

The Context of Marriage

With regard to the married life and the contemplative life specifically, the history of spirituality offers examples wherein a contemplative orientation flourished within a person during years of marriage and then blossomed into a vocation to the contemplative life after the death of a spouse and the fulfillment of parental responsibilities.

Marie Guyart (1599–1672), in religion known as Marie of the Incarnation, foundress of the Ursuline Sisters in Canada, and Louis Martin (1823–94), the father of St. Thérèse of the Child Jesus, may be two cases in point. After a brief but happy marriage, Marie Guyart became a widow at the age of nineteen. She was left with a young son whom she entrusted eventually to the care of her sister and brother-in-law in view of what she discerned to be her contemplative vocation. Needless to say, as a widow and single mother, her separation from her child entailed delicate matters of conscience and heart-wrenching grief. Marie entered an established cloistered community and went on to become a missionary and a mystic. After Louis Martin's wife of many years had died and all their children were pursuing their own vocations, he lived a solitary life in his family home at Lisieux until his final illness.

Both Marie Guyart and Louis Martin were already widowed when they entered what might be considered the contemplative life. The principles of vocational discernment in the case of a surviving spouse who has fulfilled in good conscience parental responsibilities are essentially the same as for celibate and single people with an emerging contemplative vocation.

It is possible for God to call a married person to live a contemplative life within the context of marriage itself. One expression of that vocation is that of a husband and a wife called *as a married couple* to a contemplative lifestyle. At the acceptable time in their marriage, they discern that the Spirit is prompting them to embark together upon a contemplative life. Some such couples take on a work or a cause as a facet of their contemplative mode of living, for instance, starting a small organic farm, maintaining a wildlife sanctuary on their property, or collaborating in creative writing endeavors. The usual principles of discernment for the contemplative life are generally applicable also to this vocational situation.

For the remainder of this chapter, we address this rare situation involving a contemplative vocation within the context of a marriage: One spouse discerns a calling to live the contemplative life, while the other spouse has no such interior leanings. Nonetheless, the couple believes that God wants them to remain together as committed marital partners and as a family unit.

It is difficult, if not impossible, to imagine a true contemplative vocation breaking up an authentic Christian marriage. That situation would imply that grace destroys grace. If a marriage does break up, that dissolution would be most likely due to other causes. If the marriage endures, then we have to consider a vocation (contemplative life) *within* a vocation (the marriage), not outside it, in spite of it, or parallel to it.

The following are certain key principles relevant to vocational discernment in that situation:

First, if God indeed calls a person to both Christian marriage and the contemplative life, God will surely grant also the means for that person to integrate the two vocations appropriately and to live them both fruitfully.

In this case, both vocations not only coexist in a person's life, but also interrelate in such a way that the marriage remains the matrix of the contemplative life. The calling to Christian marriage is the basic lifestyle from which emerges the contemplative vocation and into which that contemplative calling must be integrated.

Second, stability of the marriage itself is a precondition for the aspiring contemplative's movement toward a contemplative lifestyle.

Third, the communal aspect of a married person's contemplative life would consist primarily of a spousal relationship and membership in a family unit.

Fourth, an in-depth and prolonged vocational discernment, which would include input from the spouse, their children if any, and a spiritual director, is a necessity. Most likely, the aspirant's spouse also would need spiritual guidance throughout the discernment process.

Fifth, this pivotal question presents itself: Is it possible for the aspirant to secure within the framework of marriage and family life the silence and solitude necessary for a veritable contemplative lifestyle?

If that degree of silence and solitude is not available, then in all probability God is not calling the married person to the contemplative life—at least not yet.

The vocation to marriage remains the basic Christian lifestyle, and therefore holds a certain priority. Consistently unmet needs of the spouse and children for the aspirant's presence with them would constitute signs that God wants the aspirant to foster a contemplative orientation to life, but without entrance upon the contemplative life as such.

Sixth, a decision by an aspiring contemplative to begin living a contemplative life on an experimental basis within the household must be accompanied by the explicit consent and ongoing support of the spouse and family. That agreement lays the groundwork for the couple and the family to move forward together in peace and harmony.

Seventh, an aspirant's neglect of the responsibilities specific to marriage and family life or the existence within the aspirant of a dichotomy between contemplative life and married life is contraindicative of a contemplative vocation within the context of marriage.

Eighth, the aspirant has to balance necessary silence and solitude with a generous investment of time and energy in spousal and parental relationships. Furthermore, the aspirant would need to make provision for involvement in family and extended-family activities and events, although perhaps on a more limited basis than in the usual circumstances of marriage and family life.

Finally, the aspiring contemplative has a responsibility to provide assistance and encouragement to the spouse and children, if any, in their vocational quests. They have their own spiritual directions to follow and their own paths of life to pursue.

CHAPTER 14

A Contemplative Vocation within an Apostolic Institute

PEOPLE WHO WANT TO live a contemplative life are unlikely to request admission into an apostolic institute or society, nor would such a group be inclined to receive them as prospective members. While complementary in the Body of Christ, the apostolic life and the contemplative life represent two distinct vocational charisms and follow separate trajectories.

Still, a vocation to the apostolic life and a vocation to the contemplative life can interconnect within a person or a group in amazingly creative ways. One such example is that of an experienced member of an apostolic congregation whom God calls at some point to live a contemplative life within the same apostolic community. That person could be, for example, a member of the Sisters of St. Joseph, the Presentation Sisters of the Blessed Virgin Mary, the Society of Mary, or the Missionary Oblates of Mary Immaculate. In this chapter, we take up precisely that vocational experience.

The Initial Response of the Apostolic Community

Typically, the first reaction of certain members of an apostolic community to the possibility of a brother or sister having a contemplative vocation is bewilderment, fear, and denial. It is not unusual to hear from them remarks like the following: "Such a vocational change does not fit into our mission and lifestyle. Therefore, how can it be?" "The contemplative life may be fine in monasteries, but it is not part of our charism." "The member should either knuckle down to our usual way of life or leave us."

Those sentiments, though somewhat understandable, do not take sufficiently into account the following truths:

First, God is utterly free to bestow a contemplative vocation upon whomever God wishes—when, where, and however God wants.

Second, the apostolic life contains within itself a profound contemplative orientation. Therefore, although rare, it is not unusual for God to call to the contemplative life a person initially called to the apostolic life.

Each apostolic institute or society has as its foundation a unique charism, at the core of which is receptivity to God. That contemplative thrust inherent to an apostolic congregation's charism is the wellspring from which God brings forth in an experienced member a calling to the contemplative life. The contemplative orientation innate to the group's core mission expresses itself distinctively in that person. A contemplative lifestyle is in this case a normal outgrowth of the member's apostolic life.

Third, since God causes the contemplative vocation to spring forth from within the unique charism of the congregation, the contemplative's continuation of membership in the group witnesses to an essential aspect of the apostolic institute's identity. The first supposition in vocational discernment then is that God desires the development of the member's contemplative lifestyle to occur within the same apostolic congregation. As it is written, "Let us walk by the same road that has brought us to where we have arrived" (Phil 3:16). Therefore, the apostolic community's initial attitude should not be "Get out!" "Go away!" or "Transfer!" but rather "Thanks be to God!" "Welcome!" and "It's about time!"

The call to the contemplative life within an apostolic community is a normal, although rare, personal vocation within a corporate charism. It is a call within a call.

Leadership's Difficulty in Discernment

The possibility of a community member having a contemplative vocation poses formidable difficulties for those persons responsible for the leadership of an apostolic institute or society.

The greatest challenge is the discernment of the authenticity of this grace. Religious superiors, spiritual moderators, and formation personnel in apostolic communities are unaccustomed to this area of vocational discernment. Most likely, none of them has ever lived the contemplative life, nor is God calling any of them to do so. To complicate matters further, it is not unusual to find in any apostolic institute or society a few unsettled members who relish using the claim of a contemplative vocation to procure their own will, lifestyle, or "thing" from those persons in positions of authority.

Is the aspiring contemplative a special grace to the community or a malcontent? That question can be excruciatingly difficult for leadership personnel to answer, especially when signs of both possibilities exist. Most community leaders know what the contemplative life is *not*, but they are unable to say exactly what it *is*. Thus, those leaders, while quite capable of detecting misfits in their midst, sometimes flounder in discerning a community member's attraction to the contemplative life.

Three Initiatives in the Discernment Process

The following three initiatives on the part of leadership personnel can help establish a framework for discerning with a community member a possible contemplative vocation:

First, encourage the member to seek competent spiritual direction from a person who has experience in contemplative living and in ministry to contemplatives.

By and large, it takes a contemplatively inclined person to discern a contemplative vocation. To find such a skilled spiritual director may require considerable effort and substantial expense. However, the addition of such a person to the discernment process is invaluable to both the member and the apostolic group.

Second, invite the member to utilize resources available for psychological and personality assessment.

The results of that evaluation can never indicate the existence of a vocation, but they can unmask immaturities and disorders that point more toward isolation than solitude. Grace builds on nature. Therefore, an institute's leaders have a right to expect of the aspiring contemplative a strong, maturing, and vibrant self-identity.

Living the contemplative life in an apostolic setting is in many respects more emotionally, mentally, and spiritually demanding than in a contemplative community. The support systems in the two contexts are usually quite dissimilar. The aspiring contemplative in an apostolic environment will be in the position of living a lifestyle basically different from that of other communal members. That person will not have the encouragement and the challenge available in a life shared with other contemplatives. The existence of a strong sense of self-identity is essential for perseverance in that circumstance.

Third, encourage the aspiring contemplative to live the contemplative life on an experimental basis for an extended time.

Grass always seems greener on the other side of the fence. Let the member have a firsthand taste of the contemplative life and see what emerges from that experience.

Possible Contemplative Living Situations

Basically, three living situations exist in which a member of an apostolic institute or society could pursue the contemplative life on a prolonged experimental basis:

- If the apostolic institute or society has its own contemplatively oriented house of prayer, retreat house, or spirituality center, the member could reside at that facility.

- The member could live a contemplative life in a suitable local community of the institute or society, while the other members of that group continue their apostolic life.

- The member could live for a period of time in a canonically recognized contemplative institute or in an alternate form of contemplative community.

The first two options present at least two major drawbacks. *First*, in most cases neither the leadership in an apostolic community nor the membership as a whole has the expertise to discern in full measure what in the details of the member's daily life is positively indicative of a contemplative vocation. *Second*, a dearth of competent guidance and necessary challenge might exist with regard to the person's ongoing spiritual formation as a contemplative. Assistance from a wise spiritual director and insight from persons already living the contemplative life at another location could offset those drawbacks.

Whichever choice of living arrangement proves fitting, the member must continue in dialogue with a spiritual director and community representatives without fear of making mistakes and always ready to start afresh. All participants in the process will profit from clarifying their expectations of one another. Moreover, all participants will need to have at least a rudimentary appreciation of the nature of a contemplative vocation.

Pastoral Recommendations

When a person's experimental period of living yields affirmation of a probable contemplative vocation within an apostolic community, new challenges arise for the religious institute or society. Those persons in leadership will have to decide upon the long-term future relationship of the group and the member.

The simplest course would be to make arrangements for the member to go off to a contemplative group: "We will support you morally and financially. You can even retain your membership with us, but please go elsewhere." That approach could manifest goodwill. It might resolve some difficulties, but it may not be what God is asking of the apostolic institute or society.

Integration of a member's contemplative vocation into an apostolic group rests upon these premises:

- God brought the member's contemplative vocation to birth out of the contemplative thrust integral to the congregation's charism.

- God desires the member to live the contemplative life within the apostolic institute or society in which that calling came to birth.

- God wants the person with the contemplative vocation to retain all rights, privileges, and responsibilities pertinent to membership in the apostolic institute or society.

The implementation of a direction based on those foundations requires creativity and daring. We offer the following guidelines to assist both the member and leadership personnel as they continue to discern the intricacies of the situation:

First: Other members of the institute or society require periodic blocks of time away from their usual apostolic settings for the purpose of ongoing spiritual formation and education. In a similar manner, the contemplative must have blocks of time alone each day for prayer and study.

Second: Although the contemplative life and the apostolic life are distinct lifestyles, the contemplative life as such does not preclude a person's involvement in limited apostolate. In fact, within bounds certain ministries are quite in order. Activities of a quiet and solitary nature have appeal to many contemplatives. They prefer, for example, taking a portion of the night shift in the infirmary rather than the day shift, doing part-time archival work rather than full-time teaching, and engaging in one-to-one spiritual direction rather than numerous directed retreats with many large groups. Ministries of another nature, like computer programming or financial planning, also could be fitting for those contemplative members who have the talent and skills to engage in those works for the benefit of the community.

Third: In terms of a twenty-four–hour day or a seven-day week, what constitutes a "block of time for solitude" or "limited ministry"? A block of time designates two or three hours daily at a stretch. Limited ministerial activity entails approximately five to six hours a day, thirty to thirty-five hours per week.

The time element, although important, is not the only factor for consideration. The toll that various activities and responsibilities take on the member is also important. A person's energy output, intensity of involvement in an activity, and amount of unscheduled overtime work need careful assessment. The cumulative effect of daily activities depends to some extent upon individual personalities, gifts, and limitations. What might be natural to one contemplative might be a back-breaker for another. A member of an apostolic community who seeks to discern a contemplative vocation need not be treated with kid gloves. At the same time, all parties involved in the discernment must respect the exigencies and limitations of the aspiring contemplative.

Fourth: The location of living quarters for a contemplative in an apostolic community is a crucial issue. Since a contemplative vocation places a person on the fringes of society, living accommodations tend to be situated on the outskirts of the community's physical space, for example, at the secluded end of a corridor, in an unoccupied wing of a building, in an attic room, or in a cottage apart from the main residence.

The living space itself requires careful attention, since the contemplative spends so much time within that residence. It has to be a home, not a prison. It must be a prayerful and peaceful milieu, not a place of forced confinement. Human at-homeness anywhere on this earth is relative and limited. Yet, in order for a person to live the contemplative life fruitfully, a basic at-homeness somewhere is a necessity.

Fifth: A contemplative in an apostolic community requires time and space for aloneness and solitary prayer, but that solitude does not preclude all communal prayer. On the contrary, community members could expect the contemplative's participation with them in the daily Celebration of the Eucharist and possibly portions of the Liturgy of the Hours. Depending upon personal spiritual needs, the contemplative's attendance at other forms of communal prayer such as the rosary, the stations of the cross, or group meditation may or may not be appropriate.

Sixth: A contemplative within an apostolic community would ordinarily attend most communal meetings and participate in discussion of communal issues, particularly those bearing on the spiritual animation of the religious institute or society.

Seventh: In-depth study is integral to the contemplative life. Thus, the contemplative must have an adequate library, or access to one, plus sufficient time and energy for study. A contemplative member of an apostolic group might find study of the institute's charism and spirituality especially meaningful. The sharing of the fruits of that study with other members in classes or seminars would make a valuable contribution to the spiritual growth of both the contemplative and the community.

Eighth: It is not unusual for God to call a contemplative within an apostolic institute or society to exercise the ministry of spiritual direction for the benefit of people both within and outside the apostolic group. That ministry could extend also to directing retreats and to being a behind-the-scenes spiritual animator for the apostolic group both locally and at large.[1] The extent appropriate to those involvements varies from contemplative to contemplative.

For the leadership of an apostolic community, the presence of a member called to live a contemplative life is more a blessing than a headache or a heartache. If leaders take the attitude that a contemplative is not a problem to be solved, but rather someone to let go, to let live, to let be, they will discover in their midst a hidden treasure and a subtly powerful influence for spiritual growth.

A Final Recommendation

Most apostolic institutes and societies have personnel boards or committees for the purpose of overseeing ministries and renewal. Why not also have a committee to serve those members who think that they may have a contemplative vocation? Or in what is more common, why not have a committee to minister to those members who experience a need to accentuate the contemplative dimension of their lives as they continue their apostolic work?

Leadership personnel in apostolic institutes and societies do need a process for discerning the deeper spiritual exigencies of their members. Many apostolic communities make excellent health care available to members who are physically or emotionally infirm. They make abundant provision also for the continuing education of members engaged in ministries. They offer annual vacations and periodic home visits to the membership. They encourage even an annual religious retreat. Meanwhile, members struggling in some of those communities to deepen the contemplative dimension of their relationship with God meet with annoyance, misunderstanding, and on occasion outright derision.

When God calls forth a contemplative vocation from within an apostolic institute or society, God asks something of both the community and the member. The apostolic community receives a calling to welcome a full expression of its own innate contemplative thrust, which God is accentuating in the contemplative member. The person whom God calls to

1. See *Spiritual Direction*, 33–66, 193–212; *Spiritual Journey*, 143.

the contemplative life embodies the contemplative dimension inherent to the community's founding apostolic charism. The contemplative life of the member called to it by God and the apostolic life of the other members remain complementary. All persons work together to build up the same Body of Christ, according to each one's gifts (Eph 4:11–12).

CHAPTER 15

Contemplative Receptivity to God

WE HAVE CONCENTRATED THUS far upon vocational discernment prior to a person's entrance upon a contemplative lifestyle. The apostolic life is the milieu in which aspirants to the contemplative life, whether they are celibate, married, or single, undergo that phase of discernment.

The simultaneous presence of the following signs and conditions offers positive affirmation that a person living the apostolic life could have a calling to the contemplative life:

- a qualitative being-in-love with God, which manifests itself in a profound, intimate, loving relationship with Jesus and in a sense of the indwelling Trinity;

- communion with God in daily life, which becomes observable in these ways: movement beyond discursive meditation to contemplation, a distinctive contemplative approach to all aspects of life, and peaceful acquiescence in mystery;

- a history of being born out of the womb of society into solitude—carefully, patiently, and after long delay;

- a desire to live a life of silence and solitude in affiliation with a community.

When the above traits are sufficiently manifest, an aspiring contemplative's next step is to live the contemplative life on an experimental basis for an extended span of time. Henceforth, our focus is upon discernment during that interval. Since this phase of vocational discernment involves a person's immersion in an actual contemplative lifestyle, we will refer to the individual as a candidate rather than an aspirant.

What does "extended span of time" mean in relation to experimental contemplative living? There may be external factors that determine the amount of time. Most contemplative orders, for example, designate in their formation guidelines a specific number of years. At the end of that period, a candidate is expected to be either ready for permanent commitment or ready to pursue another vocational lifestyle elsewhere. Yet time frame relates above all to an interior process. Its duration depends upon the workings of the Spirit within each candidate and upon a candidate's responsiveness to God. From that perspective, a person keeps on testing the possible calling until he or she reaches a peaceful decision.

During an experimental period of living a contemplative life, the candidate's perseverance in the lifestyle, together with continuing personal growth while doing so, requires careful deliberation.

Strong-willed people could conceivably force themselves to endure something resembling the contemplative life for quite a while, but not without their self-made lifestyle adversely affecting them. Inevitably, toxic stagnation and perfunctory routine, devoid of the vitality of true perseverance, would prevail in the lives of these persons. While they might persist in that condition for a lengthy time, God alone causes authentic perseverance in the contemplative life.

True perseverance, however, is not abstract. The signs of a possible contemplative vocation that emerged prior to the person's transition to a contemplative lifestyle continue to have immense importance throughout the experimental period of contemplative living. Thus, perseverance manifests itself in the candidate's further progress in these areas: christocentric and trinitarian love of God, communion with God in all aspects of life, movement into increasing solitude, and participation in community (chapters 10–14).

In this chapter and for the remainder of this section, we take up additional signs and conditions of perseverance in the contemplative life; specifically, contemplative receptivity to God, a contemplative stance in activity, basic emotional maturity, and interpersonal relationships.

We begin with contemplative receptivity to God. We explore the effects of contemplation upon these five aspects of a candidate's communion with God: an integrating prayer life, solitary prayer, silence and solitude, simplicity of heart, and stability in life. We examine the other three additional areas related to perseverance in subsequent chapters.

An Integrating Prayer Life

An integrating prayer life consists of much more than complementarity between the various forms of prayer that might punctuate a contemplative's day; for example, communal and private, oral and silent, devotional and liturgical. It refers to more than the needed integration of prayer, study, work, and recreation. The basic factor integrating all of life into prayer is contemplation itself.[1] The contemplative communes immediately and directly with the indwelling Trinity in all things; for instance, silence and speech, stillness and activity, aloneness and social interaction. That abiding communion between the contemplative and the Father, Son, and Spirit constitutes the integrating prayer life.

In contemplation God and a person indwell each other twenty-four hours a day, seven days a week. Contemplation at that depth is not something to turn on or off like a water facet or an electric light switch. It is continuous. As loving communion, contemplation integrates all components of a contemplative life into a life of prayer. It awakens the contemplative ever more fully to the mystery of God becoming all in all (1 Cor 15:28).

In beholding the risen Christ, a contemplative experiences each aspect of daily life as a way of praying—whether solitary prayer, study, ministry, personal encounters, the natural world, meetings, or recreation. The prayerful quality of each undertaking depends also upon its appropriate balance with all the other facets of life. Each dimension of life, when in harmony with the other elements, becomes not only a way of praying in itself, but also a pathway to other forms of prayer. For instance, the quality of solitary prayer enhances activity as prayer, and vice versa. Conversely, imbalance in one area produces imbalance in other realms. Too much work could shortchange solitary prayer. Excessive time alone might detract from sufficient presence to other community members.

The balancing of all ways of praying does not imply absence of tension in the contemplative life. To the contrary, it takes a certain creative tension to hold in unity the diverse elements of life. That form of tension promotes interior peace.

A contemplative might feel anxiety or frustration and still remain interiorly peaceful. Sometimes clashes in community, surges of the storms related to the dark night,[2] personal immaturities, and sinfulness become intensely stressful experiences. Even in the midst of those trials, a true contemplative abides in the peace that the world cannot give and cannot take away (John 14:27).

God's providence purifies and refines the quality of an integrating prayer life often by means of unanticipated events and unexpected setbacks. An indigent person who requires assistance appears on the doorstep just when the contemplative is ready to seek out time alone. Or perhaps

1. See *Contemplation*, 125–40.
2. See *Contemplation*, 85–96; *Spiritual Journey*, 108–13, 167–98.

the contemplative is engaged in a project that seems to run into obstacle after obstacle, never reaching a satisfactory completion. Confronted with such events and setbacks, the contemplative learns to let go preconceived plans for prayer and to let those unforeseen situations become themselves ways of praying.

A truly integrating prayer life implies flexibility and adaptability. Rigidity in any shape or form is contrary to contemplative living. One expression of rigidity is the compartmentalization of the various aspects of daily contemplative life. These are two examples:

Some candidates move through their communal activities in a disjointed manner. They exhibit no sense of a unifying influence that weaves together all a day's happenings into a life of prayer. Instead of having a sense of the interrelatedness of their undertakings, these persons find only a series of disconnected events. This attitude can prevail even when they perform their duties reasonably well.

Other candidates find meaningfulness in their contemplative life solely in the areas of solitary and communal prayer. They set up a split between what they deem to constitute prayer and what they judge to have no import in regard to prayer. Thus, they tend to look upon manual labor, interactions with people, or recreational opportunities as intrusions upon their prayer life. They view those necessary activities and responsibilities as obstacles to eliminate so that they can return to what they consider their spiritual pursuits.

Solitary Prayer

Although every aspect of the contemplative life is a potential way of praying, contemplation of God occurs in a most unique, immediate, and direct manner during solitary prayer. Therefore, the following questions need careful attention when discerning a candidate's perseverance in contemplative living:

Is the candidate faithful to daily solitary prayer? Does the person remain in loving attentiveness to God when contemplation is arid, dark, or empty? Does the candidate pray in solitude regularly or only on an erratic basis? Is there an abandonment of solitary prayer intermittently or for lengthy intervals? When tangible results or warm feelings are not forthcoming during solitary prayer, does the candidate become unduly discouraged or even give up praying altogether? Does the person too readily forego solitary prayer with the rationale that the time would be spent more profitably at work, recreation, or reading?

A lack of fidelity to solitary prayer needs thorough discernment. On the one hand, the behavior could relate simply to a need for guidance or encouragement with a practical difficulty in prayer. On the other hand, a disinclination toward contemplation or an avoidance of solitary prayer could suggest lack of a vocation to the contemplative life.

Contemplation awakens within a person called to the contemplative life a desire for increasing aloneness with God. Does the candidate yearn for more time alone to contemplate God? Does the candidate feel a certain incompleteness—a kind of inner frustration—when a period of prayer has to be cut short or omitted, even if for a good reason? For a contemplative, that feeling of incompleteness and frustration is not the result of guilt but of deprivation. It is caused not by mere absence but by a lack of something essential.

While a contemplative might long for more solitary prayer, the presence of that desire does not mean automatically that God wants the person always to receive extended time for solitary prayer. The longing itself is often the means by which God leads the person into new depths of contemplation.

Silence and Solitude

Jungian psychology makes reference to extroverted and introverted personality types. Each human being has tendencies toward both extroversion and introversion, with one trait exerting dominance. A dominant extroverted or introverted trait pertains to a person's natural preference in relating and adapting to the world.

Many people associate contemplatives primarily with introverted personality types. Of itself, the introverted attitude toward the world has nothing to do with contemplative solitude. The fact that a person persists in living in a quiet, out-of-the-way place implies an aloneness, but that persistence does not ensure that the individual has entered contemplative silence or solitude. The contemplative mode of living is the fruit of a special grace and it is a vocation. God draws both extroverted persons and introverted persons to be contemplatives. To cite two examples, St. Teresa of Jesus seems extroverted, while St. John of the Cross appears introverted.

Extroverted people have by nature a preference for an environment wherein they interact constantly with people and engage in myriad activities. Consequently, candidates who are extroverted could have substantial difficulty adapting to contemplative silence and solitude. That difficulty has a positive dimension. It is living proof that their perseverance in the quietude and aloneness is in response to God's initiative and not of their own making.

Conversely, candidates who are introverted by nature may adapt effortlessly to exterior silence and aloneness. The adaption may be in fact too easy, more from themselves than from God. Their attraction to quietness and aloneness could originate from what is naturally familiar and comfortable to them rather than from a calling to the contemplative life. The natural preference for aloneness and introspection, while positive in itself, differs from contemplative solitude.

The Matrix of Communion

In the contemplative life, silence and solitude constitute a hallowed milieu for communion with God and compassion for all creation. The quietude and aloneness form a blessed matrix of conversion. The stillness and the seclusion become a furnace of purification and transformation in God. In silence and solitude, the risen Christ reforms contemplatives in his own Spirit and frees them gradually from their compulsions. There the old self dies and the new self comes to birth, develops, and matures.

Jesus himself was forever going off to some solitary place where he could be alone and pray (Luke 5:16). Following his example, each contemplative person has favored solitary places. Those locations go by a variety of designations: a dwelling place, a cell, a room, a cottage, a cabin, an oratory, a seascape, or a mountain top. A contemplative needs a physical space in which to taste and to feel silence and solitude. There the contemplative soul learns its gift and grows in appreciation of the interior solitude wherein God dwells. Exterior silence and solitude foster interior communion with the Trinity. In physical silence and solitude, the contemplative "hears" silent music and "sees" mystery face to face.[3]

Some people have a desire for a contemplative life, but that desire originates in something other than a calling from God. When these people seek out and attain prolonged external aloneness, they find themselves often exceedingly restless. Instead of facing God in the emptiness and detachment that solitude requires, they try to fill up life with distraction and diversion.

Even persons called to the contemplative life indulge in distractions and diversions from time to time. Some people take unnecessary excursions outside their place of solitude; for example, frequent trips to town, protracted visits with family or friends, repeated attendance at cultural performances, browsing around stores. These people are always on the go,

---

3. See *Spiritual Canticle,* especially stanzas 14–15, 35–40; Merton, "Epilogue: *Meditatio Pauperis in Solitudine*," 407–23, *Thoughts in Solitude,* 79–124, and "Notes for a Philosophy of Solitude," 177–207.

taking trips here, there, and everywhere, whenever the slightest excuse presents itself. Other people escape solitude through voluminous letter writing, texting, or emailing. Still other persons engage in prolonged phone conversations or in entertaining an endless stream of visitors.

None of those activities is in itself "wrong" for a contemplative. Each encounter, pursuit, or recreation could have a place in a contemplative lifestyle, dependent upon the specifics of a person's calling and when engaged in with moderation. Nonetheless, beyond a certain point such involvements begin to detract from contemplative living. How much is too much? It all depends upon God's will here and now for each contemplative.

Self-Knowledge

In silence and solitude, the Spirit reveals to contemplatives the truth of themselves. Committed contemplatives have a willingness to undergo the self-knowledge that emerges from encounter with God. They work to accept both their giftedness and their poverty. They have gratitude for all their blessings and they accept when necessary their need for reconciliation. As their hidden selves grow strong by the grace of God, they let the Spirit gradually and painstakingly strip away their egocentrism and dispel their illusions.

Does the candidate manifest readiness to receive and to undergo the self-knowledge that God reveals in silence and solitude? Is the candidate receptive to further personal growth in transforming union with God?

The Quality of Silence and Solitude

Even in a close-knit community, contemplatives remain silent and solitary as they interact and go about their routine. They avoid seeking out other community members for trivial conversation or gossip.

Can the candidate actually remain silent? Is the person at home and at ease in being silent, whether alone or in the presence of other people? Or, in general, is the candidate simply unable to refrain from talking, despite sincere efforts to do so? Does the candidate talk compulsively?

Does the candidate make a positive contribution toward maintaining communal silence and solitude? Is the person cooperative and helpful in preserving a silent and solitary ambience within community? When it is necessary to speak at a time or a place designated for silence, does the candidate respect the spirit of quietude? Or is loud, boisterous, and disruptive behavior the norm? Does the candidate respect the privacy of the other members of the community? Or is the candidate constantly seeking out the latest rumors and meddling in the lives of community members?

There is a child within each adult—an inner child who needs to play, to frolic, and to have fun. Some people satisfy that need on occasion by acting silly or kicking up their heels. That type of high-spirited enjoyment has its place in the contemplative life. Contemplatives need to relax, to laugh, and to play at times. Childlike playfulness differs though from continually clowning around. A candidate's incessant efforts to be comedian-in-residence or trickster-at-large would raise questions concerning suitability for the contemplative life.

Silence is far more than absence of talking. Silence is a quality that permeates a contemplative's personhood and manner of presence toward God and creation. While being verbally silent, does the candidate nonetheless undermine communal silence with a frequent barrage of strategies designed to draw attention; for instance, exaggerated facial expressions, an affected manner of walking, loud sighing, or constant yawning? In doing communal chores, is the candidate forever slamming doors, banging around kitchenware, or leaving machinery idling, with sounds reverberating throughout the entire living quarters?

How does the candidate cope with the extensiveness of silence and solitude? Is there an effort to be attentive to God in whatever the present moment holds? Or, do constant flights of fantasy and daydreaming provide the means of escape from the exigencies of silence and solitude?

Any indication of significant difficulty in the practice of silence and solitude and any tendency toward isolation in response to prolonged quietude and aloneness require thorough consideration in vocational discernment.

Simplicity of Heart

The contemplative is par excellence a person whose heart is set upon the "one thing necessary" (Luke 10:41); that is, upon being loved by the triune God and loving God in return, together with all creation in God. That simplicity of heart finds reflection in the contemplative's outer world. Consequently, simplicity in all things is a further sign of a candidate's perseverance in contemplative receptivity to God.

Simplicity of heart implies using only what is necessary to commune in love with God. In solitary prayer, for example, contemplatives remain content to love the Beloved and to be loved by him immediately and directly.[4]

---

4. See *Contemplation*, 21–26, 36–43.

They do not clutter their prayer with nonessentials. They employ words, images, and gestures only when and as the Spirit moves them to do so.

Simplicity is evident also in having only basic necessities. Contemplatives do not hoard. They do not fill up their living space with superfluous clothing, books, gadgets, and mementos. The latest fashion trends and the niceties of the cosmetic world have no place in their lives.

Simplicity postulates frugality in the use of material possessions, whether one's own, those of another person, or those belonging to the community. Contemplatives spontaneously refrain from wastefulness of any kind. They strive to exercise prudence and conservation in the use of food, water, money, electricity, and fuel. They try to maintain a basic orderliness and cleanliness in their private space and in communal property that pertains to their responsibilities.

Simplicity of heart is manifest above all in the ability to be oneself and to grow in at-homeness with one's unique identity in God. Simplicity of heart thus enables contemplatives to remain wholesomely open and vulnerable before God and creation. They can live without putting on airs, without having to assume roles, without camouflage, subterfuge, or envy.

Is the candidate then becoming increasingly attentive to "the one thing necessary" and moving toward ever greater simplicity in all things?

Stability in Life

Two sayings in particular from the desert abbas and ammas exemplify the importance of stability for a contemplative's communion with God. One saying states that just as a hen that fails to sit on her eggs will produce no young, so the contemplative that moves from place to place will grow cold in the faith.[5] Another saying notes that just as it is impossible for a continually transplanted tree to bear fruit, so a contemplative that moves from place to place cannot become virtuous.[6] Stability in contemplative living provides an ambiance wherein the contemplative can for the love of God be still (like a hen sitting on her eggs) and put down deep spiritual roots (like a tree planted in the earth).

Persons with a contemplative vocation have a need for both exterior and interior stability.[7] Most contemplatives want to settle down in one place for a prolonged time, if not for the remainder of their lives. They desire to participate in the common life and form relationships in community with

5. *The Book of the Elders*, 104. *PG*, 65.424.

6. Ibid, 114. *SC*, 387.743.

7. See *RB 1980: The Rule of St. Benedict*, 169–171.

their brothers or sisters. They commit themselves to practice obedience to God according to the charism and the constitutions of their community. Those external forms of stability help sustain an interior grounding for their contemplation of God. Stability of place and stability of relationships foster growth in stability of heart.

What contemplative groups refer to as the cloister or the enclosure is a means of promoting stability in life. Most contemplative communities have a designated area of physical space in which members dwell together and in which the community as a whole remains separate from society. Some communities legislate this space in a meticulous manner, while other communities maintain their spatial boundaries in a more informal and flexible way. Although the construct of a cloister or enclosure differs somewhat from group to group, those communities share in common the recognition of the value of a private space reserved for solitary living. Even contemplatives who live in contexts other than a contemplative community carve out spontaneously an external space for aloneness that has the spirit of a cloister or enclosure.

A contemplative cloister or enclosure is not for withdrawal or isolation. It is not a wall around a person for the purpose of keeping out the world or of keeping oneself confined within a space. It is not an end in itself. The purpose of a contemplative cloister or enclosure pertains to the biblical themes of hiddenness, privacy, and aloneness with God, which are echoed in these passages: "Your life is now hidden with Christ in God" (Col 3:3); "When you pray, enter your private room and having closed the door, pray to your Father in secret" (Matt. 6:6); "Jesus was always going off to desert places where he could be alone and pray" (Luke 5:16).

Stability in life, together with supportive components such as the cloister or enclosure, promotes a milieu in which contemplatives have all the freedom necessary for loving attentiveness to God. Stability invites contemplatives to be receptive to whatever the current moment holds and to ponder with depth the mystery of God in the here and now. Stability in life is a catalyst by which the Spirit teaches contemplatives how to live in the present and how to see as God sees.

When God calls a person to the contemplative life, the practice of stability does not leave the contemplative stunted in personal growth. Rather, stability is a dynamic quality, urging the contemplative toward creativity, change of heart, ever greater depths of transforming union with God, and communion with all creation in God. Stability represents a narrowing down of a path in order to enter through a gateway into the deep mysteries of God.

Therefore, the following questions help explore stability in life as an indication of contemplative receptivity to God:

Does the candidate experience stability in life as a positive value? Does the person view the ability to abide, to remain, to be still, and to stay put—both interiorly and exteriorly—as essential to contemplative living? Can the candidate accept the stability of communal life as a matrix for encounter with God?

On the whole, does the candidate seem at home, peaceful, and content in the stability of communal life? Or does the person appear to be mired down in endless boredom and lifeless routine? Are repetitive tasks, the unchanging daily schedule, the ordinariness of life, and the encounter with the same people day in and day out having a deadening effect upon the candidate's personality and slowly eroding all zest for life?

Candidates act sometimes in ways counter to stability. Is the candidate seeking out inappropriate diversions within or outside the community?

Has inner unrest escalated to the point that the candidate is now devising avenues of escape from the usually preferred modes of diversion? Is the person exhibiting on a habitual basis emotional agitation, inability to be physically still, undue loudness and unruliness, all of which can indicate difficulty in coping with stability? Is stability in the contemplative life promoting overall growth in the candidate? Or is it driving the person to increasing distraction?

Does stability provide a secure haven in which to undergo the challenge and chaos essential to growth in faith, hope, and love? Or is what passes as stability merely an excuse for mediocrity and complacency?

Is the candidate able to discuss difficulties related to stability in life with a spiritual director and with communal leaders? Is the candidate willing to engage with those persons in sorting out which issues pertain to the question of perseverance in the contemplative life and which struggles pertain to areas that require personal growth, irrespective of vocational lifestyle?

Once a contemplative vocation reaches a certain threshold of maturation, that calling endures for the remainder of a person's life. An authentic contemplative does not move in and out of contemplation or the contemplative life. Some contemplatives have responsibilities that require considerable activity and interaction with people over protracted periods—as in the cases of St. Bernard of Clairvaux, St. Teresa of Jesus, and St. John of the Cross. Yet, those contemplatives never cease growing in their contemplative calling. Their stability in life remains intact, even as they fulfill their responsibilities. The activities and interactions that go with their communal responsibilities are fruits of their contemplation, not distractions or diversions to evade their vocational lifestyle. Those activities and interactions are also catalysts by which the Spirit deepens in those contemplatives their transforming union with God.

CHAPTER 16

A Contemplative Stance in Activity

LOVING COMMUNION WITH GOD the Creator, the Word-made-Flesh, and the Spirit is the leitmotif of Christian contemplative life.

In the previous chapter, we focused upon areas that exemplify a candidate's perseverance in an attitude of loving receptivity to God. Those areas include the following: an integrating prayer life, solitary prayer, silence and solitude, simplicity of heart, and stability in life.

Each Christian vocational lifestyle requires a balance between its receptive and active elements. On the one hand, unless a person has a profoundly receptive stance toward God, activity degenerates into mere busyness. On the other hand, without earnest effort and fidelity to daily responsibilities, a person tends toward inertia or pseudo-quietism rather than receptivity. Therefore, in this chapter we explore the quality of a candidate's activity for signs of perseverance in the contemplative life.

A candidate has to be able to maintain a contemplative stance in activity. The preposition *in* denotes both *in the midst of* activity and *toward* activity. A contemplative stance *in the midst of* activity refers to remaining loving the Beloved no matter what one is doing. The contemplative stance is also *toward* activity in that the actual doing—the action itself—is a mode of loving encounter with Jesus. *Maintaining* a contemplative approach accentuates steadfastness, persistence, and faithfulness as one goes about various undertakings.

Perseverance with a contemplative stance in activity becomes especially discernible in these four aspects of the contemplative life: leisure, study, manual labor, and ministry.

Leisure

Leisure is essential to the contemplative life. Leisure is a way of being which permeates all contemplative activities. As such, it has nothing in common with laziness or idleness.

Leisure refers to the ability to be oneself and to remain at peace in God. It pertains to the aptitude to be as one is, with all that exists, here and now. It relates to the capacity to go calmly about one's activity with a realistic sense of eternity. Leisure is thus a mode of being-becoming in which a contemplative and God remain mutually present to each other. Leisure is a condition required for loving attentiveness to God in all dimensions of human life, including prayer, relationships, study, work, and recreation.[1]

Laziness or idleness, on the contrary, is a lack of presence to one's true self, to other people, to creation, and to God. Laziness or idleness entails inertness, destructive passivity, submission to entropy, withdrawal into oneself, isolation from the world. It is the opposite of loving attentiveness.

Leisure awakens a carefree attitude in a person. From one viewpoint, to be carefree is *to be free from care*. It is to relinquish excessive worry and undue anxiety. It is to cast off any tendencies toward a savior complex. It is to let go unrealistic expectations of oneself and other people. From another perspective, to be carefree means *to be free to care*. It is to care so passionately about "the one thing necessary" (Luke 10:42) that all other concerns are in relation to that One. Carefree contemplatives are deeply compassionate persons. They care about all things with the patient caring of God. They care as Jesus cares (John 15:12; 1 Pet 5:7), which is as the Father himself cares (John 15:9; Luke 6:36; 12:31).

Leisure requires of a person maximum effort in responding to God. Laziness or idleness refuses that effort. Leisure promotes unity and wholeness in the contemplative life. In so doing, leisure demands of each contemplative tremendous interior and exterior discipline. Laziness, on the other hand, tends toward dissipation and disintegration. In leisure a person is deified, divinized, spiritualized.[2] In laziness or idleness, a human being becomes ever more fragmented, scattered, lost.

Is leisure then a value for a candidate in living a contemplative life? Does the candidate nurture a spirit of leisure in all dimensions of life? Or is what the candidate considers leisure just a cover for laziness or idleness?

---

1. St. John of the Cross uses the Spanish *ocio* quite positively in the context of perseverance in contemplation (for example, *Dark Night*, I, 10, 5). Unfortunately, some translators render *ocio* as "idleness" or "ease" rather than "leisure" or "carefreeness."

2. *In otio, deificare*. See St. Augustine, *Letter X*, PL, 33, 71.

People exhibit laziness in numerous ways. These are practical examples: Paint remains splattered across the floor. A meal is just slapped
together. Laundry is returned in an unclean and crumpled state to community members. Dirt, dust, and smudge marks are left indefinitely after
a repair project. Personal belongings clutter up space designated for group
gatherings and activities.

True, some persons are naturally more organized and meticulous than
are other people. Yes, contemplative leisure has to let go of some things for
a while. It must bear with a certain creative chaos and disorder. It has to live
with some incompleteness and unfinished business. Nonetheless, a pattern
of continuing laziness in relation to a candidate's activities requires assessment. The candidate could be ill, in crisis, or exhausted, and consequently
overwhelmed by the demands of life. In those circumstances, compassionate
assistance could go a long way toward resolution of the matter. When those
conditions do not exist, outright narcissism could be the issue. At the very
least, the candidate's conduct indicates a lack of care and courtesy toward other people. It disrespects the needs and rights of other community members. It
is to the detriment of a candidate's own personal development.

Persistent laziness or idleness eats away at a certain disciplined
rhythm necessary to a contemplative life. That methodical flow of life
differs from a compulsive adherence to schedules or a rigid arrangement
of material things. Rather, it reflects both ascetic and aesthetic aspects
of contemplative living. It manifests interior simplicity, together with
simplicity in physical surroundings. It bespeaks inner wholeness and
wholesomeness. It embodies singleness of heart and harmony of spirit.
Its source is the "pure of heart" of the beatitudes: "Blessed are the pure of
heart; they shall see God" (Matt 5:8).

Study

The contemplative life is a "life in faith, faith in the Son of God" (Gal 2:20).
Yet in-depth study of the Scriptures, theology, spirituality, and related fields
is integral to contemplative growth in faith.[3] This pondering of the mysteries
of faith helps contemplatives formulate the direction of their lives so as to
respond with increasing freedom to the divine initiative. It raises their consciousness of God and of God's loving interaction with creation. Moreover,
study is a practical way in which contemplatives balance receptivity with
activity, listening with resourcefulness, mystery with knowledge.

3. See *Contemplation*, 131–33.

The effort that candidates exert in study can reveal attitudes ranging from a latent complacency to a resolute pursuit of truth. Some candidates complain that the content of their reading is too dense, heavy, and complex. They want to put it aside and do something less demanding. The diligent effort and the eager enthusiasm that other candidates expend in their study indicate an insatiable search for God who is beyond all that they know or grasp.

There are those people who believe that study has no place in the contemplative life. They insist that contemplatives should pass their years with eyes closed, ears plugged, and never crack open a book—except possibly the Holy Rule, the Bible, and a few authors carefully selected by religious superiors. That attitude springs from misguided reasoning and undermines growth in contemplative living. It is not that a contemplative community has to be an institution of higher learning or that every contemplative has to be a scholar. Nonetheless, faith seeks understanding and that understanding in turn opens candidates to an ever-deepening faith in Jesus.

Does the candidate then demonstrate an interest in study, not just in browsing or in eclectic reading? Granted, some persons are naturally more studious than other people. Some persons rate higher than other people on intelligence or aptitude tests. However, comparison of natural abilities among individuals is not the issue at hand. This is the pressing question: Are there signs within the candidate of a sincere and cultivated searching into divine mystery?

How does the candidate study? Contemplative study requires extensive time, concentration, and commitment. It is more than casual reading or the superficial scanning of a mass of material. Does the candidate ponder the mysteries of faith with discipline and persistence? Is the approach to study deep and penetrating or superficial and slipshod? Some people read relatively little subject matter yet study intensely. Other persons read voraciously and study little or not at all. Still other people have the ability to integrate both extensive reading and profound pondering of the mysteries.

Manual Labor

Physical work is another activity essential to the contemplative life. We refer not to wage-earning employment outside a community, but to the routine chores necessary for smooth functioning within a community, such as cooking, cleaning, dishwashing, gardening, preparing rooms for guests, upkeep of mechanical equipment, property maintenance, and financial oversight. So many diverse tasks require attention in community living—sewing, laundry, directing the choir, singing in choir, preparing liturgies, paying bills, and so on.

Physical work is an expression of a contemplative's spirit of self-giving and connectedness to the earth. The Scriptures make reference to the necessity of people earning their daily bread by the sweat of their brow (Gen 3:19; 2 Thess 3:10). Each person has to give back something in return for life's blessings. Contemplatives are no exception to that mandate. They have a responsibility to work in exchange for the basic necessities of life. In fact, the simplicity and frugality so characteristic of the contemplative life demand extensive labor on the part of each contemplative. It takes immense work to keep life simple.

Hard, earnest manual labor is salutary in the contemplative life. It is necessary for the stability and the growth of a community and its members. It contributes to each person's health and well-being. It is a positive physical outlet for anxiety and stress. To the degree that it can, a contemplative community takes care of its own needs without hiring help. Working together to sustain the community reminds members of their oneness in Christ and of their vocational interdependence.

Work assignments in a contemplative community should aim to match each member's talents with a task that requires the use of some of those personal gifts for the benefit of the group as a whole. That approach to the designation of tasks provides optimal opportunity for each member to nurture self-development and to assist in the creation of a vibrant contemplative milieu for all members. Moreover, manual work possesses its own intrinsic value. The work itself contributes to the building up of the Body of Christ and to the advancement of God's reign.[4]

Therefore, in relation to manual work, these qualities in a candidate need appraisal: personal initiative, dependability, creativity, thoroughness, cheerfulness, willingness to follow specific instructions on occasion, ability to collaborate with other members when necessary, practicality, common sense, generosity, and completion of assigned tasks.

Ministry

God calls contemplatives to be contemplative to other persons who are contemplatively inclined. All authentic ministry by those called to the contemplative life is a specific response to that missionary impulse.

---

4. See *Divine Milieu*, 17–43; *Contemplation*, 135–36; *Spiritual Journey*, 55–74.

Contemplative Ministries

Within a contemplative context, daily manual work is of value in itself. Yet it has also a ministerial dimension. The work of each member is a service to the whole community. The labor of all members serves to provide an inviting ambiance for each member. A candidate's responsiveness to the needs of individual members and to the community as a whole is a sign of a persevering love in action.

Other ministries also have an appropriate place within the contemplative life. Those ministries extend to the world outside the community and involve service to persons beyond the circle of community membership. Those ministries are of two kinds. One form pertains to the ministry of an individual contemplative. A contemplative with the appropriate gifts and training might develop a limited ministry to spiritual seekers. That service could entail, for example, proclamation of the Word, spiritual accompaniment, spiritual direction, directed retreats, or theological research and writing. The second form of ministry pertains to an income-generating work or project that a contemplative community as a whole undertakes for its own benefit and also for the good of a segment of creation.

Depending on the charism of a group and the nuances of each member's vocation, certain projects can constitute ministries suitable for a contemplative community. That communal undertaking might take the form, for example, of a farm, a bakery, a printing shop, a bookbindery, or hospitality services to spiritual pilgrims. Whatever the specific project, the extent of involvement for each member and for the community as a whole has to be determined in light of the raison d'être of the contemplative life.

Of course, a contemplative community would do extensive discernment prior to committing itself to a specific enterprise. Even when the project has become well-established, discernment of God's will would continue. Moreover, leadership personnel in the community would have to be responsive to the contemplative needs of members who participate in the venture.

Contemplative communities take on a work or a project usually for the purposes of financial independence and stability in life. The income generated from a project contributes to communal stability in several ways. It enables the institute to have the financial means to sustain a way of life true to its charism. It provides for the material needs of the members. It helps maintain a spiritual milieu in which the members can continue to contemplate God.

Financial independence to the extent that it is possible within the communal circumstances is in the best interests of a contemplative community. Most contemplative communities in contemporary western societies have a primary means of financial self-support. Many of them supplement that income through seeking alms or donations. History teaches convincingly that whoever controls the purse strings eventually dictates the regimen. Generous benefactors are a blessing. Nevertheless, if a community is too financially dependent upon them, certain benefactors attain the power to intervene in the internal affairs of the community and to exercise undue influence in shaping its direction.

When a contemplative community decides to undertake a project for the purpose of its own financial support, the group would be wise to choose a project that accords with its distinctive mode of contemplative living. It is crucial for the members to approach the work as a contemplative ministry, not as an extraneous job or an add-on task in their lives.

Projects designed for community financial support are not the equivalent of private businesses. The contemplative life is geared toward primary goals and values different from those of a business. There is no evading that truth, no matter how much for profit-making reasons a community might wish to rationalize a venture. Certainly, business acumen and administrative skills are important to the success of a project, but a contemplative community should never turn a financially self-supporting undertaking into a business in the Wall Street sense of the term. While incorporating a component of service, a business is out to make as much profit as possible in a competitive market. A ministry, by contrast, is primarily a service inspired by the gospel—a service of each member to the community, a service of the community to other people, a service that could enable the community to be modestly self-supporting.

During the period of living the contemplative life on an experimental basis, a candidate must begin to consider how God might be calling him or her to be contemplative to other persons who are contemplatively inclined. What personal gifts in that regard does the candidate feel drawn to use? Are persons already seeking out the candidate? If so, what exactly are they seeking from the candidate? Does the candidate experience participation in routine chores and communal works as a form of contemplative ministry? Is the candidate able to integrate limited involvement in communal ministry with other facets of the contemplative life?

Contemplation as Ministry

God is utterly free to call a contemplative or a contemplative community to any number of contemplatively oriented ministries. However, contemplation itself—daily contemplative prayer—remains par excellence the ministry of the contemplative and of the contemplative community within the church and to the world.[5]

Contemplation as a ministry does not consist of continual intercessions to God for specific needs. The ministry of contemplation is that of remaining loving the Beloved and being loved by him. Adoration, praise, contrition, and thanksgiving are all epitomized in that wordless, imageless prayer of the heart.[6] In that simple act of communion, the love of God is mysteriously operative not only *within* the contemplative, but also *through* that person for the benefit of the church, the world, indeed all creation.

Generally, a contemplative sees little or no visible results of this ministry of contemplation. Yet experienced contemplatives have in faith an unshakable conviction of its value. In fact, they possess a sense of being sent forth by the Spirit to serve God and creation by means of contemplation. Over a prolonged period of living the contemplative life then, does the candidate experience contemplation as ministry? Can the person find ministerial fulfillment in prayer above all?

Many Christians perceive a general ministerial dimension to their prayer, whether discursive or contemplative. Nonetheless, praying is not the quintessence of their ministry. Prayer—even contemplation—is surely a priority, but it is not "above all." Theirs is a calling to the apostolic life. They do not have a vocation to the contemplative life as such.

5. See *Contemplation*, 141–46.
6. See *Contemplation*, 21–43.

CHAPTER 17

Emotional Maturity in the Contemplative Life

TO AN OUTSIDE OBSERVER or a casual visitor, the contemplative life can look like a laid-back mode of existence, a perpetual vacation, or even a piece of heaven on earth. Contrary to superficial appearances, it takes immense effort and discipline for people to live the contemplative life in a faithful manner. The love of God challenges contemplatives to the core of their being. Consequently, perseverance in contemplative living requires an uncommon degree of emotional maturity. Unless that emotional maturity exists within candidates, isolation and stagnation rather than solitude and growth tend to prevail in the day-to-day experience.

In this chapter, we explore emotional maturity as indicative of perseverance in the contemplative life.

Stress Management

Stress refers to a persistent force or energy that tends to alter a person's equilibrium. A certain positive stress holds in balance all the shifting elements and circumstances of a person's daily life. Other forms of stress have the potential to diminish human well-being and quality of life.

Each Christian lifestyle and every situation in life exert specific forms of stress. Those stressors can trigger within a person mental anguish, emotional anxiety, cognitive difficulties, and physical maladies. Stress management is not directed toward total removal or complete avoidance of all discomfort and tension. Rather, its aim is to lessen or to eliminate the undue anxiety that people heap upon themselves. Above all, healthy stress management promotes the development of skills and strategies that enable people to stay grounded amidst the pressures of life. It fosters the ability to confront difficulty. It encourages people to claim their inner strength. It directs human energy toward a good outcome in the circumstances. It challenges people to work creatively with the instability and the unpredictability of human existence.

In the contemplative life stress arises from many quarters. It occurs as a contemplative endures feelings of loneliness and hurt. It surfaces in reaction to boredom and monotony. It emerges as an individual undergoes the poverty, darkness, detachments, and renunciations inherent to each contemplative vocation. Stress results from personal immaturities, limitations, vulnerabilities, and sinfulness. It stems from conflict in significant relationships or in communal living. Frequently, stress is related to discrepancies between a contemplative's inner needs and the external conditions of life.[1] For a contemplative immersed in silence and solitude, God's transforming, enlightening, and purifying love itself is a formidable source of tension, conflict, and bewilderment.[2]

A contemplative's emotions have significance in relation to their origin, intensity, and management. Human emotions are in themselves neither good nor bad. They simply are. Feeling one's feelings and feeling one's way through those feelings open a contemplative to increasing self-experience and self-knowledge, which in turn point the way to deepening experience and knowledge of God and of all creation in God.

How then does a candidate for the contemplative life cope with a troublesome person or a disturbing event? What are the candidate's usual reactions to stress: aggression, withdrawal, anxiety, fear, repression, anger, tears, frustration, defiance, equanimity? What is the significance of a specific reaction? For example, an outburst of tears, on the one hand, could be symptomatic of an inner healing of a hurt and a cathartic release of pent-up feelings. On the other hand, crying endlessly or at the drop of a hat could signal self-pity, depression, a persecution complex, or some other emotional disorder. Can the candidate recognize, accept, and work creatively with sources of stress, together with emotional reactions to them?

What strategies or techniques does the candidate employ in managing stress? Some people handle stress best by promptly confronting its source. Other people need to back off for a while so that grace and time can work their healing effects. When the source of stress is loneliness, boredom, or monotony, it is not enough for the candidate merely to suffer it passively. The energy invested in that emotional experience has to be reoriented toward personal growth.

Over the course of time, does the candidate show signs of an ability to sustain emotional balance? Or are extreme mood swings a regular

---

1. See *Contemplation*, 97–109.
2. See *Contemplation*, 85–96; *Spiritual Journey*, 99–113, 163–98.

occurrence? Do the candidate's coping strategies lead eventually to a peaceful resolution of a problem or at least to a sense of peacefulness in living with the difficulty?

Certain Contraindicative Traits

The presence of any of the following traits raises concern about a candidate's emotional ability to persevere in the contemplative life:

- a generally negative, judgmental, and critical attitude toward self, other members of the community, and/or the community as a whole;

- an unremitting need to be right all the time;

- an inability and/or a refusal to share pertinent thoughts and feelings in the context of discernment with leadership personnel, community members, a spiritual director, and other significant persons;

- an inability to cope with conflict or confrontation;

- unacknowledged or unresolved issues related to family of origin or to abusive adult relationships;

- unexamined or unresolved trauma and grief resulting from military service or from ministry in violent areas of the world;

- a history of pent-up anger and resentment;

- a persistent need for a form of affirmation that the contemplative life by its nature is unable to provide.

Persons discerning the possibility of a contemplative vocation need to work intensively, with the assistance of their spiritual guides and psychological counselors, on any above difficulty that might assert itself. The groundwork would best be done before a person embarks upon the contemplative life. If the individual makes basic progress with the difficulty and if sufficient signs of a contemplative vocation exist, work on the issue could continue after entering the contemplative life. For some people though, it takes the silence and solitude of the contemplative life itself in order to come to even initial awareness of a problem.

Questions relevant to the above contraindicative traits include the following: Does the candidate manifest signs of growth in overcoming the tendency or resolving the issue? What, if any, positive virtues are emerging as the candidate gains freedom from the difficulty? For example, as the candidate lets go negative judgments, is there growth in tolerance, forgiveness, and compassion toward people? Would an apostolic lifestyle rather than the contemplative life provide a more supportive context as the candidate contends with the difficulty?

A person may have come to terms with a problem such as food, drug, or alcohol addiction, sexual promiscuity, deep-seated anger, or severe lack of self-love and self-esteem. However, lingering effects of the disorder could render the contemplative life inadvisable for that individual. Continued well-being and further growth may necessitate sustained interaction with people, involvement in many activities, variety in daily events, and frequent social engagements. Those forms of support and challenge, when necessary, are more readily found in the apostolic life.

Certain phobias can impede a candidate's ability to live a contemplative vocation peacefully in specific locales. For example, someone with an irrational fear of wild animals, insects, or physical darkness would find it practically impossible to live in a contemplative community located in a desert or a wilderness.

Peculiarities of dress and eccentricities in demeanor on the part of a candidate raise questions. Do these things represent merely experiments in self-discovery and attempts at self-expression? Or do they indicate a social disconnect that is contrary to the contemplative spirit?

Scruples pertaining to religious matters or ethical issues also detract from qualitative contemplative living.[3] Despite all protestations to the contrary, candidates afflicted with scruples possess immense self-centeredness. Instead of acting from the freedom of the Spirit, these persons react with anxiety toward an array of people, issues, and events. They want absolute assurance that they are right in their decisions and judgments. They become preoccupied with adherence to religious customs, rules, and regulations, either of their own making or handed down by an authority. The intense silence and solitude of the contemplative life make it difficult for these candidates to cope successfully with the indecisiveness, guilt, and confusion that their scruples cause them to feel. Peace of mind and heart eludes them.

Holistic Growth

It takes uncommon emotional balance to persevere in the contemplative life. Equally true is the fact that faithful living of this lifestyle itself facilitates continuing emotional development. Perseverance enhances immeasurably the identity and the integrity of the person called by God to this way of life.

---

3. Strictly speaking, scrupulosity is a psychological diagnostic criterion for obsessive-compulsive personality disorder. The difficulties that we mention lean heavily in that direction.

If the contemplative life is indeed a God-given vocation, an innate affinity will exist between the lifestyle and the recipient of the calling. The candidate will ease into the contemplative life and feel at home. If over time personal stress increases, negativism rises, phobias escalate, and eccentricities proliferate, that trajectory of events could indicate effort by a candidate to fit into a lifestyle foreign to his or her true identity and spiritual direction.

Lack of appreciable human growth and spiritual development during the period of experimental contemplative living constitutes a significant indication that a candidate's authentic vocation could be other than the contemplative life. God never demands the impossible of a person on any level in any manner, shape, or form. God never asks something that is destructive to a candidate's unique identity in Christ Jesus. The grace of each vocation is necessarily holistic. A calling to the contemplative life catapults a person in the direction of happiness, well-being, and life, "life to the full" (John 10:10).

CHAPTER 18

Love of Neighbor in the Contemplative Life

JESUS IDENTIFIED FOR HIS disciples the first and the greatest command-ment as love of God with full heart, soul, mind, and strength (Mark 12:30). In conjunction with that imperative, Jesus called his disciples also to love their neighbor as they love themselves (Mark 12:31). On another occasion, he went beyond self-love as the norm for love of neighbor. He taught his disciples that their love for each other must be an extension of the love with which he loves them—that love being the same love as that of the Father for the Son (John 15:9, 12). Thus, Christians must love one another as Jesus loves them, which is as the Father loves the Son. They are to love each other with God's own love.

On the spiritual journey, an ever-increasing love of neighbor affirms a person's deepening love of God. As the first letter of John observes: "Those who do not love people whom they see cannot love God whom they have never seen" (1 John 4:20). Consequently, love of neighbor is a further sign and condition of authentic perseverance in the contemplative life.

Like that of every Christian, a contemplative's love of neighbor has to be all-inclusive. It is the very nature of that love to reach out to all people, all living creatures, and creation as a whole. We focus in this chapter, how-ever, upon love of neighbor primarily in relation to the immediate circle of people whom a contemplative encounters in the course of daily living.

Love of Neighbor for a Celibate Contemplative

Celibate contemplatives living in community share solitary life together in their common quest for God. That communal milieu is the sphere in which they learn to love one another with Christ's own love. We explore signs now which indicate that a candidate who lives in a contemplative community is growing in love of neighbor. *Mutatis mutandis*, the signs pertain also to a candidate who lives the contemplative life alone, but who has a loose-knit association with some form of Christian community.

Communal Participation

The fact that a candidate has sought out official membership in a contemplative group does not automatically ensure community with those persons. Some candidates can be reasonably faithful to the external practices of the common life—for example, work, prayer, silence, recreation—and still not have a sense of belonging. Without recognizing it, they live in their little world parallel to or insulated from the community. That situation may exist through no fault of their own. God may not be calling them to the contemplative life at all, or at least not to this communal expression of it.

Therefore, has the beginner in the contemplative life wholeheartedly entered community? Does the candidate experience a basic at-homeness in the communal environment? Is this person truly a participant in the common life? Does the person have a sense of deepening bonds with other members? Does the candidate have an awareness of being united in Christ Jesus with fellow community members in a shared spiritual quest?

Contemplative Refinement

One observable sign of love among members of a contemplative community is the practice of basic social virtues. A general lack of courteous behavior on the part of a candidate could indicate movement into isolation and withdrawal rather than growth in love of neighbor.

A true contemplative possesses a certain refinement. She exudes a benevolence toward all persons. He emanates magnanimity at all times. This graciousness need not be that of a Miss Manners, an Emily Post, or an Amy Vanderbilt, but it is evangelical, Christian, and obvious. It is the result of genuine love governing the contemplative's attitudes, demeanor, and conduct.[1] For love seeks to act always with patience, kindness, delight in the truth, forgiveness, trust, hope, and endurance (1 Cor 13:1–10). Contemplative refinement flows also from a person's embodiment of the virtues that Jesus spoke of in the beatitudes. Those virtues include poverty of spirit, gentleness, compassion, hunger and thirst for justice, mercy,

---

1. See *The Cloud of Unknowing*, 224–25. St. John of the Cross's portrayal of the soul or bride in *Spiritual Canticle* and *Living Flame* is similar.

purity of heart, peacefulness, and the endurance of persecution for the cause of right (Matt 5:1–10).

Contemplative refinement manifests itself in a person's ability to be at ease and to act cordially in a wide range of social situations, for example, carrying on a conversation, sharing a meal, or assisting someone in need. It becomes evident in the contemplative's attentiveness to people's sensitivities and in compassionate presence to the travail of the world. A contemplative refinement finds expression also in simple and unassuming attire, in good personal hygiene, and in relaxed yet dignified body posture.

Are these qualities evident then as the candidate interacts with people both within and outside the community: graciousness, compassionate listening, receptivity to diverse viewpoints, and tolerance toward various approaches to life? Does the candidate share convictions, feelings, and ideas in a polite and respectful way? Is the candidate unpretentious in demeanor and appearance?

Does the candidate with a gentle spirit work for justice and seek peace? Or are gossip, destructive criticism, and power plays the preferred works? Does the candidate pit faction against faction in order to influence the outcome of an issue or to manipulate an area of contention?

A person's efforts to promote justice and peace are not always immediately pleasant and agreeable to all community members. Working in the cause of right with respectfulness for all people entails pain and suffering. Those efforts tend in the long run, though, to become a unifying force within a contemplative community.

Four Stressful Circumstances

Tensions, misunderstandings, frictions, and differences are part and parcel of the dynamics of each community and family. However, the nature and the exigencies of the contemplative life tend to magnify those difficulties. We highlight below four circumstances that contain potent sources of stress.

A *first circumstance* that contributes to heightened tensions in a contemplative community is the fact that the members did not choose to live together specifically out of liking or caring for one another. They find themselves together in the community because of obedience, vocation, chance, or divine providence. Consequently, they stay with each other for better or for worse, often till death do them part. Their common vocational lifestyle throws them together in a proximity that is difficult for an outsider to imagine.

In a contemplative community, the same people live together in the same place following the same routine day after day, year after year. Normal differences have the potential in that situation to turn easily into dislikes, and dislikes into disgust. Healthy friendships can evolve into cliques, and cliques tend to generate factions, envy, and bickering. Some communities are better known for their internal strife than for their charity, for their dissension than for their peace, for themselves than for Christ.

A member of an apostolic community who is living a contemplative life may undergo similar adversities. Some members of that group might tend to look upon the contemplative as eccentric simply because that person's lifestyle differs from their mode of living. Conversely, a few members who feel disappointed because they did not get "the same deal" are likely to cry favoritism and to reject, if not demean, the contemplative.

A *second circumstance* in a contemplative community that tends to magnify everyday struggles is the relative absence of the diversion and the mobility available in most other Christian lifestyles. Contemplatives participate in meaningful recreational activities. They go outside the community when a just reason exists. Yet they cannot hop merrily in a car and go visit a friend, attend a concert, or stroll through the park whenever they feel the need for it. The contemplative life requires coping skills different from those employed in other lifestyles. Those contemplative ways of managing stress are generally solitary and quiet, but for a person called by God to the lifestyle they are equally healthy and effective.

A *third circumstance* likely to amplify tensions in a contemplative community is "close horizons" or "small world syndrome." Spiritually, the world of the contemplative is the entire universe with Christ at its center, recapitulating all in himself (Col 1:15–20). Spiritually, the horizons of the contemplative are eternal. But in the nitty-gritty of daily life some contemplatives become short-sighted. They fall into tunnel vision. Because of the closeness of their immediate world so much of the time, that small world is all they become inclined to see. The smaller their world, the bigger ordinary things within it look to them.

Thus, these contemplatives fret continuously over one matter or another. On occasion, an issue may be genuinely important, but they occupy themselves excessively with it. More often, they pick something of very little consequence and inflate it far beyond its importance. They make mountains out of molehills. Fixated upon their exaggerated concerns, they become petty, narrow-minded, and judgmental toward other people. They plummet into ever greater loss of contemplative carefreeness.

A *fourth circumstance* that occurs with some frequency in community living is the experience within a contemplative of, on the one hand, an

ardent affinity toward one member and, on the other hand, a strong antipathy toward another member. Each human being has likes and dislikes.
At times (and often for no apparent reason) those feelings become quite
forceful. Several factors converge in a contemplative milieu to make coping
with those intense feelings a formidable undertaking: the perimeters set
by the cloister or enclosure in which members live; the close proximity of
members to each other, possibly until death do them part; the pervasive-
ness of silence and solitude; and the infrequency of contact with people
outside the community.

St. Thérèse of the Child Jesus observed that in her contemplative life
coping with those emotional extremes was a heavy cross. As a member of
a close-knit Discalced Carmelite community, she found within herself a
potentially overpowering affection for at least one member and a possibly
overwhelming natural aversion toward at least one other person.[2] To love
joyfully and productively, without being overwhelmed by either extreme, is
a daunting challenge for most contemplatives.

Therefore, the following questions pose themselves in vocational
discernment:

Does the candidate maintain a spirit of freedom and detachment in
dealing with a natural affinity toward a community member? Or does the
affection lead to preoccupation with the loved one? Is the affinity mutual? If
so, do the two persons keep their friendship open to and inclusive of other
members? Or does the relationship lean toward being a closed world for
two? Is the friendship a force for unity or a cause of division within the
community?

Can the candidate handle constructively an aversion toward a community member? Does the candidate cope adequately with dislike from
a member? Or does an interpersonal conflict cause such disturbance that
neither the candidate, the other person, nor the community itself can live
in peace?

If both persons with a natural antipathy or an unresolved conflict
have vocations to the same community, God's grace and the assistance of
qualified personnel can help them to accept and to transcend their differences. Moreover, a little self-discipline, sacrifice, and common sense on the
part of each person will go a long way toward letting peace prevail. The two
members will have to learn to interrelate amicably in communal gatherings. They must maintain Christian charity and civility toward one other
whenever they meet. Occasions for togetherness need to be balanced with
times of separation. Distance from each other, when the normal daily flow

---

2. See Thérèse, *Story of a Soul*, 222–25, 237.

of communal life provides it, will be to the benefit of each of them and the community as a whole.

If God is not calling to that community one or both of those persons, their conflict will erode harmony within the group. The probable outcome in that situation will be the departure from the community of one or both of the members.

Poverty of Spirit

The communal aspect of a vocation to the contemplative life is a gift from God. Each sister or brother is a blessing to a contemplative community and the whole community is a catalyst of God's grace for each member. Yet the persistent close proximity with the same people confronts a contemplative inevitably with his or her immaturities and sinfulness, with the deficiencies of each member, and with the dysfunctional aspects of the community itself. That experience of personal and communal poverty of spirit becomes a powerful instrument of God's transforming, enlightening, and purifying love.

Some contemplatives attempt to evade the truth of their poverty of spirit by concocting an endless stream of diversions. Overindulgence in an activity that in itself is appropriate to the contemplative life cannot assuage poverty of spirit. Nor will engagement in activities counter to the nature of the contemplative life serve to block out awareness of frailties, faults, and failings. In the long run, such diversionary pursuits lead only to an increase of dissipation and frustration. The irritations and frictions arising from poverty of spirit produce trying times, but similar struggles exist in every Christian life. Contemplatives are beset by all the foibles and vicissitudes of any other group of pilgrims striving to live the gospel. In an imperfect world, exercising forbearance when faced with some strife is a necessary spiritual practice for contemplatives.

The first letter of John proclaims that out of love Jesus laid down his life for his disciples. As he did for them, so they are to do for one another: "This has taught us the meaning of love: that Jesus Christ laid down his life for us. And we too have to lay down our lives for our brothers and sisters" (1 John 3:16).

Poverty of spirit is a catalyst in the process of a contemplative's daily dying and rising in Christ Jesus. The Spirit bestows upon a person called to the contemplative life the ability to accept poverty of spirit and to transcend it by love. The letter to the Ephesians expresses well the mandate to love and to put love into action within community: "Walk worthily of the calling you have received. Bear with one another in love, with all humility, gentleness, and patience. Be eager to keep the unity of the Spirit in the bond of peace" (Eph 4:1–3).

In contrast, a candidate's persistent inability to practice love by bearing with faults and failings could imply unsuitability for the contemplative life. Some beginners in a contemplative lifestyle become mired down in resentment, jealousy, and pettiness or in hurt feelings and self-pity. Most of their energy and time becomes consumed not in seeking God but in dwelling upon unresolved conflicts. Those candidates can become so preoccupied with the strife and dissension that they jeopardize their health and well-being.

An inability to cope with poverty of spirit differs from a beginner's transition from idealism to realism. That transition is one that each maturing candidate necessarily undergoes in the contemplative life. Most candidates enter the contemplative life with somewhat romantic and idealistic notions. Upon their arrival, they expect perfection at once from everyone. Consequently, the ordinariness that surrounds them shocks them. Their sudden disappointment and frustrated naiveté trigger cynicism and negativity toward their lifestyle and community. If their vocation is authentic, that reaction passes. It gives way to a more realistic and balanced perspective. These candidates develop a fresh way of seeing that incorporates both the strengths and the weaknesses of themselves, each member, and the community as a whole.

Authority in the Community

Discernment of perseverance in love of neighbor includes appraisal of a candidate's relationships with members who hold positions of authority within the contemplative community.

Community members duly elected or appointed to positions of office provide the candidate a significant means of insight into God's will. The contemplative community as a whole and a candidate's spiritual director also have a certain authority vis-à-vis the candidate.[3] They have in the discernment process a charismatic, moral, and spiritual authority.

Is the candidate respectful toward members in various positions of authority? Are they in turn courteous, caring, and responsive toward the candidate? Does the candidate exhibit an openness to suggestions, observations, and corrections from them? Can the candidate truly listen to them? Is the candidate able to ponder the insights and the concerns that they

---

3. See *Spiritual Direction*, 175–77; *Contemplation*, 97–109.

express? Or does the candidate persistently reject the truth contained in other perspectives? Does the person remain in matters of dialogue usually calm and responsive or mostly hostile and reactive?

Without direct rebellion against authority, a candidate can be resistant in more subtle ways. Some candidates conform externally to the wishes of those persons in leadership positions, even as these candidates seethe interiorly in defiance and resentment. Other candidates retaliate against leadership personnel by avoiding encounter with them, by withholding information from them, or by making caustic remarks about them to other people. In those situations, self-protection and self-interest, not love and altruism, motivate a candidate's behavior.

When repeated conflict with leadership personnel occurs, there could be within the candidate an underlying "authority problem." In this case, a candidate reacts irrationally to another person simply because that individual holds a position of authority. The candidate has an overwhelming fear that anyone in a leadership position is out to curtail individual freedom and self-determination. This candidate dreads the possible loss of self-identity and of a meaningful life by means of the will and the actions of people in leadership. The candidate's personal feelings of powerlessness and insecurity collide with what he or she perceives to be their power and control. Consequently, the candidate reacts toward authority figures with unwarranted withdrawal or unprovoked aggression. That dysfunction in relationship can deteriorate to a point wherein the candidate misconstrues virtually everything that an authority figure or a leadership team says, does, believes, or values. Trapped in that mind-set, the candidate judges even the slightest observation or correction from those persons with authority not as a casual remark or an invitation to growth, but as a deliberate infliction of suffering.

The problem is not always a candidate's immature responses or unfounded fears in relation to legitimate authority. Persons in positions of authority have their own immaturities and make their own mistakes in relation to community members. Moreover, sooner or later most candidates run into instances of an abuse of authority. Leaders and entire communities fail sometimes to listen to a contemplative's genuine spiritual needs. They refuse on occasion to accept the challenge that God offers them through a nonconforming member.

In a situation of abuse by someone in authority, the candidate needs to confront the issue. What are the available options? Who might be willing to offer assistance in the matter? What recourses or procedures do the community's constitutions and directives offer for resolution of conflict and reconciliation between members? Is the Spirit leading a candidate to remain in the community, provided that personal spiritual growth can continue in that context? Or, is the Spirit prompting the candidate to move elsewhere?

Love of Neighbor for a Married Contemplative

We referred earlier in this work to a few situations in which God might be calling persons to the contemplative life within the context of their Christian marriages. Vocational discernment for these people proceeds from the fact that marriage is their basic vocational lifestyle. A contemplative calling evolves out of and in relation to marriage. The vocational lifestyle of marriage and family life remains a primary point of reference in the development of a married contemplative's mode of living.

When the candidate is a married person living the contemplative life on an experimental basis, the practice of "love of neighbor" applies above all to relationships with the spouse and their children, if any. It extends also to those people with whom the candidate has direct interaction.

The expression of love in action meets with many challenges in the unusual situation of one spouse and parent having a possible contemplative vocation, while the other spouse and the children do not. During a period of experimental contemplative living, the consent, understanding, and support of the spouse and family continue to be crucial for the candidate. A healthy and growth-filled atmosphere for all family members must persist in their home, since they too have their vocations to follow. Their maturation cannot be stunted for the sake of the contemplative member. They have to be free to live and to evolve in a style and a direction appropriate for them, even if that means the one who desires to live a contemplative life must postpone a transition to it. God's calling to one family member does not impede the vocation of another member. All vocations within the family unit are interrelated. There must be give and take on the part of all members in order to discover what is in the best interests of each person and the family unit as a whole.

Prudence is especially necessary when children are involved. Their normal environment is anything but a silent and solitary one. Most children are spontaneously rowdy, rambunctious, and loud, at least at times. They need to be free to talk, to play, to run in and out of the house, to socialize with each other, and to invite friends to their home. Constantly cautioning them to be unduly quiet could cause in them emotional withdrawal and loss of a feeling of at-homeness under their own roof. Furthermore, should the contemplatively oriented parent remain too much apart from them for the sake of solitude, the children could perceive that parent as being cold, distant, or uncaring. The children could consequently feel unloved, abandoned, or rejected. Whatever God wants, it is surely not a dysfunctional family under the guise of a contemplative vocation.

Otherwise, married persons who are living a contemplative life on an experimental basis practice love of neighbor in ways similar to those of celibates with a contemplative calling. Those married contemplatives seek to let the love of God guide them in their being and their doing. They strive to develop a sense of belonging within their home, family, and local community. They try to let a contemplative refinement govern their demeanor and actions in relation to people. They show respect toward people by their practice of the basic social virtues. They make great effort to accept their spouses and children as they really are. They do their best to come to terms with their personal poverty of spirit and bear with the immaturities of their loved ones. They celebrate with joy and gratitude the life that they share with their loved ones. They make the effort to be responsive and adaptable to unanticipated requests and events. They foster in themselves a willingness to let God form them through their spouses, children, extended family, friends, spiritual guides, and local communities. Whatever they do for people or creation, they seek to do with love and in communion with the risen Christ.

CHAPTER 19

Concluding Pastoral Observations
on the Contemplative Life

THROUGHOUT THIS SECTION, WE described core characteristics of Christian contemplative life. Furthermore, we presented principles of discernment indicative of the presence of a possible contemplative vocation. In this chapter, we offer a synthesis of the vocational discernment process, together with some final pastoral observations.

Readiness to Enter the Contemplative Life

The existence of the following signs and conditions in aspiring contemplatives—whether they are celibate, married, or single—affirms readiness to pass from an apostolic life and to embark upon the contemplative life for an extended time of further vocational discernment.

First, the love of these persons for God has decidedly christocentric and trinitarian dimensions. Those qualities of love become evident in the profound, intimate, tender relationship that these people have with Jesus and the indwelling Trinity. For many aspiring contemplatives, the Eucharist is a uniquely meaningful symbol of their communion with the loving Creator, the Word Incarnate, and the Holy Spirit. The Eucharist is the sacrament of the indwelling presence of God manifest in Christ Jesus.

Second, these aspirants experience communion with God in the whole of life. That communion manifests itself specifically in at least the beginning of a transition from discursive prayer to contemplation, in an explicit contemplative orientation to all facets of daily living, and in an ability to acquiesce peacefully in mystery.

Third, over the course of time, these aspirants experience a transformation of their way of relating to creation. They have a personal history of being born "carefully, patiently and after long delay"[1] out of the womb of society into solitude.

Fourth, these aspirants desire some form of community with other persons who are contemplatively inclined. That community could be a canonically recognized contemplative institute 4or society of consecrated life. It could be a contemplative group of another sort, such as a contemplative house of prayer. When God calls a person to live the contemplative life in a private or independent way, community for that individual could consist of a loose-knit affiliation with a Christian community of one form or another. In the case of a person called to live the contemplative life in an apostolic institute or society, the communal setting could consist of a small group of persons who are living an apostolic lifestyle, but who welcome a contemplative in their midst. In the case of a person whom God calls to live a contemplative life within the context of marriage and family life, the primary community would consist of the spouse and children, if any.

Transition to the Contemplative Life

When married, celibate, or single persons actively involved in an apostolic life manifest preliminary signs of a possible contemplative vocation and are ready to begin living the contemplative life on a prolonged experimental basis, their vocational experiences fall within one of four general patterns.

A first pattern: These people had from an early age a clear sense of vocation to the contemplative life and a firm resolve to proceed eventually in that direction. They intended from the outset that their participation in the apostolic life would be on a provisional basis, for example, only until completing college, gaining certain human experiences, or fulfilling a familial obligation.

A second pattern: The desire of these people wavered for many years between the apostolic life and the contemplative life. Throughout that lengthy period of vacillation, they continued to live the apostolic life until a vocation to the contemplative life became clearly discernible. Thus, these persons experienced a prolonged indecision with regard to both lifestyles prior to reaching a definitive vocational option.

A third pattern: These people embarked wholeheartedly upon the apostolic life with no serious thought of a contemplative vocation. They persevered faithfully in ministry, all the while growing in experience and wisdom. Their solitary prayer progressed gradually beyond discursiveness to contemplation, and their overall contemplative orientation to life

1. Merton, "Notes for a Philosophy of Solitude," 204.

flourished. Without seeking a contemplative vocation or directly adverting to it along the way, they experienced in due course a calling to the contemplative life. That contemplative attraction reached such an intensity that they experienced a spiritual imperative to leave the apostolic life and pursue the contemplative life.

A fourth pattern: These persons, while engaged in apostolic endeavors, may or may not have aspired to the contemplative life. In the course of their spiritual journey, they came eventually to the threshold that marks the beginning of contemplation.[2] They interpreted that threshold initially as a probable vocation to the contemplative life. Upon more careful discernment, they came to understand the situation in a different light: God was indeed drawing them to an enhanced depth of loving communion in solitary prayer. God indeed willed that they allow the contemplative thrust inherent in life to develop more vigorously. Yet, God's desire was that they pursue those directions as they continued to be an apostle, to have an apostolate, and to live the apostolic life.

Of the above scenarios, the fourth one is the most common. Many maturing Christians have difficulty distinguishing the call to contemplation from the call to the contemplative life. They tend to confuse the transformation of their communion with God, especially as evident in their practice of solitary prayer, with a possible vocation to the contemplative life. The outcome of discernment for most of these people is the recognition of a calling to become increasingly contemplative, but not to enter the contemplative life. Their vocation is to let their intimacy with Jesus deepen as they go on living their apostolic life.

The first, second, and third patterns described above have in common the presence of an emerging contemplative vocation. But, practically speaking, how do these people move forward to the contemplative life?

In the case of persons who have made perpetual vows in an apostolic institute or society and who believe that they have now a calling to a specific contemplative order or congregation, one course of action is to seek a canonical transfer from the apostolic community to the contemplative group.

When it is the case of single persons, entrance upon a contemplative lifestyle will be rather straightforward. They will eventually make some form of celibate commitment. They will either live the contemplative life independently, seek admission to a contemplative order, or form an association with another type of Christian community.

In the case of committed celibates without membership in a religious institute or society, entrance upon a contemplative lifestyle will be relatively

2. See *Spiritual Journey,* 39–52, 75–113, 135–43, 227–31.

uncomplicated. These people have no preexisting binding commitment in church law to an institute or society of consecrated life. Thus, they have already the freedom to embark upon a contemplative life in the manner that they discern to be according to God's design.

Persons in an apostolic institute who have not yet made any profession of vows or who have made only temporary religious vows are also in a position of considerable freedom to pursue the contemplative life. They can leave the apostolic group and live the contemplative life in whatever way they discern that God wants.

When the second and third patterns above occur in the case of a spouse discerning a possible vocation to the contemplative life within the context of marriage, then obviously a delicate and complex situation exists. If the married person truly has a calling to the contemplative life, God will show the way toward integration of the two lifestyles.

Should the second and third scenarios involve a celibate who has taken perpetual vows in an apostolic religious institute or society and who now wants to live the contemplative life within that group, then a number of specific challenges arise. In this case also, nothing is impossible to God.

Perseverance in the Contemplative Life

Once aspirants have entered the contemplative life on a prolonged experimental basis, they are considered candidates for the contemplative life. They continue to discern with their spiritual guides their progress in the above "prior to entrance" signs of a possible contemplative vocation. An additional principle of discernment also requires wise assessment: that is, a candidate's perseverance in living a contemplative lifestyle, together with continuing personal growth while doing so. In that respect, candidates and their spiritual guides profit from giving attention to these dimensions of the lifestyle:

- Contemplative receptivity to God: Perseverance in contemplative living becomes apparent in an integrating prayer life, in fidelity to solitary prayer, in a preference for silence and solitude, in simplicity of heart, and in stability.

- A contemplative stance in activity: Leisure is an activity which permeates all activities in the contemplative life. Contemplatives participate in endeavors such as study, manual labor, and limited ministry as means of encountering their Beloved and of advancing God's reign. They see contemplation itself as the ministry par excellence of the contemplative life.

- Emotional maturity: Contemplatives manifest on a consistent basis an emotional equilibrium as they enjoy life and manage the stresses of life.

- Love of neighbor: Contemplatives grow not only in love of God, but also in love of neighbor; that is, community members, friends, families, acquaintances, indeed all living creatures and creation as a whole.

It takes time, effort, and patience for beginners in the contemplative life to form a cohesive personal experience of the lifestyle. Prayerful reflection upon that process disposes candidates to receive insight into the quality of their perseverance in the contemplative life. When there is an authentic vocation, perseverance shows itself in an integration within a candidate of two apparent opposites: on the one hand, increasing awareness of gifts, talents, and goodness; on the other hand, heightened consciousness of immaturity, selfishness, and sinfulness. Moreover, the candidate comes to receive a depth of inner peace, joy, and happiness that cannot be explained or even imagined apart from God's direct activity. That peace is Christ's own peace (John 14:27). That joy is his joy (John 15:11). That happiness is the blessedness of the beatitudes (Matt 5:3–11).

Together with the principles of discernment for a contemplative vocation that we have described, contemplative communities have their own additional signs. Those further principles emerge from the uniqueness of their respective charisms. Carmelites, for example, look for certain specific traits in their candidates and members, as do Benedictines, Trappists, and Poor Clares.

Commitment in Faith

As valid as all the principles of discernment for a contemplative vocation remain, they do not in themselves give absolute proof that a person has in fact received a calling to the contemplative life. The signs and conditions that we have explicated in the above chapters do not constitute a clear-cut checklist. The candidate, spiritual director, or community leaders cannot slide down the margins, check off lists of yes or no, more or less, or one to ten, and then at the end come up with a precise score. Some people may be relatively strong in all those principles. Other persons may be only moderately so. Still other people may appear rather weak in most of them. Nevertheless, each person could have a contemplative vocation. Those candidates or members who appear to be outstanding in most areas are not thereby "better contemplatives" or "more holy" than other persons. It is even possible that an individual who is well-endowed in all respects has no calling at all to the contemplative life.

The ultimate key to perceiving a vocation to the contemplative life is faith—a faith that imbues the wisdom, intuition, and common sense of all those persons involved in a discernment process. After all is said and done, only a leap in faith enables an individual to pass from considering the *possibility* of a contemplative vocation to affirming the existence of an *actual calling* to the contemplative life.

The ultimate sign of a contemplative vocation is the candidate's faith experience of this calling as an existential inability to become otherwise. The principles of discernment that we have identified help the person's faith seek some understanding of that vocational imperative.

Emancipation

At some point, a person with a contemplative vocation will make a permanent commitment to God in and through the contemplative life. From thereon out, a contemplative advances in the direction of increasing emancipation.

In common parlance, to emancipate means to free. Emancipation denotes liberation from the restraint, bondage, or control of other entities, whether they are societies, groups, authorities, cultural mores, or one's own inordinate attachments. In a vocational sense, to become emancipated is to appropriate fully to oneself the responsibilities of one's calling and to act with the freedom of the children of God. It is to grow up.

Emancipation is a hoped-for effect of maturation. Optimally, in human development a person evolves from dependence to independence to interdependence.[3] An infant or a child, for example, is completely dependent upon the parents. Then, throughout adolescence and early adulthood the individual assumes a stance of independence from direct parental care. Finally, toward midlife the person develops a rapport of interdependence with the parents. The adult child and the parents recognize their mutual reliance upon each other. That sense of interdependence establishes a new grounding for their relationship.

An analogous process occurs in the relationship between a member and a contemplative community. Initially, a candidate is understandably dependent upon the community. Like a nurturing parent, the community models in its daily life what for the beginner are as yet untested values and untried ways of values actualization. Gradually, the candidate attains

3. See *Spiritual Direction*, 169–73.

a certain independence in relationship to the community by means of as-similating those values and learning to implement them in an appropriate contemplative way. Similar to a child gaining a sense of identity separate from a parent, the candidate establishes a differentiated sense of self vis-à-vis the community. That shift from dependence to independence in relationship could in dysfunctional groups be of a harsh or an antagonis-tic nature. Such a community might perceive the candidate as becoming disobedient or individualistic. In healthy communities, the change occurs in the manner of a peaceful rite of passage and a celebration of growth. Eventually, with further experience, the candidate and the community reach interdependence. They recognize that they need each other on the spiritual journey, even as they relate to one another with the freedom of the children of God. The contemplative who is capable of interdependence in relation to a community sees fellow community members as both leaders and followers, animators and animated, accountable to each other and to God in a diversity of responsibilities.

Perseverance in the contemplative life necessarily invites emancipa-tion, liberation, and freedom. Life pushes relentlessly forward. Yes, parents remain parents. Their children remain their children. But just as the quality of their rapport matures over the years, so too the contemplative's relation-ship with the community evolves with the passage of time.

A candidate's growth from dependence through independence into in-terdependence is vital to the freedom, carefreeness, and spontaneity essential to the contemplative life. Therefore, perseverance in this lifestyle postulates significant maturation and emancipation on all levels of personhood: spiri-tual, emotional, cognitive, relational, social, psychosexual, and so on. True perseverance does not mean maintaining what stood as the status quo at the time of a candidate's entrance into the contemplative life. On the contrary, authentic perseverance in the contemplative life requires that a person pass through and beyond everyone and everything to God. In God, the contem-plative communes with all creation in a mutually dependent way.

The Contemplative Vocation as Mystery

Many people find the contemplative life perplexing. Why does God call a person into solitude out of a much needed and successful ministry? Why does the Spirit transplant a highly efficient and deeply appreciated social worker from the crying needs of Latin America to a monastery? It is much the same bewilderment that prompts people to ask why God allows a young effective missionary to drown in the Amazon or to die of typhoid fever in Africa.

The age-old question of sacrifice throws some light on the mystery of a contemplative vocation. Why did the Mosaic Law require for sacrifice first fruits of the earth and heifers in their prime? Why not sacrifice what is of inferior quality and utilize for the common good what is most productive? Why not sacrifice the last fruits or the weak animal and sell, enjoy, or eat the best? Yes, that is the logic of Wall Street, the wisdom of Silicon Valley, the spirit of Las Vegas. But if to sacrifice means to do something or to abstain from something that apart from love we would never do or abstain from, then to sacrifice a gift is to use it eminently, especially if it is for God. From that perspective, to sacrifice an aptitude means to take a quantitative entity or good, and cause it to pass into the realm of immeasurable quality and unimaginable value.[4]

The most striking example of sacrifice is Jesus's giving up of his life in order to draw all creation to God. Jesus loved to the end (John 13:1). The prologue to the Johannine gospel laments that while some people accepted the value of that act, other persons did not do so: "He came into the world . . . and the world knew him not. He came to his own, and his own did not receive him" (John 1:10–11).

St. Paul also struggled with the contradiction of the complete self-giving of Jesus and his rejection by so many people: "While the Jews demand signs and the Greeks seek wisdom, here we are preaching a crucified Christ; to the Jews, a stumbling block, to the Greeks, foolishness" (1 Cor 1:22–23). According to human judgment, God's way seemed to many people so foolish and powerless. But, as St. Paul acknowledged, the truth remains otherwise: "God's foolishness is wiser than human wisdom. God's weakness is stronger than human strength" (1 Cor 1:25).

Some people still judge God's ways to be absurd, especially in reference to a contemplative vocation. Ultimately, God's purpose in calling a person to the contemplative life pertains to divine mystery. A contemplative vocation is entirely from God and not from oneself, any other person, or any group (1 Cor 1:26–31; 2 Cor 4:7). Moreover, that gift is bestowed for God's qualitative designs and not for humankind's quantitative appraisals.

The contemplative life embraces a host of paradoxes. Those persons called by God to a contemplative lifestyle embody this delicate balance of opposites:

---

4. See *DVMCS*, 143–45.

Contemplatives are drawn irresistibly into solitude,

> yet remain warmly sociable.

They are generally reserved,

> but intensely loving and sensitive.

They are deeply prayerful,

> while remaining thoroughly children of their times.

They are serious-minded,

> yet wholesomely playful and witty.

They are self-effacing,

> but ready and able to speak out when necessary.

They know how to weep,

> and they know how to laugh.

They are staunchly resolute,

> while yet profoundly open and adaptable.

They are capable of penetrating study and research,

> even as their prayer is increasingly imageless and wordless.

They yearn for silence

> but can prove talkative and entertaining when occasion permits.

They are creative, resourceful, and spontaneous,

> even as they remain steady and stable.

They are deep and mysterious,

> while also down-to-earth and practical.

They can be forceful,

> yet free and freeing.

They are sinners,

> but also humbly repentant.

They have no idea where they are spiritually,

> and they would rather not know.

They have an insatiable zest for life,

> but consistently prefer the desert, frugality, and simplicity.

They enjoy people and the natural world immensely,

    yet cannot rest in anything.

They are passionately in love,

    but suffer aridity and emptiness.

They live on the fringes of society,

    yet abide in Christ at the heart of the world.

Part Four: The Eremitic Life

The Process of Being Born into Eremitic Solitude

OVER THE PAST CENTURY western Christianity has witnessed a resurgence of interest in the eremitic life. Unfortunately, a general lack of in-depth understanding of this vocational lifestyle and considerable uncertainty as to how to proceed in its discernment have accompanied the renewed interest. What exactly is this calling? How does one go about discerning a possible eremitic vocation? What signs indicate the existence of a calling to this lifestyle?

In this section, we explore a vocation to the eremitic life. As in our deliberations upon the contemplative life, we approach this calling from two successive points of view: *first*, the principles for discernment prior to a person's transition to the eremitic life (chapters 20 and 21), and *second*, the principles of discernment that pertain to a person's perseverance in living this lifestyle (chapters 22 to 26). We conclude this section with a brief synthesis of our insights and with some final pastoral observations (chapter 27).

Toward a More Accurate Use of Certain Terms

The terms "solitary," "recluse," "anchorite," and "hermit" have been used interchangeably in many contexts. Nonetheless, the designations do refer to four unique vocational modes of living. While they share common features, significant differences exist among them.

Solitary

The word "solitary" has its origin in the Latin *solitarius*. "Solitary" came into the English language probably through the French word *solitaire*. In French, *solitaire* refers to a bachelor or to an unmarried woman.

Solitary can describe anyone who lives alone. A solitary could be single or celibate. A solitary might inhabit an apartment in the city, a house in town, a cottage on the beach, a cabin in the woods, or a cave in the mountains. A solitary might live alone for one of several reasons, for example, a spiritual motive, a natural preference for aloneness, or a predilection for isolation and social withdrawal.

Every hermit is necessarily a solitary, but certainly not every solitary is a hermit.

Recluse

The word "recluse" is a transliteration of the Latin *reclusus,* which denotes someone sequestered, sealed off, or secluded.

Reclusion accentuates a confined existence within four walls. A recluse rarely ventures out of that abode. A solitary, in contrast, is likely to be seen with some frequency by other people.

Like a solitary, a recluse could be single or celibate. The motives for living a reclusive life also can range from spiritual aspirations to outright isolation. In a positive religious sense, a recluse has more in common with an anchorite than with a hermit.[1]

Anchorite

The word "anchorite" is derived from a compound Greek verb, *anachōrein,* meaning to retire or to retreat to the periphery of an entity.

Traditionally, anchorites are persons who inhabit solitary abodes for the purpose of devoting themselves to a distinctive form of Christian life. They are committed to Christ as celibates. Historically, their habitats are adjacent or attached to a church, a monastery, or similar structure. Usually, anchorites live in cells, not hermitages as such. The living quarters consist of a single room, which the anchorite rarely, if ever, leaves. The cells of many anchorites are located in cities or other relatively populated areas. The lifestyle of some anchorites is ascetical and penitential. That lifestyle may or may not also be contemplative.

---

1. An exception to that fact is the Camaldolese understanding of "recluse." A Camaldolese recluse is one who, with the permission of religious superiors, moves beyond the usual form of Camaldolese eremitic life into a life of greater silence, solitude, and freedom for the purpose of contemplative union with God. Reclusion in the Camaldolese tradition is thus an extension of an eremitic lifestyle.

Dame Julian of Norwich was an anchorite, a contemplative, and a mystic.

Hermit

In a religious sense, a hermit is a contemplative who dwells both interiorly and physically alone with God.

The word "hermit" comes from the Greek *erēmos*, meaning uninhabited area; hence, desert or wilderness. While populated areas provide the location for cells of anchorites, places apart from human habitation offer sites for hermitages. Most persons called to the eremitic life have a strong attraction toward a desert or wilderness location. Yet for practical reasons some hermits opt to live at secluded sites in or near a town or on the grounds of a monastery or a convent.

The process of movement into eremitic solitude and the principles of discernment that we describe throughout this section refer primarily to hermits and not necessarily with equal vigor to anchorites (and, a fortiori, recluses or solitaries). Radical silence and aloneness are foundational to the vocational lifestyles of solitaries, recluses, anchorites, and hermits. From spiritual, theological, and pastoral perspectives, however, those modes of living do not represent identical vocations.

Two Prerequisite Vocational Experiences

Ordinarily, the following experiences constitute the grounding for a calling to the eremitic life: *first*, a vocation to celibacy, and *second*, passage through the apostolic life and the contemplative life.

A Call to Celibacy

A calling to the basic Christian lifestyle of celibacy for the sake of Jesus and the gospel underlies virtually all eremitic vocations. The intensity of eremitic solitude is ordinarily incompatible with the necessary togetherness of conjugal living. Even so, a few couples have described themselves as married hermits living together in silence and solitude.[2] The modality of eremitic intimacy with God impels a hermit beyond the single life as such.

---

2. See Fredette and Fredette, *Consider the Ravens*, 94–95, 168.

Passage through the Apostolic Life and the Contemplative Life

A history of passage first through an apostolic lifestyle and then through the contemplative life gives indication of a person's readiness to embark upon the eremitic life. We refer here primarily to *a process of growing into the eremitic life* by living first a distinctive apostolic life, followed by a clearly distinguishable contemplative life. This does not mean that the person desiring to be a hermit has to have lived an apostolic life or a contemplative life with official recognition by church law or in a specific ecclesial structure.

The contemplative life does not necessarily or even usually lead to an eremitic calling. The contemplative life is a unique vocation in its own right. A genuine eremitic call remains nonetheless a radical intensification of a contemplative vocation. A hermit is essentially a contemplative. Consequently, a wise spiritual director would not even consider beginning the discernment of a possible eremitic vocation until the aspirant has persevered for some time in a vibrant contemplative mode of living.

In most monastic traditions, the monk or the nun with a possible eremitic calling receives permission to move into a hermitage only after having fruitfully lived contemplative life in a communal setting for many years. *The Rule of St. Benedict*, for instance, takes that approach for contemplatives who follow the Benedictine tradition.[3] Even in the Camaldolese Congregation and the Carthusian Order—two eremitic institutes of consecrated life—spiritual formation personnel discern carefully aspirants' ability to be at home in the communal dimension of contemplative living before encouraging them to enter the solitude of a hermitage.

What of the case of a celibate man or woman who is already in an apostolic institute or society, who has not lived a contemplative life, and who professes to have a vocation to live an eremitic life as a member of that congregation? Should this celibate first pass through a period of contemplative living before embarking upon an eremitic life? Assuming that the apostolic community considers an eremitic vocation within the scope of its charism, it is advisable that the member indeed do so. For every person called to be a hermit, living a contemplative life is an integral phase of the movement into eremitic solitude. Thus, it is within a contemplative lifestyle that the member of an apostolic group would test first a possible calling to be a contemplative and then later discern a possible vocation to embark upon the eremitic life.

3. See *RB 1980: The Rule of St. Benedict*, 169–171.

Contexts for Living the Eremitic Life

Before entering an eremitic life, a contemplative has to give consideration to the type of solitary setting in which to live. Most aspirants lean toward one of these three options:

- Remain a solitary hermit living alone in a hermitage at a secluded location.

- Become a member of a laura of hermits. (A laura refers to a group of hermits who reside within their individual hermitages on a shared tract of land, who live the eremitic life independently of each other, and who meet together on occasion for the material and spiritual good of the group.)

- Seek membership in an eremitic institute of consecrated life. (With this option, hermits live a vowed life in separate hermitages situated at some distance from each other around a central building, as in the Camaldolese Congregation, or in hermitages separate but adjacent to each other, as in the Carthusian Order).

With regard to monastic institutions, the 1983 Roman Catholic *Code of Canon Law* makes no direct reference to hermits. The Code assumes that most monastic communities have provision in their constitutions for an experienced contemplative member to become a hermit, should that contemplative discern with those in authority the existence of an eremitic calling.

With regard to hermits who are not members of a religious institute or society and who seek ecclesial recognition as persons dedicated to God in a consecrated life, the Code requires of them devotion to praise of God and salvation of the world by means of "a stricter separation from the world, the silence of solitude and assiduous prayer and penance."[4] Additional stipulations for ecclesial recognition of their lifestyle as a consecrated life include their public profession of vows received by the diocesan bishop and their observance of a personal plan of life under the guidance of the bishop.[5]

As a point of interest, Canon 603 of the Code begins with the statement that the church recognizes "the eremitic or anchoritic life," thus apparently employing the qualifiers *eremitic* and *anchoritic* in an interchangeable way. However, from a pastoral perspective, questions remain. Toward which solitary vocation is a seeker drawn? What specific solitary lifestyle is a spiritual director assisting a person to discern?

---

4. Canon 603 (1).
5. Canon 603 (2).

Some persons who are not members of religious institutes or societies use Canon 603 as a kind of last resort in their efforts to attain recognition by church law for their "dedication to God in a consecrated life." Given their actual mode of living, these persons appear to be seeking recognition for a lifestyle other than eremitic or even anchoritic. A few of those people live independently an expression of the contemplative life. Many of them reside alone, either as celibates or single persons, and faithfully live an apostolic life.

A person's lifestyle may accord profoundly with an authentic calling from God, but has the person accurately named that calling? Is the lifestyle indeed eremitic? Those are crucial questions in vocational discernment. It takes sufficient vocational consciousness and personal freedom to make a long-term commitment to God, whether privately or through public profession of vows or promises. To what exactly is the person saying "yes"? Does Canon 603 really apply to the lifestyle under consideration?[6]

Not all hermits desire ecclesial recognition of their eremitic life. For a variety of reasons, some hermits live their vocation hidden with Christ in God, without public profession of commitment or official approval from ecclesial authorities.

Movement into Eremitic Solitude: Four Phases of Transition

A person called to the contemplative life must be born carefully, patiently, and after long delay out of the womb of society into solitude.[7]

A contemplative called to the eremitic life has to be born into a solitude that exceeds even that of the contemplative life.

Therefore, this principle of discernment provides an important indication of a possible eremitic vocation: a history of being born into progressively more solitude brings the contemplative at a critical point to the silence and the aloneness of a hermitage.

In chapters 10–14 of this book, we discussed the passage from the apostolic life to a contemplative lifestyle. Now, we describe four consecutive phases in the transition from the contemplative life to the eremitic life.

---

6. Canon 604 recognizes also "the order of virgins" as a form of dedication to God in a consecrated life. Canon 605 leaves open the possibility of approval by the Holy See of "new forms of consecrated life."

7. See Merton, "Notes for a Philosophy of Solitude," 204.

Phase One: Using Available Opportunities for Solitude

Most contemplatives discover at some point a growing need for more alone-ness with God. With consciousness of that desire comes also the realization that many unused opportunities for solitude exist within daily life. Work-free days, cancelled events, and early completion of projects, for example, offer occasions for silence and solitude. The initial step for the contempla-tive who seeks more aloneness with God is to begin making use of those readily available, but as yet untapped opportunities.

In the course of utilizing those possibilities, the contemplative has to in-tegrate each advance into solitude with all other aspects of the contemplative life. Moreover, perseverance for a while in a newly established equilibrium is necessary before seeking out more aloneness. The contemplative needs to exercise patience and to endure what seems at times to be long delay. Only after the gradual integration of all opportunities for solitude available in the ordinary flow of contemplative life is it prudent for the person to pass on to the second phase of being born into increased solitude.

During the first phase, it can happen that a contemplative genuinely wants more aloneness and God desires that the person have that solitude. Yet the individual either misuses or does not make any effort at all to utilize readily available opportunities to be alone with God. Inability to actualize those possibilities and to integrate them gradually into daily contemplative life indicates that the person is as yet ill-prepared to benefit from the soli-tude of a hermitage.

Phase Two: Seeking out Further Opportunities for Solitude

The need within some contemplatives for more aloneness with God eventu-ally surpasses the amount of solitude available to them in the usual flow of communal life. Even so, they continue to feel drawn irresistibly to further solitude.

Thus begins a second phase of being born into increasing solitude. The contemplative continues to live the common life, but leadership personnel permit the person opportunities for solitude beyond those ordinarily avail-able in the communal environment. Instead of the contemplative engag-ing in conversation at the main meal with members of the community, for example, those in leadership could give permission for this individual to eat in silence once in a while, a few times a week, or even on a daily basis. They could excuse the contemplative from certain group recreational activi-ties in view of a need for greater solitude. They could assign the person a responsibility that entails working alone rather than with other community members. They could give the contemplative several consecutive days of solitude weekly or monthly.

The choice and the actualization of those additional opportunities to be alone with God depend upon the nuances of each vocation, the needs of the community, and the options available to those in leadership. The contemplative's recurrent cycles of securing more aloneness, establishing a new contemplative equilibrium in daily life, and patiently waiting upon God while desiring yet more solitude continue throughout this second phase.

A contemplative begins this second phase only after all significant persons involved in the discernment process affirm that a desire for more solitude is probably from God. Moreover, throughout the second phase a person's discussions with a spiritual director, leadership personnel, and community members continue. Participants in the discernment need not be overly fearful or excessively cautious about giving the contemplative the freedom to respond to authentic movements of the Spirit. Nor do they have to lend their support hastily or indiscriminately to the contemplative's every whim and fancy.

The role of all those assisting the contemplative in discernment is to prepare the way for the Spirit to give wisdom and insight. To that end, they affirm in the contemplative what they perceive as emanating from God and they challenge what smacks of isolation, individualism, or stubbornness. They let God have the utmost freedom in the contemplative's life. They trust God's transformative activity and the contemplative's responsiveness to the divine promptings. They allow the contemplative to learn by trial and error. They give the person the chance to crash or soar, to sink or swim. They stand firm in their conviction that should the contemplative go astray, the Spirit will provide guidance back to the path of life. They abide with faith that God's intent will manifest itself in due time through the contemplative's experience. Thus, like Gamaliel they take this approach as they seek to discover God's calling: "If this movement or this work is of human origin, it will come to nothing. If it is of God, not only will you be unable to destroy [it]; you will find yourselves fighting against God" (Acts 5:38–39).

Throughout phases one and two of the process of being born into more solitude, the gradual increase of aloneness with God occurs within the context of the contemplative life. The person remains in the contemplative life, but with an emphasis on the solitary aspect of communion with God. Most contemplatives reach the limits of the solitude to which God is calling them somewhere in the course of those two phases. They recognize those limits intuitively by faith and by the fruits of their solitary experience.

In the case of a contemplative with a vocation to the eremitic life, the movement into solitude throughout these two phases is a necessary preparation for life in a hermitage.

Phase Three: Living in a Hermitage on an Experimental Basis

When a contemplative has an eremitic calling, the conclusion of the second phase of being born into increasing solitude marks a vocational crossroads. This contemplative comes to realize that utilizing additional opportunities for solitude within the context of communal life still does not satisfy. Thus, the contemplative experiences an interior imperative to enter a depth of aloneness with God that surpasses what is possible in communal contemplative life. Moreover, the contemplative knows that not to proceed in that direction would impede progress in transforming union with God. Thus, God's calling and the human response to it attain a critical threshold that marks the contemplative's departure from one lifestyle (the contemplative life) and entrance into another mode of living (the eremitic life).

First, the contemplative successfully utilized all the opportunities available for solitude in the ordinary rhythm of communal life. Then, the person exhausted all possible additional opportunities for increased solitude within the communal life. Now, with the affirmation of a spiritual director, community leaders, and community membership, the contemplative is ready to test the authenticity of an eremitic call by living in a hermitage on an experimental basis.

During the vocational testing period, the contemplative lives apart from the community, free from most of the duties and structures of the common life. Mistakes are inevitable in the course of experimentation, and at times the person will entirely miss the mark. A wide range of feelings will surface and the individual will have to discover how to maintain consistent emotional equilibrium. It will take time for a suitable rhythm of eremitic life to emerge. Throughout this phase, the contemplative continues vocational discernment with the assistance of all significant persons. God will indicate in the favorable time the presence or absence of an eremitic vocation. The truth will become evident through the contemplative's experience and through the insights of other participants in the discernment.

This phase of experimental living in a hermitage lasts from approximately one to three years. Less than a year for this initial eremitic formation is too short. If the person is still indecisive after a three-year period, an eremitic vocation is probably lacking.

Even should a genuine eremitic calling exist notwithstanding a candidate's inability at the end of Phase Three to perceive its presence, intense vocational indecisiveness and accompanying anxiety could make continuation in the hermitage an unwise course for the candidate. As an alternative, the candidate could consider the option of leaving the hermitage and returning to the common life of a contemplative community, which at least for the immediate future might better correspond to God's grace. The person could resume at a later time life in a hermitage and discernment of an eremitic vocation, if the Spirit were to indicate the appropriateness of proceeding again in that direction.

Phase Four: Moving into a Permanent Hermitage

Having successfully passed through the one- to three-year experimental period, the contemplative is ready to move into a permanent hermitage or else to live in the present hermitage with an attitude of permanency toward the eremitic lifestyle. The contemplative has completed a first or primary formation in the eremitic life. Now the time has come to embark upon more thorough formation.

Affirmation of a lifelong calling to the eremitic life and final eremitic commitment to God are likely still a few years down the road. When time and further experience confirm an eremitic vocation, the hermit undertakes that commitment with the encouragement of a spiritual director. When the hermit is a member of an institute of consecrated life or a person who seeks canonical recognition as a hermit from the bishop of a diocese, the permission of appropriate ecclesial authorities also is necessary prior to profession of the commitment.

For the present, however, the positive signs of an authentic vocation are strong enough to warrant living the life fully and unequivocally. The one dimension lacking at the outset of this phase four in the discernment process is the person's long-term perseverance in the eremitic life. That sign of an eremitic vocation takes many years to establish. How many? No one can know in advance or even hazard a guess. When the proper time comes, all participants in the discernment will recognize it and respond accordingly. Until they know in faith, they wait.

CHAPTER 21

An Increasing Solitary Thrust in Life

IN THE PREVIOUS CHAPTER, we identified four successive phases through which a contemplative is born into the solitude of the eremitic life. Passage through phases one and two proceeds in the direction of an increasing solitary thrust. Yet neither of those phases constitutes an eremitic lifestyle as such. In this chapter, we focus upon discernment of a person's growing need for increasing aloneness with God in the context of the contemplative life.

The Yearning for More Solitude

Throughout phases one and two, a contemplative frequently wants more external silence and solitude than accords with God's desire. The Spirit draws forth from the person immersed in that perplexing situation further loving surrender to the divine initiative. Although no increase in physical aloneness occurs, interior solitude intensifies.

A contemplative's thirst for more solitude, even when it accords with God's desire, is not without distress and anxiety. The yearning to be alone often conflicts with other preferences. The contemplative would like to fit in with the community, but cannot do so entirely. The person wants to rest in the security of approved customs and procedures, but something deep within that individual prevents it. The contemplative desires to conform to a certain routine, but instead searches always for something more, "an-I-don't-know-what."[1] That interior restlessness and inability to be satisfied, together with the accompanying doubts and concerns, could indicate a contemplative's realistic awareness of the darkness, unknown, and risk intrinsic to deepening encounter with God in mystery.

Progression in aloneness with God occurs gradually. It follows a long and winding course. Success and advancement alternate with setbacks and

---

1. St. John of the Cross uses this expression (Spanish: *un-no-sé-qué*) to describe God as mystery. See *Spiritual Canticle*, stanza 7 and commentary.

delays. Yet, all things work together to facilitate a contemplative's birthing into the solitude of God.

Eremitic Solitude

Most contemplatives who long for more aloneness with God do not have their hearts set on living as hermits. Rather, their burning desire for more intimacy with God guides them day by day in a progressively solitary direction, even as they stay grounded in their contemplative lifestyles. The majority of these contemplatives remain called by God to persevere in a contemplative life. Only a few of them discover in their need to be alone with God an awakening sense of vocation to the eremitic life.

When God is leading a person beyond the contemplative life into the eremitic life, the perplexing restlessness for more aloneness endures. The yearning for solitude not only persists, but also inexplicably increases. The irresistible longing to be totally alone with God is unquenchable. It cannot be satisfied.

Thus, an obvious question arises. How can a contemplative discern whether an indomitable attraction toward silence and solitude is indeed from God and not from another source?

Positive Signs

A contemplative who is being born into eremitic solitude manifests consistently throughout the discernment process these characteristics:

- sincerity;
- a need for more solitude than is currently available;
- openness to the input and the guidance of participants in the discernment process;
- forbearance with delay;
- willingness to wait upon God;
- continued examination of personal motivations underlying the desire for aloneness;
- ability to integrate existing exterior solitude with the other aspects of daily contemplative life.

The lack of any of those characteristics, or a significant deficiency in their quality, requires careful assessment of the contemplative's solitary orientation.

Countersigns

The existence of any of the following attitudes or behavioral patterns casts grave doubt upon the authenticity of a contemplative's pursuit of physical solitude.

Unhappiness in Community

Contemplatives who are dissatisfied in the communal life will be unhappy also in the eremitic life. Poor communication skills, tendencies to be non-assertive, propensities toward aggressive behavior, dislike for the practical inconveniences of communal living, unresolved conflicts with a community member, and problems with those in authority can become incentives to seek out more aloneness. Those motivations lead some people to use aloneness as a cover-up for their inability to cope with difficulties. Aloneness of that sort does not lead people to communion with God in all life, but rather to withdrawal from life. Persons with such motivations would do best to remain in the midst of people and to learn to relate to them more maturely.

Withdrawal and Isolation

Withdrawal designates the act of cutting oneself off from a person, a community, or a situation. Isolation denotes the state of being that results from the act of withdrawal.

Propensities toward withdrawal and isolation are diametrically opposite to a vocation to eremitic solitude.[2] Withdrawal and isolation result from a person circumventing or severing ties with creation. The process of being born into solitude presumes a passionate involvement with creation, not a circumvention or a negation of it. That movement into aloneness with God requires of the contemplative convergence upon Christ by passage *through* the created, not by alienation from it.[3] If a person exhibits consistent withdrawal and isolation in the context of contemplative community, those tendencies will assert themselves again should the individual move into a

---

2. See *Contemplation*, 98–99.

3. See *O Blessed Night*, 47–56; *Spiritual Journey*, 55–74, 89–95.

hermitage. Increasing narcissism—not loving surrender to God—will likely characterize life in the hermitage.

Rugged Individualism

Aloneness with God differs from rugged individualism. Solitude is for the purpose of loving communion with Christ Jesus. Its objective is not to let one's ego reign supreme. Its goal is not to go it alone, to have no need for people, or to be in control of life. A contemplative's persistent efforts to be completely autonomous bespeak withdrawal and isolation rather than growth in communion with God and with all creation in God.

The all-embracive receptivity to God essential to the eremitic life indeed requires an uncommon degree of self-reliance, self-sufficiency, and independence. But those qualities, when they are mature and healthy, balance with a compassionate solidarity with the world, a realistic knowledge of one's own needs, and an abiding sense of interdependence with all creatures.

Inability to Persevere in Exterior Solitude

Despite good intentions and sincere effort, some contemplatives experience a distressing inability to persevere in the degree of solitude that they have procured. That inability constitutes a convincing sign that they have exceeded the limits of the quietude and aloneness to which God has called them. With any vocation, God gives the grace to respond. Without that grace, perseverance is impossible to sustain.

An inability to persevere in solitude becomes observable in basically two ways: Some persons stay put and remain alone, apparently in solitude. However, instead of becoming more open to God and creation, they become preoccupied with themselves. They become trapped in introversion and introspection. They entomb themselves in their narrow, closed world. In contrast, other people find excuses to leave their place of solitude. They become lonely gadabouts, always on the move here or there.

Some contemplatives do not realize that they are in fact unable to persevere in their current measure of solitude. They insist to their community leaders and spiritual guides that God is calling them to even more physical aloneness and proceed to demand further opportunities for solitude. In this instance, spiritual guides and community leaders have the following options:

A First Option: They delay making a decision. They hope that in the meantime the contemplative will have a change of heart and withdraw the request for another increase of quietude and aloneness.

A Second Option: They give their consent for further solitude, aware that the person already has too much aloneness. They hope and pray that through additional experience the contemplative will come to see the truth.

A Third Option: They draw a line in the sand, so to speak. They refuse the request for more solitude and urge the contemplative to accept this decision in a spirit of obedience. If they are convinced of the wisdom of that direction, they must then stand firm, even if the contemplative threatens to leave the community and go elsewhere.

The Spirit active within all participants will direct them to the approach that is appropriate for a specific person, time, and circumstance.

Fixation on the Eremitic Life

Some people develop a fixation on the eremitic life. Preoccupation with procuring more aloneness or obsession with becoming a hermit is usually symptomatic of a pursuit of solitude for its own sake rather than a quest for God in solitude. A person can become so inordinately attached to being alone that the desire for solitude itself constitutes an obstacle to the Spirit's work. That attachment to aloneness leads to rigidity and isolation instead of loving encounter with God and with creation in God.

A fixation on the eremitic life manifests itself in these ways:

A First Scenario: A person who joins a contemplative group views the communal life solely as a means to an end. Constantly projecting into the future, the individual thinks only about getting past the common life and becoming a hermit. The level of preoccupation with that goal becomes so consuming that the person never truly enters into contemplative life or forms bonds with community members.

A Second Scenario: A person undertakes a contemplative lifestyle of some sort. In the initial phases of vocational discernment, it becomes clear that this individual cannot live the contemplative life, whatever its modality. Although the person admits the lack of a contemplative vocation, he or she insists nonetheless on the existence of a calling from God to become a hermit.

In effect, this individual perceives no connection between the contemplative life and the eremitic life. Yet a hermit is fundamentally a contemplative. A person grows into eremitic solitude by passing through the contemplative life. The eremitic life is an extension and a transformation of a contemplative lifestyle.

A Third Scenario: A person gives positive indication of a vocation to a contemplative life with a solitary orientation. In vocational discernment, it becomes evident that an eremitic life itself exceeds the scope of that orientation to solitude. Nevertheless, the contemplative keeps on demanding permission to move into a hermitage.

Persons who are obsessed with becoming hermits display at times a certain irrationality when their spiritual guides express concerns or raise questions. They have a quick and ready answer to every hesitation or query raised by participants in the discernment process. Moreover, some aspirants entertain a highly romantic attitude toward the eremitic life, imagining it to be an ideal way to holiness or the perfect solution for their every ill.

When people are obstinately determined to secure increasing aloneness, their quest reveals itself over time to be something other than an authentic response to the Spirit's inner promptings. Rather, in advance these individuals have created their own master plans. They have plotted their own course. They have charted their exact moves to achieve their preset goal of becoming hermits. And heaven help anyone who gets in their way!

Rather than journeying by faith, hope, and love, they force themselves into a way illuminated by the false light of their misguided desire. These people are often thoroughly convinced that they are following God's will. So absolute is their certainty that when a spiritual guide or a community member presents to them honest reservations or sincere objections, they proclaim in effect: "The Lord told me that he wants me to be a hermit, and I am going ahead with it regardless of what anyone says or thinks!"

When the quest for deepening solitude is an authentic response to God's call, contemplatives face always into darkness and mystery. They do not know where they are going or even how they have arrived at the present.[4] They strain forward to God by means of faith, hope, and love, along a solitary way that they cannot possibly understand.[5]

---

4. See Merton, *Thoughts in Solitude*, 83.

5. See Merton, *Contemplative Prayer*, 111–19.

CHAPTER 22

Life in a Hermitage

OF THE FOUR SEQUENTIAL phases in a transition from the contemplative life to the eremitic life, we have considered discernment in reference to phases one and two. Most contemplatives find within their contemplative lifestyles ways to attain sufficient personal solitude. A few contemplatives, though, experience a still insatiable longing for further aloneness as they reach the end of phase two. Those persons desire to embark upon the eremitic life.

In this chapter, we suggest practical pastoral approaches pertinent to a candidate's experimental living of the eremitic life (phase three). We describe also some practical aspects of life in a hermitage, whether the candidate resides in the hermitage on experimental basis or has moved on to an attitude of permanency toward eremitic living (as in phase four). We thereby set a framework for discernment of the candidate's perseverance in the eremitic life throughout both phases three and four (chapters 23–27).

Practical Pastoral Approaches

Residence in a hermitage for a prolonged testing period is the discernment context for the third phase. This phase of being born into the solitude of the eremitic life ranges from one to three years. During this experimental period, a contemplative gets a firsthand taste of the eremitic life, undergoes initial formation in the lifestyle, and continues the discernment process.

Among the significant persons involved in the discernment during this third phase, the spiritual director and the candidate work together most closely. We offer the following suggestions for the spiritual director:

To begin with, for approximately the first six months remain as non-directive as possible with the candidate. Make virtually no suggestions and avoid for the most part giving specific instructions. Do not put ideas about the eremitic life into the person's mind. Ask a few questions perhaps, but basically just listen. Let the candidate learn by trial and error. If this way of life is the fruit of an authentic vocation, the Spirit will guide the candidate to a daily eremitic routine and to creative solutions for difficulties.

Then, after sufficient time for initial experimentation, begin a detailed discernment with the candidate. Go step by step–principle by principle–through all that pertains first to solitude in the contemplative life (chapters 10 through 19 above) and then to solitude in the eremitic life (chapters 20 through 27). Discussion of those matters would extend usually over a period of at least several months.

Next, after the candidate has had a firsthand taste of life alone in a hermitage and has pondered thoroughly the principles for discernment of an eremitic vocation, encourage the person to remain living in the hermitage for approximately another year. That extension would be for the purpose of additional eremitic formation and further discernment in the crucible of experience.

Finally, toward the end of that period, invite the candidate to write on a single page a personal rule of life.

The rule of life is an expression of an already lived, tested, and discerned eremitic experience. Thus, the candidate cannot write it before having a prolonged taste of living in a hermitage. The rule is not a schedule or an horarium. It is not even the statement of a goal to attain. It is not equivalent to what some communities would term their "constitutions." The rule is a simple and concise synthesis of the principles, values, and practices that constitute the core of this hermit's unique vocation. If the rule is longer than a single page, it is too long. If after the passage of a reasonable time, the hermit is still unable to compose a personal rule of life, the quality of the eremitic experience and possibly also the authenticity of the supposed vocation need to be reexamined.

Depending upon a candidate's situation, a document supplementary to the personal rule may be necessary. In relation to Canon 603 on the eremitic life, for example, most bishops and their councils require a legal agreement between a diocese and a hermit with regard to provision for the hermit's present and future material needs.

The fourth phase of being born into eremitic solitude begins with the candidate moving into a permanent hermitage or taking on an attitude of permanency in what has been the temporary hermitage. At the acceptable time during phase four, the candidate makes a permanent commitment to God through this lifestyle. The duration of the fourth phase is open-ended. In phase four a person is not only born more deeply *into* the solitude of the eremitic life, but also over the course of time born *through* eremitic solitude into the fullness of God in eternal life. Thus, if an authentic eremitic vocation indeed exists, a person could quite possibly remain in that hermitage until death.

Daily Life in a Hermitage

In the ensuing chapters of this section, we present principles for the discernment of authentic perseverance in the eremitic life. By way of preparation for that endeavor, we describe now certain practical features of daily life in a hermitage.

A Typical Hermitage

Each eremitic vocation is unique. Consequently, it may seem pretentious to speak of what constitutes a hermitage or a hermit's daily schedule. If we were to approach the subject in terms of proposing "the ideal hermitage" or "the best schedule," we would indeed be presumptuous. Our intention, however, is merely to offer a few candid observations that have emerged from our ministry of helping persons discern a possible eremitic calling.

Silence, solitude, contemplation, and self-surrender to God form the matrix of an eremitic lifestyle. The hermitage is the symbol of that reality. So important is the hermitage that one desert abba gave this advice: "Stay in your cell and your cell will teach you all things."[1]

So, what might a typical hermitage look like in the twenty-first century?

Due to their circumstances, some contemplatives who embark upon an eremitic life have to find a way to revamp an existing structure into a hermitage. That type of renovation can be quite appropriate, provided that the makeover conforms to the purpose of a hermitage. Other contemplatives live in dwellings designed and built intentionally as hermitages.

The main characteristic of a hermitage, besides the presence of a hermit, is a room or space designated for contemplation. Hermits affiliated with Christian denominations that emphasize liturgical celebration of the sacraments tend to have that prayer area take the form of a small oratory with the Eucharist reserved in a tabernacle. In addition to a space set apart for prayer, a hermitage would comprise a kitchenette, a bedroom/study, a bathroom, and an open porch, screened or not depending on local conditions. If the hermitage is a newly built structure, the total floor space, including the porch, would be roughly 400 square feet (approximately 20' x 20').

---

1. Abba Moses of Scete, *PG*, 65:283–84. *Spiritual Direction*, 33–50.

For practical reasons, it is best that the entrance and the porch of the hermitage face the direction of the prevailing spring and summer breezes. The location of the hermitage could be in a desert, a wilderness, or another green-space environment. The porch itself would face out, preferably toward a clearing of some size. A hermitage completely surrounded by tall trees, high brush, or gigantic boulders tends to create a closed-in feeling or a claustrophobic ambiance. Hermits do not want to feel confined. They like to have a sense of reaching out to the world and of opening out to the vastness of creation.

As a general guideline, no one need ever come to a hermitage except its hermit. A hermitage should never become a place where people visit, congregate, or make pilgrimages. Meetings of whatever sort—even with other hermits—are most appropriately conducted at another location. A flow of visitors tends to violate something of the privacy and solitariness of the hermitage, which by its nature is a one-person cloister in the wilderness. Nonetheless, there can be commonsense exceptions to the policy of no visitors to the hermitage. Workers will have to come once in a while to attend to maintenance issues. A family member or a close friend may want to visit the hermit at the actual hermitage site. The hermit's spiritual director, religious superior, or spiritual moderator may have occasion to come to the hermitage.

A hermitage would always exemplify the aesthetic values of simplicity and austerity. It would not have to look like a dilapidated shack or a shanty. It would be more substantial and self-contained than a tent or a hut. It would have electricity, running water, and indoor plumbing. It would be well-insulated and have some means of adequate heating for winter. Availability of air conditioning during the warmer seasons would depend upon the climate and the hermit's health needs. A hermitage designed in this way would provide the freedom for its occupant to focus on the spiritual life rather than survival issues.

A Day in the Life of a Hermit

What might a hermit's typical day look like?

True hermits know intuitively that neither the "typical hermit" nor "a typical hermit's day" exists. There are only individual hermits and the uniqueness of each day. Nevertheless, people who are not acquainted directly with the eremitic life may welcome some idea of the rhythms of an ordinary day in a hermitage.

Three pivotal activities punctuate any day in a hermit's life: prayer, study, and work. Approximately four to six hours of solitary personal prayer, two to four hours of study, and four hours of manual labor or limited ministry to people would round out the day. That routine would leave another twelve hours for meals, relaxation, and sleep. Some hermits find it meaningful to attend daily or weekly Celebration of the Eucharist or to participate occasionally in another form of communal worship.

Some limited ministry and part-time projects are compatible with the eremitic life. The hermit can perform many of those works in the hermitage or in a nearby facility, for example, beekeeping, bookbinding, vestment making, furniture repair, or computer tasks. Other eremitic works take the hermit away from the hermitage for brief periods, for instance, offering spiritual direction, teaching weekly adult spirituality classes, or guiding directed retreats. The hermit needs to remain as solitary as possible in making a living or in helping other people. Therefore, it would be wise for a hermit to arrange to have another person or a group do any necessary marketing or selling of products. More than roughly twenty-four hours per week at work or ministry would seem excessive.

Hermits must have a means of minimal financial support. From early Christian times, it has been an unwritten law of the desert that hermits earn their daily bread. That custom is a practical application of St. Paul's counsel: "If someone does not wish to work, neither should that person eat" (2 Thess 3:10).

Hermits are not freeloaders. When they are members of a community, they contribute in an eremitic way to that group in return for the basic necessities of life. When they have benefactors, hermits assume their responsibility by giving an eremitically oriented service to a community of their choice. When they have neither a community nor a benefactor, they have to be totally self-supporting. Many hermits provide for their material needs through a combination of earned income and donations from benefactors.

If a hermit is not judicious in efforts at self-support, that work can jeopardize the spirit and the quality of the eremitic life. Earning too much money, working too many hours, and taking on too many income-related projects are constant temptations for hermits who have to provide for themselves.

Like every human being, a hermit needs to spend some time each day in enjoyable recreation. For a hermit, recreation is of a solitary nature. Some hermits jog, write letters, read light material, or play solitaire. Others hike in the woods, follow the news or other informative programs, plant gardens, or play their guitars. Once a week, a more extended period of recreation is in order. Moreover, what is relaxing for one hermit could be dissipating for another.

A hermit undertakes specific ascetical practices only at the Spirit's prompting and after careful discernment. The eremitic life is the most solitary form of the *contemplative* life, not of the ascetical or penitential life. Overemphasis on asceticism inevitably militates against contemplation. Neither fasts, vigils, nor hair shirts characterize Christian hermits. There is no need for them to be unshaven, unkempt, or unbathed. They do not have to look like drifters, vagabonds, or wizened elders. Hermits do not even necessarily wear a distinguishing garb, such as a veil, a soutane, or a neck chain with a symbol. One might pass a hermit in a supermarket or sit next to one on a bus and not know it. The eremitic life lived to its fullest contains within itself a formidable ascesis—as does every other authentic Christian lifestyle. Unless God clearly indicates a specific penitential work, the hermit need not add ascetical practices onto those that flow from the life itself.

Qualities that must characterize a hermit's daily life, however, are simplicity, austerity, and frugality, together with self-discipline, sincerity, compassion, faith, hope, and love. Those virtues represent the true ascetical practices of a hermit.

The Reservation of the Blessed Sacrament in a Hermitage

The Reservation of the Blessed Sacrament is of special significance to hermits who practice their Christian faith in liturgical traditions that incorporate celebration of the sacraments. Some of these hermits have in a designated space or room within their hermitages a tabernacle that contains the reserved Eucharist. They obtain permission for this reservation of the Blessed Sacrament from their local diocesan bishop and/or from religious authorities within their institute or society of consecrated life. When hermits are not ordained priests and it is not possible to attend Mass, they have the option of receiving communion from their eucharistic reserve.

Why do those hermits so treasure having the Eucharist reserved in their hermitages?

First, the need for the presence of the Blessed Sacrament is intimately linked with the process of being born out of the womb of all forms of society into deepening aloneness with God. Hermits become increasingly marginal to society in that process. They undertake an inner journey that is solitary, uncharted, and full of risk. In seeking God alone in the vast desert of the human heart, hermits become acutely aware of the unfathomable depths of their dependencies, limitations, and vulnerabilities. The eucharistic presence then reminds them that they are solidly grounded in Christ and are not wandering aimlessly. The Eucharist is a sign to them that God and none other has lured them into this desert place in order to commune Heart-to-heart (Hos 2:16).

Second, the Eucharist re-presents in sacramental form the Passover of Jesus and a hermit's participation in that mystery. The Eucharist is a tangible symbol of a hermit's return journey with Jesus to the Father, through the Spirit: "If I go and prepare a place for you, I shall return and take you with me so that where I am you also may be" (John 14:3).

The eucharistic presence is thus a continuous visible reminder of the paschal dimension of the eremitic life and of all life. It helps focus a hermit on "the one thing necessary" (Luke 10:41).

Third, as hermits undergo the more difficult stages of the dark night, the Eucharist symbolizes the peace-filled depths of a chaotic inner world. The eucharistic presence becomes an external sign of the joy, stability, and equanimity of the divine indwelling. It is not that hermits experience the eucharistic presence as balm that soothes all discomfort. Rather, as the storms rage on, the Eucharist is a palpable symbol of God's abiding love and everlasting faithfulness. In the midst of night, the eucharistic presence echoes the promise of Jesus: "Courage, I am. Be not afraid" (Mark 6:50). It is a continuous reminder of Jesus's invitation: "Remain in me as I remain in you" (John 15:4).

Fourth, the presence of the Eucharist serves to remind hermits that in Christ Jesus they are in communion with all creation and are journeying with the entirety of creation to the fullness of life in God. The sacramental presence is a visible sign of God's love recapitulating all creation in Christ Jesus.

It is not that a hermit must pray always in the oratory directly before the Blessed Sacrament. While the Spirit does lead the hermit to pray frequently before the tabernacle, the Spirit inclines the hermit to pray also at other locations, such as the front porch, the woods, a nearby beach, or a hilltop. Since God abides within the hermit, that divine indwelling constitutes "the real presence." The Eucharist is, therefore, the external sign of the indwelling Trinity and of God's presence within all creation. It is a faith symbol. It represents a hermit's abiding communion with God and with all in God.

CHAPTER 23

Eremitic Being-In-Love with God

ONCE A CONTEMPLATIVE HAS been born into the solitude of a hermitage, perseverance in the eremitic life becomes a key emphasis in the discernment process.

Throughout the remainder of this section, we examine perseverance as it relates to a candidate living in a hermitage during an initial experimental period (phase three) and then on a long-term, possibly permanent, basis (phase four). We explore in relation to perseverance these principles of discernment: being-in-love with God, love of people, love of the natural world, and participation in the paschal mystery of Christ.

We begin with perseverance in the eremitic life as it is exemplified in being-in-love with God. Love of God inspires a hermit to be fully attentive to the person of Jesus and to embrace silence and solitude in the here and now with freedom of spirit as a means of communion with him. Thus, a person-centeredness, an acceptance of quietude and aloneness, an ability to abide in the present, and an attitude of carefreeness are indications of perseverance in eremitic being-in-love with God.

Love of God

The primary inspiration for undertaking an eremitic lifestyle comes not from a hermit's love for God, but rather from God's free and gracious love for the hermit: "This is the love we mean: not so much our love for God, but rather God's love for us" (1 John 4:10).

The love of God lures those called to an eremitic life into the desert and sustains them with steadfast intimacy throughout their solitary journey. God's word to the prophet Hosea describes eloquently certain attributes of that love: "I will lure her and lead her out into the desert, and speak to her heart. . . . I will betroth you to myself forever, betroth you with integrity and justice, with tenderness and love. I will betroth you to myself with faithful-ness, and you will come to know [me]" (Hos 2:16, 21–22).

Repeatedly in the Hebrew Scriptures, God affirms the divine covenant of faithful love. These are but two examples among a multitude: "Though the hills may be shaken and the mountains collapse, my love for you will never leave you" (Isa 54:10); "I have loved you with an everlasting love; I have drawn you with loving kindness" (Jer 31:3).

Those persons who have received an eremitic vocation put their faith in God's love for them. Because of the unique divine love that they have come to experience and to know, they cannot but abandon themselves un-reservedly to God in love by means of radical silence and solitude. God's love for them and their love for God require of them a solitary life. Their eremitic mode of living is their way of obeying Jesus's imperative: "Love the Lord your God with your whole heart, with your whole soul, with all your mind, and with all your strength" (Mark 12:30).

Hermits abide in continuous loving communion with the indwelling Trinity. That contemplation of the triune God integrates each hermit's re-lationships and activities into a life of prayer. That contemplation is itself a hermit's ministry within the church and to the world. The hermit's life of contemplation benefits the world in ways that remain hidden even to the hermit through whom the Spirit bestows those blessings.

Contemplation enables a hermit's participation in the community of the indwelling Trinity. In union with the three Divine Persons, a hermit experiences community with all creation. For it is in God—Father, Son, and Spirit—that all creation "lives, moves, and exists" (Acts 17:28). In God—Loving Creator, Word-Made-Flesh, and Breath of Love—the entirety of cre-ation abides as one body. The community of the Trinity holds within itself all community and all communities. A hermit participates in the Trinity as an integral member of the Mystical Body of Christ, for "he is the image of the unseen God and the firstborn of all creation. . . . In him were created all in heaven and on earth. . . . He holds all in unity. . . . All fullness was pleased to dwell in him" (Col 1:15–19).

In vocational discernment, these questions pertinent to love of God deserve reflection: Is the candidate for the eremitic life growing in gratitude for God's gift of unconditional love and for the ability to love God in return? Does the candidate have an experiential sense of participation in the com-munity of Father, Son, and Spirit and of community with all creation in God? Does the candidate have an appreciation of contemplation as a mis-sion within the church and to the world?

Person-Centered Focus

The decision to become a hermit in response to a God-given call is not primarily a choice of some-*thing*. Rather, it is above all an irresistible option for some-*One*. The focus of attentiveness remains always the three Divine Persons. In the silence and solitude, a contemplative's whole being turns ever more fully to God.

That Person-centeredness is in contradistinction, for instance, to the eremitic lifestyle itself as the focus of commitment. A hermit indeed chooses the eremitic life as a vocational path. Yet attention is not primarily upon the way itself, but upon God as Beloved. To illustrate the point, let us consider an analogy. You are sitting on a park bench, and you notice in the distance a person whom you love dearly. You immediately stand up and move toward that person. Your whole being strains forward in eager anticipation. All you can think about is the beloved. Without adverting to it, you intuitively follow the way that enables you to reach your loved one most quickly. So intent are you on encountering that person that you pay at best only minimal attention to the path. You just advance instinctively and spontaneously until you reach your beloved.

It is similar with those contemplatives called to become hermits. Their whole being strains forward in loving anticipation toward the Trinity abiding within them, but always beyond them. Their first concern is beholding the risen Christ, present within them, but always farther ahead. Their hearts are set upon contemplating him, even as they recognize intuitively the silence and solitude of their hermitage as their way to him. First, foremost, and always, their attentiveness is riveted upon Christ Jesus—not on the way of reaching him. Their deepest aspirations are like those of St. Paul: "All I want is to know Christ and the power of his resurrection, by communing in his sufferings and by being conformed to his death" (Phil 3:10).

Jesus is the Way, the Truth, and the Life (John 14:6). Applying that metaphor to the eremitic life, it is a way within the Way, a life in the Life. It is true only to the degree that it is called forth by Truth.

Consequently, these questions arise in the discernment of a candidate's eremitic experience: Is the candidate preoccupied with or fixated upon a "way"—be it the silence, the solitude, or the hermitage? Or, while journeying by means of an eremitic lifestyle, are the contemplative's heart, soul, mind, and strength set upon contemplating the Trinity in deepening faith, hope, and love? Is the risen Christ the love of the person's life? Is Christ alone—God alone—becoming increasingly the candidate's only desire?

Acceptance of Silence and Solitude

Silence and solitude are essential to eremitic being-in-love. A hermit goes apart from the usual flow of human society to be alone in communion with God. That radical aloneness with God lays the foundation for a vocational lifestyle distinct from, yet complementary to other Christian modes of living.

Acquiescence in Silence and Solitude

Eremitic silence and solitude pose numerous difficulties. Even the passage of time does not necessarily alleviate the effort required for acquiescence in the quietness and aloneness. On the contrary, because God lures a hermit into ever greater interior silence and solitude, the passage of time brings new challenges.

The element of permanency in commitment to God through an eremitic life generates an additional nuance to the aloneness of a hermit. It is one thing to spend some time—even a few years—in a profoundly solitary setting, while realizing that eventually there will be a return to life in the midst of people. It is another matter to remain in a hermitage, knowing that silence and solitude will endure and increase till death.

An Experience of Nada

In the acceptance of radical aloneness with God, a hermit experiences the incompleteness and the mortality that reside within all creation. The reality of transience and impermanence in the created world becomes undeniable and inescapable. While every person has to drink of those dregs, the hermit by vocation lives that existential situation in an intensely raw and at times harrowing manner.

Even in the contemplative life—especially in its more community-oriented forms—conditions appropriate to that lifestyle take the edge off aloneness. Community members live in physical proximity to one another. There exists a sense of other members nearby. Moreover, considerable non-verbal communication transpires within the group. Each member has also the security and the comfort of being around shared familiar spaces such as the kitchen, the dining room, the community room, the library, the laundry room, the sleeping area. Members have household chores that contribute to their sense of satisfaction in working for the common good.

In contrast, a person called to the eremitic life lets go for the most part the human interaction and communal activities appropriate to the contemplative life. A hermit remains alone day after day, journeying through nothingness (Spanish: *nada*) while encountering ever more deeply in the nothingness God who is becoming all (*todo*) in all. *Nada y todo* (nothing and all) work together to reveal to the hermit the risen Christ.[1]

Resistance to Silence and Solitude

The interior response to the effects of God's inimitable love influences a hermit's feelings toward silence and solitude. For instance, if the hermit is willing to confront a truth that is trying to surface through a specific inner trial, the quietude and aloneness feel familiar and friendly. If the hermit attempts to avoid the emerging insight, aloneness feels oppressive.

A hermit's resistance to God can manifest itself in the following interior behaviors: daydreaming, isolating oneself from God or from significant individuals, persisting in anger or resentment toward God or people, demanding that God make something perceptible happen without delay.

Resistance can be evident as well in a variety of external actions, for example, taking unnecessary naps, spending excessive time at recreation, engaging another person in prolonged chit-chat, or shirking daily responsibilities. A hermit could use even certain forms of prayer, study, and manual work as escapes from silence and solitude. In those instances, the hermit engages in spiritual practices as ways of passing time and evading truth.

Resistance to quietness and aloneness leaves a hermit in barren forms of darkness, turmoil, and emptiness. Loneliness, despondency, and fatigue then tend to prevail. In contrast, acceptance of silence and solitude enables the hermit to find new life in the midst of trials and difficulties. The *nada* of the hermit becomes the *todo* of God. Out of the desert emerge subtle yet undeniable peace and joy. From the depths of the night emerges a profound realization of loving and being loved by God, together with a deepening love for all creation in God.

Ordinarily, both acceptance of and resistance to silence and solitude are operative within a person. Hermits experience simultaneous attraction toward both propensities. They find themselves submitting in obedience to God and yet withholding something from God. They experience the risen Christ as awesomely irresistible and yet as too demanding. It is a question of which propensity is dominant in a specific time and circumstance.

---

1. See *Ascent*, I, 13, 6–11; *O Blessed Night*, 155–65.

The Spirit uses resistance itself as a means of drawing a hermit further into solitude of heart. God's merciful love awaits the return of the prodigal son or daughter. Tasting the bitter fruits of rebellion, the hermit learns to acknowledge the folly of deceits and subterfuges, and grows in trust of God's tender care.

Questions for Discernment

Acceptance of silence and solitude is essential to a candidate's perseverance in eremitic being-in-love with God. Therefore, these questions require reflection:

Can the candidate identify his or her usual forms of resistance to aloneness with God? When succumbing to those behaviors, does the candidate fall into self-pity, undue discouragement, and self-condemnation? Or do those failures serve to catapult the candidate into humble abandonment to God?

What is the nature of the candidate's resistance to aloneness? Does resistance occur only on occasion, or does it manifest itself as a persistent pattern of behavior? Does the resistance arise within the context of an overall acceptance of silence and solitude? Or has evasion of the intense aloneness become a way of life in itself?

Instead of a candidate's resistance representing personal failures, is the resistance Spirit-inspired? In other words, do the various forms of resistance bespeak the candidate's inmost self wisely protesting against his or her forced efforts to live a lifestyle that is not truly God's calling?

In general, does the candidate experience the silence and solitude of the hermitage as life-giving or as oppressive?

Ability to Live in the Present

It is the nature of love that two lovers relish intimacy alone with each other in the timelessness of the present moment. Similarly, eremitic being-in-love with God entails an invitation not only to solitary intimacy with God, but also to participation in the now-eternal. A candidate's ability to abide lovingly with God in the present is a further sign of perseverance in eremitic love of God. The past has gone. The future does not yet exist. All the hermit has is God as Beloved in the here and now: "Now is the acceptable time. Now is the day of salvation" (2 Cor 6:2).

An Essential Attitude

An ability to live in the present is vital for each Christian. However, the depth and the intensity of eremitic solitude make the practice of abiding in the present especially crucial. Unless a hermit remains grounded in God here and now, ordinary happenings become preoccupations. Concerns with what was or will be, what could have been or what might come, fill the human mind and erode loving attentiveness toward God.

Staying with the present helps a hermit to cope with trials and difficulties. Frequent storms, temptations, and misgivings arise in the course of life in a hermitage. Stressful situations occur. For example, a hermit becomes overwhelmed by a problem, perhaps magnifying it beyond all measure. Consequently, anxiety escalates and the person cannot engage in the daily routine. A sense of God at work in the now-eternal then rapidly diminishes.

Positive Signs

A candidate's attentiveness to God in the present manifests itself in these attitudes and actions:

- The candidate has an unwavering trust in God's providence.

- In coping with either minor annoyances or with intense trials, the candidate maintains for the most part a balanced outlook.

- The candidate is able to situate a specific difficulty within the context of the whole of life.

- In undergoing the transforming, enlightening, and purifying influences of God's love, the candidate remains generally faithful to the requirements of the current circumstances and the daily routine.

Carefreeness

Mutual love brings two lovers knowledge of each other. The experience of loving and being loved enables each one to perceive trustworthiness, care, and dependability in the other. That experiential knowledge summons the lovers to at-homeness and freedom in each other's presence. In short, their shared loving knowledge calls forth carefreeness.

The mutual love of God and a person also evokes carefreeness.[2] Thus, God's love invites a hermit to the joyful surrender of self to Christ Jesus and

2. See Merton, "A Life Free from Care," 217–26.

to the entrusting of all concerns to divine providence: "Cast your cares upon God, because God cares for you" (1 Pet 5:7; Ps 55:22). Love for God awakens a hermit's desire to receive God wholeheartedly.

Empathy, not Unconcern

Eremitic carefreeness is not unconcern or indifference. Hermits do not sit passively in a corner and let the world go by. They are not insensitive to the horrendous misery, pain, and injustice all around them. On the contrary, they empathize profoundly with all creation in its suffering, but they do so in silence and solitude, from within the heart of the world—its Sacred Heart.

Stability, not Mobility

Eremitic carefreeness does not mean gadding about all over the place. Hermits are not malcontents moving continually from one place to the next. Nor are they vagabonds, drifters, or social butterflies. On the contrary, long-term stability in a hermitage is at the core of perseverance in eremitic love of God.

Occasionally, one hears stories of "itinerant hermits"—men or women who are here today and gone tomorrow. Some of those persons even have their own vehicles, campers, tents, or sleeping bags to facilitate their travel and lodging. The designation "itinerant hermits" seems a contradiction in terms. The nature of the eremitic vocation requires that the hermit settle down in one place for the long haul. That stability in life optimizes the hermit's availability to God's love. It provides the hermit with the freedom to advance on the inner journey to God.

Freedom from Care

Eremitic carefreeness implies freedom in regard to the external world and the usual cares of most people. It is a freedom from worrying about oneself, from having to earn a huge salary, from deciding what to do next, where to go, what to wear, what to eat, or what to say.

Carefreeness is freedom from concern about self because God remains the focus of a hermit's attention. It is freedom from concern about earning lots of money because the eremitic life is so frugal and the reliance on divine providence so direct. It is freedom from concern about deciding what to do next because the basic routine remains the same day after day, month after month—not out of lack of creativity, but rather due to the inner simplicity of the life itself. It is freedom from concern about where to go because where else does the hermit need to go than to the indwelling Father, Son, and Spirit. It is freedom from concern about what to wear because there is no one to impress. It is freedom from concern about what to eat because the diet is so simple. It is freedom from what to say because the silence is so stark.

The eremitic life, when lived faithfully, produces in a hermit carefreeness in relation to all aspects of human existence. That carefreeness remains above all interior and spiritual.

Freedom for The-One-Thing-Necessary

The freedom of the eremitic life is not flight from the world. A hermit does not shirk responsibility, does not retire from all need to problem solve, does not retreat from all occupation. No, eremitic carefreeness exists so that a hermit can become totally concerned and utterly occupied with "the one thing necessary" of Luke 10:42. Moreover, this shall not be taken from the hermit.

Carefreeness empowers a hermit to care in an uncommon way for the interior and spiritual realities of existence, namely, life in God and God in life. It enables a hermit to attend sensitively to what matters more than anything else: the mystery of God's immediate and direct activity within all creation. That mystery of transforming, illuminating, and purifying love is salvation at its core. It is redemption at its purest source. It is liberation in its simplest form.

The Crux of the Issue

Carefreeness is indicative of a hermit's perseverance in being-in-love with God. Therefore, in the ebb and flow of daily life in a hermitage, does the person discerning an eremitic vocation remain carefree? Or is the candidate still "fretting, anxious, and disturbed about many things" (Luke 10:41)?

If a candidate does not have some measure of the carefreeness which Jesus observed in Mary of Bethany, then perhaps that person is not becoming a hermit after all—or at least not yet.

CHAPTER 24

Eremitic Love of People

JESUS SUMMONED ALL HIS disciples to love of God and neighbor. He taught them to love God with all their heart, soul, mind, and energy. He instructed them to love their neighbor not only as they love themselves, but especially as he loves them, which is with God's own love (John 15:9, 12). The practice of love of God and love of neighbor (Mark 12:29–31; 1 John 4:20) is imperative in each of the three general vocational lifestyles: the apostolic life, the contemplative life, and the eremitic life. Yet each vocational lifestyle evokes its own unique expression of love of God and neighbor.

In the previous chapter, we discussed being-in-love with God as indicative of perseverance in the eremitic life. We explored the following areas related to a hermit's love for God: person-centeredness, acceptance of silence and solitude, ability to live in the present, and carefreeness.

In this chapter, we take up love of neighbor in the eremitic life. "Neighbor" for a hermit encompasses every living being—human beings, nonhuman creatures, and the entire world of nature. We focus now on "neighbor" in the sense of a hermit's relationships with fellow human beings. We explore growth in love for people as another indication of perseverance in eremitic living. We highlight three aspects of a hermit's life that pertain to love of neighbor: basic maturity in human development, direct interaction with people, and intimacy with loved ones.

Basic Maturity in Human Development

Emotional instability, personality disorder, psychosis, or cognitive impairment would certainly prevent a person from flourishing in the solitude of a hermitage. However, the level of well-being necessary for perseverance in the eremitic life far transcends mere absence of severe emotional or cognitive difficulties. Certain needs or weaknesses that pose no undue struggle for a contemplative in a community or family setting work against a person living alone in a hermitage.

Basic maturity in human development is essential if a hermit is to withstand the challenges of an eremitic lifestyle. These themes pertain to that maturity: personal affirmation, self-esteem, and independence of spirit.

Personal Affirmation

A person with a vocation to the contemplative life receives extensive reassurance and encouragement from participation in the common life and from interaction with communal members. The living witness of the members inspires sustained effort and fidelity. Their love contributes to a sense of self-worth and self-acceptance. Their presence is supportive in the difficult moments of the faith journey. When those forms of communal affirmation remain necessary for growth, it would be clearly counterproductive for a contemplative to move into a hermitage—or to stay there, if the move has already occurred.

A contemplative called by God to the eremitic life does not experience the absence of communal living as a deprivation of something essential for well-being. This contemplative has been born into solitude to a point that sustained interaction with people is no longer necessary for well-being. By virtue of an eremitic vocation, a contemplative can forego the affirmation that comes from participation in community life. In fact, a person called to the eremitic life has to let go that support in order to progress humanly and spiritually. Communion with God and fidelity to the eremitic calling provide the necessary affirmation for a hermit.

Self-Esteem

A fundamental sense of self-esteem is part and parcel of being a healthy human being. Furthermore, the ability to love oneself correlates with the capacity to love other persons (Mark 12:30; Matt 22:39).

Many people, even contemplatives, struggle with intense feelings of unworthiness and inferiority. A contemplative who has substantially low self-esteem might be able to cope effectively with that difficulty in a contemplative lifestyle. That contemplative would be unlikely, however, to find in the eremitic life the supports necessary for development of basic self-love. A need for continual interaction with people as a tool in overcoming low self-esteem is contraindicative of an eremitic vocation.

It is not that a hermit must possess psychological perfection or any other kind of perfection for that matter, especially at the outset of the eremitic life. Each hermit will have to bear with certain emotional, cognitive, moral, and spiritual weaknesses until death. But, with God's grace, those debilities will not impede a hermit's overall growth in the context of silence and solitude. Moreover, as the hermit's solitude of heart deepens, God brings further healing to all inner hurts and wounds. The Spirit transforms all past and present wounds into the wound of love.[1]

Independence of Spirit

Healthy independence in relation to people contributes to perseverance in the eremitic life.

A hermit has to be capable of persisting in prayer, work, study, silence, and solitude, without the presence and affirmation of people. Although the need to consult a spiritual director arises on occasion, the hermit must have sufficient ability to discern solutions for problems that arise in daily life. A hermit must be able also to do upkeep in and around the hermitage without seeking constant assistance from people. The hermit has to be adept at making decisions without relying on other people's suggestions and opinions.

Independence is not, however, individualism or self-sufficiency. Healthy independence disposes a hermit to remain in silence and solitude with direct dependence upon God alone. Independence in relation to people and dependency upon God work together to enhance a person's perseverance in an eremitic lifestyle.

Interaction with People

God calls a hermit to persevere in radical silence and solitude. God also sets some parameters to that aloneness. In God's providential care, a hermit thus encounters certain persons for a variety of purposes.

Examples of Purposeful Interaction

A hermit may leave the hermitage in order to meet with people when necessity and common sense demand it. Acceptable reasons for a hermit to go elsewhere on occasion include participation in the Celebration of the

---

1. See *Living Flame*, commentary on stanzas 1 and 2.

Eucharist, fulfillment of an obligation of charity, a need for medical care, and management of personal business.

Sometimes the Spirit moves a hermit to be of service to other persons by contemplative presence or certain forms of work. That service could transpire in a diversity of contexts. Family and close friends feel the need for the hermit's presence with them at times. Because of insufficient personnel to cover all chores, a contemplative community might require assistance with tasks of a solitary nature from a member who lives an eremitic life. People who are contemplatively inclined might seek out spiritual direction from a hermit. Dependent upon the hermit's abilities, there may be invitations for tutoring studies in spirituality, engaging in weekend ministry, or conducting occasional retreats.

Interaction as Limited

The limits appropriate to a hermit's physical aloneness and to direct interaction with people are not rigidly set or entirely predictable. Those boundaries are constantly shifting, and thus require ongoing discernment. The uniqueness of each eremitic vocation, the hermit's closeness with family and special friends, the temperament and gifts of each hermit, and the needs of the community with which the hermit is associated have to be considered in discerning what is suitable at a specific time. As a general guideline, direct interaction with people remains at a minimum. Otherwise, the eremitic life becomes a mere abstraction, not a lived reality.

The Providential Role of Limited Interaction

The spiritual exercise of integrating a little direct human interaction with physical aloneness has a threefold providential purpose in a hermit's life:

To start with, through encounters with people, the hermit grows in self-knowledge and in knowledge of God. That knowledge enkindles in the hermit an increase of love for the risen Christ and for all creation in him. Interaction with people thus becomes a means by which God leads the hermit into deeper solitude of heart.

In addition, limited interaction with people assists the hermit in undergoing the exigencies of prolonged exterior solitude. This side of the resurrection a certain amount of matter is always necessary in order to elicit an optimum of spirit. Therefore, when God calls the hermit to be with a person or a group for a while, the companionship and the collaboration serve overall to enhance the hermit's solitude.

Finally, the balancing of eremitic solitude with limited human interaction requires flexibility and adaptation. That endeavor runs counter to any propensity in a hermit to set up too comfortable or too rigid a routine. The constantly shifting balance reminds the hermit anew each day of the need for reliance upon God alone.

Issues for Discernment

In discerning perseverance in the eremitic life as evident in a candidate's love of people, these questions invite discussion:

Does the candidate accept the fact that a little interaction with people on certain occasions is an intrinsic dimension of an eremitic vocation? A candidate's experience of necessary involvement with people as being extraneous to the eremitic life or as disruptive of aloneness with God could indicate unhealthy isolation and withdrawal rather than authentic silence and solitude.

Is the candidate truly called to engage in specific interactions? Or do they constitute forms of escape from solitude? These four signs together affirm that an involvement is probably from God:

- A person or a group presents a genuine need to the candidate.

- The candidate in turn has the ability to assist with the need.

- The candidate discerns it appropriate to help out in the situation.

- After rendering assistance, the candidate returns immediately to the solitude of the hermitage.

Does the candidate remain ready, willing, and able to take an open-ended and flexible approach to the question of integrating limited human interaction with extensive physical solitude? Or does the candidate demand a once-and-for-all definitive answer to the question of how to balance the two directions? The former approach indicates a listening heart; the latter bespeaks tendencies toward rigidity and control.

Intimacy with Loved Ones

To be in relationship and to experience intimacy are essential to being human. A unique intimacy emanates from each mode of human relationship, for example, parent to child, spouse to spouse, sibling to sibling, mentor to student, friend to friend, and lover to beloved. An absence of significant human relationships and a lack of intimacy with loved ones are counter to the spirit of an eremitic vocation.

Love as the Wellspring of Intimacy

Intimacy is to love as a flower to its roots or a stream to its source.

Love is a Spirit-enabled participation in the inner life of God. Love directs one's thoughts and affections to the loved one. It enkindles in the lover the desire to reveal oneself to the beloved. It gently urges one to transcend fear of rejection and to share with the beloved one's inmost desires and aspirations. Love awakens a longing to know the beloved more fully. It creates a willingness to endure pain and hurt for the sake of the beloved. Love empowers one to protect, to trust, to hope, to forgive (1 Cor 13:4–7).

Intimacy arises from loving and being loved. Love can be one-way, at least initially in a relationship. Intimacy, however, implies mutual love. It bespeaks two-way effort in caring, in self-giving, in willingness to share and to trust. Intimacy does admit of differences from one relationship to another and from person to person within a specific relationship. Expressions of intimacy include endearing words, palpable gestures, and tangible signs. Modes of intimacy can include heartwarming conversation, a supportive hug, an affectionate caress, or sexual intercourse. How any two people appropriately express intimate affection for one another depends largely on what is suitable in light of their God-given vocations.

Reconciliation of the Desire for Intimacy with Eremitic Solitude

The challenge to reconcile the need for intimacy with a calling to solitude presents itself in all forms of celibate living. For a hermit, the intensity of aloneness, the passage of time, and the aging process bring acutely to the fore the issue of a need for intimacy.

Jesus spoke of the disciple who has left "home, brothers, sisters, father, mother, children, and land" for his sake and for the sake of the gospel (Mark 10:29). The hermit is a disciple in that sense not only spiritually, but also quite literally. The hermit lives physically apart from everyone else—including those persons who are most beloved.

Sooner or later, each hermit feels profoundly the absence of interaction with family members and special friends. Moreover, a sense of barrenness and emptiness arises from the realization that a capacity to be wife or husband, mother or father will go forever unused. Intense feelings of rootlessness and loneliness also accompany that experiential knowledge.

The unfulfilled longing to share in love with another human being and the accompanying feelings of loss eventually have a liberating effect. By means of those experiences the Spirit awakens an increasing appreciation of the gifts of celibate consecration and eremitic life. The Spirit brings the hermit to a heightened sense of having freely chosen those vocational lifestyles in response to God's calling and for the sake of Jesus and the gospel.

A hermit's feelings of insufficient intimacy can arise from various sources. On the one hand, while yearning for intimacy reflects a natural human need, certain forms of intimacy are contrary to an eremitic vocation. The hermit may not possess clarity as to what mode of intimacy would satisfy, but there persists within the person a yearning for something other than what is. On the other hand, a hermit may not recognize the intimacy that he or she already has. Some form of intimacy exists already between a hermit and each loved one, but a craving for a form of intimacy that is lacking can blind the hermit to the reality of existing closeness with family and friends.

In the struggle to reconcile the need for intimacy with eremitic solitude, a hermit's stance has to be above all else that of receptivity to God's tender love: "You are mine. . . . You are precious in my eyes. . . . I love you (Isa 43:1–4)." God has to become all the hermit loves. As St. Augustine counsels: "Hope for nothing else from the Lord except that he himself become your hope. . . . Seek God alone. Letting go everything else, make your way to him. . . . He will be to you all you love."[2]

God alone—God in God's own self—is the fullness of the hermit's desire. In God dwell all those persons for whom the hermit has special affections. Thus, the hermit grows in loving other people as Jesus loves them, which is as the Father loves the Son (John 15:12, 9). The hermit loves those people in God with God's own love.

Positive Signs

Like every human being, a hermit treasures a variety of loving relationships. Therefore, in discernment of perseverance in the eremitic life, these questions deserve consideration: Does the candidate have significant relationships? Is the candidate able to maintain and to nurture them in ways compatible with his or her solitary life? What is a candidate's experience of intimacy in relationships, especially with family members and close friends?

2. Augustine, "Commentary on Psalm 40." *PL*, 36:437–38; *CCSL*, 38:430.

Not every candidate for the eremitic life undergoes a crisis in relation to intimacy during the early years in a hermitage. Nonetheless, the need to reconcile solitude and intimacy is always active to some extent.

A first sign of that reconciliation is the candidate's ability to weather the storm of the apparently conflicting needs for solitude and intimacy on each occasion that it arises and to come to a peaceful resolution in each instance.

A second sign consists in this: the candidate's desire for and experience of intimacy with loved ones becomes an impetus for growth in seeking God alone.

A third sign is that as the candidate's communion with the risen Christ deepens in solitude, love for each significant person matures.

Sometimes it seems to a hermit that zest for life, capacity to love, and ability to enjoy creation are formidable obstacles to perseverance in the eremitic life. In truth, that very richness of personhood is what God most desires a hermit to consecrate to Jesus. Moreover, God's transforming love itself has a humanizing effect within a hermit. Being loved by God and loving in return causes the hermit to becomes more fully human, more loving and compassionate, more capable of enjoying creation as God desires it to be enjoyed.[3] In transforming union with God, the hermit's true self in Christ emerges ever more radiantly in all its innocence, freedom, and naturalness.

3. See *O Blessed Night*, 47–68.

CHAPTER 25

Eremitic Love of the Natural World

WE HAVE EXAMINED IN depth two principles for discernment of perseverance in the eremitic life, namely, love of God and love of neighbor, in the
sense of fellow human beings.

In this chapter, we consider a third principle of discernment related to
eremitic perseverance: a hermit's love of neighbor, understood this time as
the natural world and its creatures. Actually, human beings are inseparable
from the natural world. They are creatures who belong integrally to it and
who interrelate with all its other creatures in one web of life. But in this
chapter, we refer to the world of nature as "neighbor" primarily in the sense
of its other-than-human life forms.

Each human being has a responsibility to exercise compassionate care
for the earth. The practice of what many people term nature conservation,
environmentalism, or integrity of creation is an essential Christian duty. The
content of this chapter has general application to each person's love and care
for the natural world, whatever one's vocational lifestyle or combination of
lifestyles. Nonetheless, since a hermit abides alone in a desert, a wilderness,
or a green space of some kind, that world of nature constitutes the primary
physical milieu for communion with God. There a hermit grows in love of
God, love of self, love of humankind, and love of all creation.

Thus, we focus specifically upon the eremitic experience of love for the
natural world and care for its creatures. We examine how as a participant
in the one web of life a hermit loves the natural world as a neighbor and
how that love is a sign of eremitic perseverance. In that respect, we highlight these themes: the earth as sacred grounding, encounter with creation
in God, encounter with God through creatures, renewal within nature, the
providential role of the natural world, and what Pope Francis calls the "common home" shared by the one family of God.[1]

---

1. For further study of themes related to this chapter, see Francis, *Laudato Si*, and
Johnson, *Ask the Beasts.*

Earth as Sacred Grounding

The earth, together with the entire cosmos, is sacred because it is the work of God the Creator. To God belong the earth and all that it holds, this world and all who live in it, heaven and the heaven of heavens (Ps 24:1). To be anywhere on the earth as a point of orientation for life in this cosmos is to be on holy ground, for the earth continues to be a living organism sustained by its Creator.

An authentic hermit experiences solidarity with the earth. The land upon which the hermitage is situated and the landscape surrounding the hermitage provide the physical foundation and sacred grounding for continuing maturation of a hermit's sense of community with the earth. With striking clarity, the word of God to Moses reverberates within the hermit: "The land upon which you stand is holy ground" (Exod 3:5).

As a hermit's awareness of the sacredness of the earth in the local setting increases, that consciousness extends to Planet Earth in its entirety. Not only is this piece of land holy to the Creator; all the lands of the earth are sacred to God. Indeed, the entire cosmos manifests the glory of the Creator (Ps 19:1). Thus, a hermit's maturing realization of "standing on holy ground" encompasses local, planetary, and cosmic dimensions of creation.

In discernment of a candidate's experience of the earth as holy ground, these questions come to the fore: Does the candidate experience the immediate natural world as sacred, because God is its Creator? Does the beauty of the earth evoke awe and wonder in the candidate? Does the candidate see the earth as sacred grounding for an eremitic lifestyle? Does connectedness with the natural world surrounding the hermitage awaken in the candidate increasing consciousness of the planetary and cosmic sacredness of creation? Or, to the contrary, does the candidate display disconnection from the land or lack of care for the earth? Do the candidate's actions exhibit disrespect for the earth, abuse of the land, or cruelty toward its inhabitants?

Communion with Creation in and through God

In the New Testament, the word *agapē* refers to God as love and to God's way of loving. Its meaning extends also to a person's ability to love God, self, humankind, and all creation with God's own love. *Agapē* constitutes the heart and soul of Christian contemplation and of an eremitic vocation.

Contemplation denotes direct and immediate communion in love between the Trinity and a human being. During contemplation, a hermit's attentiveness is riveted with faith, hope, and love upon God in mystery.

The hermit does not focus intentionally upon anything or anyone during solitary times of beholding God— not upon a method of prayer, not upon feelings and concepts, not even upon an image of God. Nevertheless, there are two ways in which a hermit's rapport with creation comes into play during contemplation.

The first way: A hermit encounters creation in and through God. For it is *in God* that all creatures—human beings and all life forms—live and move and exist (Acts 17:28). *Through God*, the hermit communes with the entirety of creation.

Thus, in contemplation itself a hermit discovers profound community. Contemplation enables a hermit to participate in the community of the loving Creator, the Word, and the Spirit. The more deeply the hermit communes with the Trinity, the more intensive, expansive, and personalized is the experience of community with all creation in and through God.

There is no such thing in Christian contemplation as "me and God," exclusive of creation. To contemplate God directly is also to commune in and through God with all creation. On the perceptible level of a human being, contemplation transpires for the most part without specific thoughts and distinct feelings. The practice of contemplation plunges a person into emptiness, aridity, nothingness, often even the apparent absence of God. Nevertheless, the person experiences also in contemplation a subtle intuition of universal oneness with all in God. That unity does not consist of absorption of creatures in God or loss of their identity. Rather, God remains God and creatures retain their created nature.

Is contemplation then for the candidate a wellspring of community? Does the person manifest as an integral dimension of contemplation a sense of unity with local, planetary, and cosmic creation? Is the candidate growing in awareness of community with all creatures in God?

The second way: Another way in which a hermit's rapport with creation asserts itself during contemplation pertains to the identity and the creatureliness of a human being in the act of contemplating God. A hermit approaches contemplation with the awareness of being a creature bonded to the created world on all levels of existence. In the spiritual realm, for example, the hermit shares with the entirety of creation a longing for fulfillment in God. In the biological sphere, the hermit interrelates with all creatures in a history of evolution. On a physical level, each human body comes forth from the same matter with which God formed the stars and all other creatures, and unto dust shall that body return.

"Remember that you are dust and unto dust you shall return." That proclamation has its roots in a story of creation contained in the book of Genesis (Gen 3:19). Those words are included in the liturgical rite for "the blessing of the ashes" on Ash Wednesday to mark the beginning of Lent. Many Christians think of that mandate primarily as a reminder of human lowliness, personal sinfulness, and the need for repentance. But when considered from an evolutionary world view and in the light of faith, that mandate points to evolution as God's way of creating. It accentuates the sacredness of matter. It invites recognition of the interconnectedness of all creatures and the celebration of the interdependence of all forms of life. All creation belongs to the Body of Christ. The entirety of creation is ablaze with the glory of God. Creation is one living organism in which each creature—including each human being—constitutes a unique member and, according to its distinctive nature, proceeds on a spiritual journey to the fullness of its destiny in God.

Has the candidate for the eremitic life come to acknowledge and to welcome human existence with its element of creatureliness as gift from God and precious to God? Is the candidate growing in experiential awareness of the interdependence of all creation, even on the level of physical being? After all, God became what we are so that we can become what God is.[2] Does the candidate approach contemplation as a member of the one Body of Christ?

Communion with God through Creation

During contemplation, a hermit experiences God directly and in God encounters creation immediately. Like the rest of humankind, a hermit beholds God also *through* creatures. In the latter case, creation itself becomes a point of entry into experience of God. Involvement with creatures leads a person through and beyond them to God dwelling in them.

The book of Wisdom teaches how humankind encounters God through creatures: "From the greatness and beauty of creatures, the Creator can be seen, so as to be known thereby" (Wis 13:5). In a similar vein, St. Paul sums up with these words his view of creation as revelatory of God: "Since the creation of the world, God's invisible things—the eternal power and divinity—have been clearly seen, being understood through what he has made" (Rom 1:20).

Therefore, the following questions serve as springboards for discussion in vocational discernment:

---

2. A saying of many of the early church fathers, for example, Athanasius, *On the Incarnation* (*De Incarnatione*), 54:3. *PG*, 25:192B.

Does the candidate welcome all creatures great and small as beloved of God for their own sake? Is the candidate's involvement with the natural world a means of encounter with God?

Does the candidate manifest genuine interest and tender care toward the specific creatures that live around the hermitage? Or is the person absorbed in narcissism and self-centeredness?

Is tenderness and compassion exercised appropriately toward creatures one and all? Or does the candidate accept some creatures as "good" and reject others as "bad"? A person, for example, might judge deer to be enchanting, but snakes to be appalling. All God's creatures are good. Their value does not depend upon human likes and dislikes, attractions and repulsions.

Does the candidate feel at home with immersion in the world of nature? Or is fearfulness the overriding response to the natural environment? One sign of a disconnect would be the candidate staying inside the hermitage and deliberately keeping to a bare minimum any contact with the surrounding natural world and its inhabitants.

Does the candidate integrate both modes of relating to creation in daily prayer life; that is, "in contemplation of God, communion with creation," and "through encounter with creation, communion with God"? Or are there signs of undue tension between those two modes of encounter with God and creation?

Renewal within the Natural World

Attentiveness to the natural world has the potential to enrich a hermit's communion with its loving Creator. Two areas in particular exemplify that truth: the earth's natural processes of renewal and the specificity of each creature. At the same time, these areas evoke questions relevant to vocational discernment.

The Earth's Natural Processes of Renewal

One example of a natural process of renewal is the annual life cycle of a tree. Spring brings new greenery, growth, and budding. Summer displays the tree at or nearing the peak of its glory and fruitfulness. Autumn marks harvest time, with the dying process beginning to overtake the tree's life. Winter manifests death and the hibernation of life. Then spring comes around again and that annual cycle begins afresh. Prolonged observation of a tree shows repetitive cycles of living, dying, and rebirth, but with the life of the tree always moving forward according to its nature toward a definitive end and a final rebirth.

A regenerative process is visible also in the natural recycling of a tree's waste into sustenance for its life. The dead leaves of a tree, together with broken twigs and branches, drop to the earth. There with the aid of water, air, heat, and microorganisms, the fallen matter undergoes slow decomposition. It gradually decays, breaks down, forms mulch, and finally rich compost for the earth's topsoil. The tree then draws nutrients from that soil in order to feed itself. All composting for farm or gardening use is an acceleration of that natural process.

Any pristine wilderness or desert offers a firsthand experience of the food chain operative on a broad scale. A "food chain" serves to promote life across different levels of being and myriad species. For example, soil forms, seeds germinate, vegetation grows, plants and trees synthesize nutrients that sustain herbivores. The herbivores then become food for carnivores. Throughout the food chain, production of organic waste occurs. That organic waste begins anew the process of soil enrichment and evolution of life.

Still another example of the interdependent actions of species for the purpose of promoting life pertains to maintenance of air quality. Trees take in carbon dioxide from the air, synthesize it with sunlight, and release oxygen. Human beings breathe in the oxygen in order to stay alive. They breathe out carbon dioxide as a waste product, which in turn trees absorb. The interdependence of trees and human beings is continuous. It is one of nature's ways of filtering, purifying, and refining the quality of the earth's air so that the planet has the capacity to sustain life.

Is the candidate in tune with the repetitive natural cycles of birthing, living, decaying, death, and rebirth in creation? Does the candidate observe affinities between human life cycles and nature's processes of regeneration? Does the candidate have an expanding sense of participation in the one community of all creatures on earth? Does seeing those awe-inspiring natural processes at work point the candidate toward beholding the Creator?

The Specificity of Each Creature

The biodiversity that comes forth from the hands of the Creator is exhilarating to behold. No two trees even of the same species are identical. No two leaves of any one tree have precisely the same design. Within a species of birds or mammals, each creature has its unique temperament and traits. Although profuse similarities exist within a species, each member of the group has certain distinctive modes of relating to the world around it. Each and every creature has its own form of beauty and intelligence. Each creature great or small has its specific life cycle and makes its contribution to the propagation of its species.

God brings forth into being-becoming each creature of the natural world as a unique being of immense value. Every living being is beloved of God. Each one gives glory to the Creator. As Pope Francis noted, "The fleeting life of the least of beings is the object of God's love, and in the few seconds of existence, God enfolds it with his affection."[3]

Is the candidate attuned to the uniqueness of creatures in the natural world surrounding the hermitage? Does the candidate seek to respect each living being as cherished by God? Does seeing the biodiversity of creation enhance the candidate's sense of the magnificence of the Creator?

The Providential Role of the Natural World

God's creation provides a continuous feast for the human senses. Each day the natural world within the vicinity of a hermitage is present to behold. Creatures of nature are providential in an eremitic life in these ways:

First, each creature within the natural world reveals something of God by its existence, its traits, its actions, its beauty, and its interdependence with other creatures. God bestows upon each creature not only natural life, but also a reflection of God's own self. God beholds each creature and sees that it is very good (Gen 1:31). God thus imparts to all creatures some ability to participate in God's own life and to witness within the limits of their nature to the presence of the Creator. Each creature holds within itself a trace of Christ Jesus, the Beloved Son of God.[4]

Does the candidate try to see each creature and creation as a whole in the way that God sees it? Does the candidate seek to love the natural world with God's own love?

Second, although a hermit catches joyous glimpses of the Beloved through creatures, those chance sightings do not satiate desire. Rather, they intensify longing for God alone and yearning for consummate communion with all creation in God. A hermit's relatedness to creatures of the natural world becomes in that way a mode of loving encounter with God. In turn, the experience of God through creation has the effect of stirring up within the hermit ever deeper desire for the One who remains utter mystery in both the divine immanence and the divine transcendence.

3. Francis, *Laudato Si*, 77.
4. See *Spiritual Canticle*, commentary on stanzas 5 and 6.

Does the candidate experience immersion in creation then as ripe with opportunities for encounter with God? Is the candidate still longing and yearning for God alone and for consummate union with all creation in the fullness of God?

Third, creatures of the natural world can be spiritual teachers for the hermit, as they were for Jesus himself.

It is clear in the Scriptures that Jesus experienced closeness to the natural world and received wisdom from it. The winds and the sea taught him about the valor of faith (Matt 8:22–27). The fig tree without fruit spoke to him of the need for patient waiting upon growth (Matt 21:18–23). How the sight of a hen gathering her chicks under her wings must have touched him! He drew upon that experience in expressing his lament over Jerusalem (Luke 13:34–35). Yeast and mustard seeds were signs to Jesus of the potency of the reign of heaven (Matt 13:31–33). The birds of the air and the flowers of the field witnessed to him of trust in divine providence: "Look at the birds of the air. They neither sow nor reap, yet your heavenly Father feeds them . . . . Look at the flowers of the field. They never have to work or to spin. Yet I tell you that not even Solomon in all his glory was clothed like one of these" (Matt 6:25–29).

So too in the daily life of a hermit, all creatures great and small speak words of wisdom by their being, their beauty, their silence, their sounds, and their actions. Through them, the Spirit gives spiritual direction for the hermit's journey. That direction could consist of challenge, comfort, encouragement, or affection, depending upon the hermit's need at the time.

Does the candidate for the eremitic life keep a listening heart toward God's creatures of the natural world? Is the candidate receptive to and cooperative with their providential role in eremitic living? Does the candidate assimilate their teachings and put them into action?

One Family of God Sharing a Common Home

A person called by God to an eremitic life goes apart from human society for the purpose of loving communion with God. A hermit occupies a place of silence and solitude in a desert, a wilderness, or other green-space location. In that environment creatures of all kinds and shapes abide: mammals, birds, fungi, algae, worms, insects, reptiles, and microorganisms. Diverse forms of vegetation protect the earth's topsoil, as nature's elements enrich it. The hermit abides on land that is holy and participates in a community of life that is sacred. There the hermit continues to grow in appreciation for the gift of each living being and in respect for life in all its manifestations.

The presence of God within creation, together with all creation pointing beyond itself to the Creator, sustains and nurtures a hermit in the silence and solitude of the eremitic life.

The ordinary daily experience of a hermit holds within itself a gateway to the universal and an opening to the divine. What the person perceives spiritually in a hermitage and in its natural surroundings is a microcosm of the whole. Within the limitations of time and space, the hermit undergoes an ever-deepening experience of transforming union with God and of communion with creation on all levels of existence: local, planetary, universal, and cosmic. The hermit abides within the risen Christ at the heart of all matter.

A hermit's perseverance in the eremitic life bears fruit in a sense of the unity of all life and the interconnectedness of all creation, even on a visible physical level of existence. The hermit realizes that ultimately there is but one ecosystem, one web of life, one body in which each creature is unique and all creatures are interrelated. That recognition occurs not merely in an abstract or an intellectual way. It is the fruit of spiritual experience. The hermit beholds the natural world through the eyes of faith, hope, and love. An increasing sense of the interconnectedness and interdependence of all aspects of creation in the immediate environment around the hermitage enables the hermit to see each creature as "neighbor" and all creation as one family embraced in God, our shared dwelling.

The life of a hermit is a witness to the unity and community of all creation in God. A hermit passionately loves God's creation. That love manifests itself especially in actions of tender care toward creatures and in the practice of frugality in the use of created things. With gratitude for all God's gifts in and through creation, the hermit gives praise to God. The hermit's presence in silence expresses solidarity with creation as both beloved of God and as fragile. The hermit's silence is itself a word. And at appropriate times a hermit's words out of that silence become a voice for the voiceless creatures of the natural world.

CHAPTER 26

Participation in the Paschal Mystery

FROM AN EVOLUTIONARY AND relational faith perspective, the phrase "paschal mystery" embraces the whole of Jesus's life: his incarnation, passion, death, and resurrection.

The spiritual meaning of *paschal* or Pasch originates in God's "passing over" the homes of the Israelites to protect them from death and destruction as they prepared to leave Egypt and to begin the journey to the promised land (Exod 12–13). The word *mystery* reminds us that God, God's love, and God's salvific plan for creation remain forever beyond the grasp of human wisdom, understanding, and insight. The paschal mystery is central to Christian faith because it symbolizes the fullness of God's saving, redeeming, and liberating plan for creation in Christ Jesus.

The crux of the eremitic life consists in a hermit's experience in silence and solitude of being loved unconditionally by God, of loving God wholeheartedly in return, and of loving all creation in God. That loving communion with God and creation unfolds by means of a hermit's participation in the paschal mystery of Jesus. In union with the risen Christ, a hermit undergoes a spiritual incarnation, passion, death, and resurrection.

Incarnation refers to the hermit's full immersion in creation and increasing freedom in relation to created realities. The hermit progresses in ardent love for all creatures and in openness to nurturance from them, without clinging to them or becoming enmeshed in them. Dwelling in the Spirit with the risen Christ at the heart of the cosmos, the hermit thus abides at the qualitative center of an evolving universe rather than on its periphery.

Passion signifies that the hermit undergoes in solidarity with the entire cosmos the struggle, suffering, and pain necessary for Christ to become all in all (that is, christogenesis).[1]

Death denotes that process of detachment in which the hermit relinquishes gradually whatever impedes communion with the risen Christ.

---

1. See *O Blessed Night*, 155–65.

Transforming union with God and communion with all creation in God is the context for the hermit's daily dying to self, up to and inclusive of his or her personal death.

Resurrection means that with each detachment the hermit rises up a little more transformed into the image and likeness of Christ. In dying to self, the hermit becomes a new creation and sees a new creation taking shape in this world (2 Cor 3:16–18, 5:17; Gal 6:15).[2] Thus liberated, the hermit experiences a progressively more qualitative share in the freedom of the children of God. The grace of rising anew in Christ continues until in death the hermit is "filled with the utter fullness of God" (Eph 3:19).

In this chapter, we turn our attention to participation in the paschal mystery of Jesus as indicative of a person's perseverance in the eremitic life. We highlight four critical areas in which a hermit encounters the paschal mystery: acceptance of the cross, self-knowledge, acedia, and insatiability.

Acceptance of the Cross

Love is an evolving reality. The only cure for true love is to love more deeply. In order to welcome God in love, to surrender to God wholeheartedly, and to love all creation in God, a hermit has to die to self in the process. It takes a lifetime—perhaps even an eternity—to learn to love as God loves and with God's own love. There is nothing in this mortal life more transforming and purifying, nothing more uplifting and crucifying, than love.[3] Thus, a hermit's life exists profoundly in the shadow of the cross of loving to the end.

Love to the End

Jesus loved and revealed his love "to the end" (John 13:1)—*to the end*, in the sense of loving simultaneously *unto death* and *unto perfection*. Actually, "unto death" is the cost of loving "unto perfection." Conversely, "unto perfection" occurs only when one loves "unto death." Death and dying constitute the cathartic aspect of loving unto fullness. As a follower of Jesus, each hermit has a desire to love to the end.

Every advance in loving communion has a cost. Each movement into new depths of union requires a relinquishment. For example, being born into the solitude of a hermitage requires increasing physical separation from human society. Movement into aloneness with God necessitates a "stricter

---

2. See *Spiritual Journey*, 212–19; 223–26.

3. See *O Blessed Night*; 86–87; *Spiritual Journey*, 191–98; 206–8; 212–14.

separation from the world"—to use the terminology of canon law. That separation represents the sacrifice and the detachment necessary if a person is to plumb new depths of loving communion and transforming union with God by means of an eremitic lifestyle.

The contemplative or mystical aspect of an eremitic lifestyle, together with the corresponding ascetical dimension, endures for the remainder of a hermit's life. The attraction toward fullness of love and life requires that a hermit let go gradually not only inordinate attachments, but also those cherished created realities that have sustained and nurtured personal development. Movement toward the future entails letting go all that is. Intensifying union with God necessitates effort, labor, patient waiting, faithfulness, and self-surrender. Paradoxically, whatever of value is let go, the hermit rediscovers in God.

Kenosis

Kenosis is a metaphor often used to describe the process of dying to self as a consequence of love.

The word "kenosis" is derived from the Greek verb *kenoō*, which means to empty, to evacuate, or to divest oneself of one's privileges. Biblically, the term refers to Christ emptying himself of his divinity in order to become human (Phil 2:6–7). While Christ emptied himself, a Christian is emptied of self by the Spirit.

Two dynamics in particular shape a hermit's experience of kenosis:

First, God remains a mystery to each person. The Spirit leads a hermit beyond the sensate dimensions of communion with God to immediate and direct encounter with the Beloved in faith, hope, and love. That gift of contemplative communion is profound and awesome. On some occasions, a hermit misinterprets the encounter with the divine presence in contemplation as absence of God or as abandonment by the Beloved. The truth prevails eventually, especially during the mature stages of the spiritual journey. The indwelling Spirit, "the living flame of love," has by then so transformed, purified, and enlightened within a person the "deep caverns of sense" that they give back to the Trinity God's own "heat and light."[4] Nonetheless, God still transcends all human desire, feeling, and understanding.

Second, transformation in God requires that a person be emptied of all that is counter to God. To that end, the Spirit slowly and painstakingly breaks down a hermit's egocentrism, illusions, and defense mechanisms. That aspect of kenosis continues until the hermit is left denuded of all but

4. See *Living Flame,* stanza 4 and commentary.

God. God alone becomes all for the hermit. The Spirit does this kenotic work directly from within the hermit, as well as by means of people, the natural world, and the ordinary circumstances of daily life.

Self-denial, self-discipline, silence, and solitude are constants in the eremitic life. They are privileged catalysts for kenosis. Yet, as a hermit dies to self, a shift of accent occurs in his or her consciousness. A more intuitive awareness of Christ becoming all in all (1 Cor 15:28) emerges. A clear perception that nothing exists in the desert of solitude apart from God presents itself. The insight that growth in communion with God is possible only by dark faith, yearning hope, and selfless love dawns with new light. Consequently, in undergoing kenosis, the hermit's attentiveness becomes ever more passionately riveted upon the risen Christ at the heart of creation, recapitulating all in himself (Col 1:15–20).

Dying and Rising in Christ Jesus

The presence of an eremitic vocation immerses a person in a work of "loving to the end"; that is, of dying to self in loving surrender to God. In that process, the hermit undergoes a veritable living death, a spiritual martyrdom, for the sake of Christ and the gospel. At some point, the realization dawns upon a hermit that henceforth the journey will be, metaphorically speaking, with Jesus from the garden of Gethsemane to Mount Calvary. In undergoing that passionate dying of love, the hermit participates in the interior struggle of Jesus to surrender to the Father: "Now my soul is troubled. What shall I say? Father, save me from this hour? No. It is for this reason that I have come to this hour. Father, glorify your name" (John 12:27–28).

Thus, the hermit commits to journey with Jesus unto death. In the fullness of time the person becomes one with Jesus crucified on the cross, ready and waiting to abandon himself completely to the Father. There in the act of complete self-surrender, the hermit discovers new life, eternal life, the life of God.

All creatures participate somehow in a universal process of coming to birth, living, dying, and rising. All creation strains forward on its evolutionary journey to ever more complex and refined levels of being, even in its biological and physical dimensions. The sound of all creation groaning in that one great act of giving birth to new life (Rom 8:22) impresses itself profoundly upon the hermit's listening heart. Moreover, the hermit becomes increasingly able to situate his or her own spiritual journey in relation to that cosmic experience. As the hermit lives, suffers, dies, and rises in Christ Jesus, creation offers strength and comfort. In community with all creation yearning for freedom and fullness of life, the hermit journeys forward in God, going "from glory to glory" (2 Cor 3:18).

Questions for Discernment

Acceptance of the cross is a sign of a hermit's participation in the paschal mystery of Jesus. Therefore, it can be fruitful to explore these questions in vocational discernment:

Is the candidate's life truly under the sign of the cross? Or is the candidate concerned primarily with seeking the delights and consolations of God? Does the person's eremitic lifestyle witness to a participation in the incarnation, passion, death, and resurrection of Jesus? Can the candidate take up the cross daily in following Jesus (Matt 10:38)? In the midst of suffering and pain, does the person experience communion with Christ crucified? Or does the candidate feel utter despair and abandonment by God?

Does the candidate believe that God can draw forth good from all suffering? Or is suffering seen as a waste, a punishment, something to avoid at virtually any cost?

In the midst of undergoing kenosis, does the candidate remain lovingly attentive to God? Or do narcissism and forgetfulness of God prevail?

Generally, does the candidate exude peace in carrying the cross? Or is there indication of excessive anger, despondency, or introspection?

Self-Knowledge

God's transforming, purifying, and enlightening love effects in a hermit at times an almost overwhelming experience of night, of the cross, of inner poverty. At times the interior struggle between Christ indwelling a hermit and the hermit's resistance to the divine presence erupts with full force in the silence and solitude. With Christ ever gaining the ascendency, a hermit's endurance of that conflict thus bears fruit in self-knowledge.

Poverty of Spirit

In Christ, the Light and the Truth (John 8:12; 14:6), a hermit comes to see hitherto unimaginable depths of inner poverty. There bursts forth within the person a striking awareness of moral, psychological, and spiritual limitations, as well as of unresolved hurts, regretted behavior, and actual sinfulness. That self-knowledge stirs up anguished sentiments akin to those of the psalmist: "Save me, God, for the waters have risen to my neck. I am sinking into swampy depths" (Ps 69:1–2); "Have mercy on me, Lord, in your unfailing love. . . . Create in me a pure heart and a steadfast spirit renew within me" (Ps 51:1, 10).

The hermit's encounter with inner poverty leads to a further jolting enlightenment. Inclinations toward greed, lust, envy, aggression, arrogance, and the like do not belong to the hermit alone. Humankind as a collective entity contends with those propensities. All people possess them and contribute to their harmful effects. The hermit sees that the personal experience is but a microcosm of the "sin of the world" (John 1:29). The natural world of creation also undergoes its distinctive form of inner struggle: that of a propensity toward entropy, which runs counter to its longing for God.

Hope in the Cosmic Christ

The experience of profound inner poverty has roots in a deeply positive reality. God indwelling the hermit bears down intensely upon personal limitations, immaturities, and sinfulness. The love, truth, and light of Christ cause those contrary propensities to become agitated, to break loose, and to surge into consciousness.[5] In undergoing that poverty of spirit, the hermit lets God purify all vestiges of "bitterness and anger . . . along with every other kind of evil" (Eph 4:31).

It is precisely because a hermit is in communion with God that purification occurs. God remains faithful throughout the process. The divine presence impresses itself upon the hermit's consciousness, especially when all seems lost. The words of Jesus in calming the storm reverberate through the turmoil: "I am. Be not afraid" (John 6:20). The risen Christ takes hold ever more securely and firmly. He enables the hermit to persevere through the raging inner storm. With a heart overflowing with thanksgiving to God, the hermit beholds the salvific power of Jesus: "Who will save me from this body doomed to death? Thanks be to God, through Jesus Christ our Lord" (Rom 7:24). Thus, the hermit discovers in poverty of spirit unconditional and healing love from a God of tenderness and compassion.

Moreover, the hermit recognizes by faith that God's transforming and purifying love is operative within each person and within humankind as a collective entity. It is as a member of the human family that the hermit undergoes the struggle to let Christ prevail. What happens in the hermit happens to the whole of humanity. What happens to the whole of humankind

5. See *Contemplation*, 85–96; *Spiritual Journey*, 108–13, 167–98.

happens in the hermit. With knowledge of personal weakness and frailty, the hermit is able to empathize with all human beings in their poverty.

The hermit's consciousness expands in still another direction, namely, in the recognition that Christ is becoming ever greater not only in the poverty of each person and of humanity as a collectivity, but also within the entirety of creation. The risen Christ secures ever more firmly his blessed hold upon the whole cosmos. Christ's transformative presence intensifies within the entirety of creation as it waits with hope to be set free from decay and, together with all God's children, to enjoy the freedom of life in God (Rom 8:21).

Pertinent Questions

Self-experience and self-knowledge give indication of the quality of a candidate's participation in the paschal mystery of Jesus. Therefore, these questions come to the fore in discernment of perseverance in the eremitic life:

Does the candidate recognize with gratitude blessings received from God? Is being unconditionally loved by God integral to the candidate's self-experience, even in the midst of limitations, infirmities, and sinfulness?

Does that self-knowledge awaken in the candidate a compassion of cosmic magnitude? Or does knowledge of the dark side of self and of life lead to isolation, hardness of heart, and self-pity?

Does the candidate in the struggles of life feel solidarity with humankind and with creation as a whole? Is the candidate embracing life at the heart of the world where Christ is becoming ever greater? Or has the person become a prisoner of narcissism? Has the candidate given in to defeat and become an isolationist?

Is the candidate a person who hopes in God or one who is falling into despair?

Acedia

A hermit spends year after year immersed in the same hermitage, the same locale, and the same regimen. In truth, that milieu changes from hour to hour, day to day, season to season. Each morning the hermit awakens to a subtly new creation. Artists who paint a scene repeatedly but at different times and in varying atmospheric conditions capture glimpses of the progression of delicate changes that occur in a physical locale. Consider, for example, Claude Monet's series of canvases on lilies floating on a pond in his garden, bundles of hay in a field, or the façade of Rouen Cathedral. The living world offers always more to behold. The longer a hermit remains in a hermitage and its surroundings, the more opportunity exists for appreciation of the awesome richness and the exquisite diversity of creation.

However, at times the human senses become dulled and the spirit deadened. Then the dominating force becomes preoccupation with what the hermit judges to be lack of variety and absence of diversion. Monotony, boredom, and weariness quickly ensue in the silence and solitude.

Early Christian writers used the word "acedia" to refer to that condition. Evagrius Ponticus, a fourth-century monk, identified these indications of acedia in a hermit: a sense of time standing still or barely moving; feelings of disgust with the hermitage and the surroundings; distaste for eremitic works; feelings of loneliness and abandonment; strong desires to go elsewhere in order to find diversion; a longing for one's former life and for being with family and friends; discouragement with the hardships of the daily routine; daydreaming to escape the monotony; and the temptation to give up the solitary life altogether.[6]

Acedia epitomizes a cluster of everyday ordinary struggles in the eremitic life that occasion considerable pain and suffering. Acedia is for a hermit an occupational hazard, so to speak. Contending with acedia requires a hermit to exercise daily vigilance and self-control. Therefore, this question arises in vocational discernment: Is a candidate for the eremitic life able to maintain discipline in thoughts, feelings, and actions? Or does the person succumb to the inner turmoil?

Discipline that flows from the indwelling Spirit's inspiration differs radically from human willfulness that initiates aggressive behavior. Is the candidate's discipline representative of the grace to be faithful and to endure? Is the practice of self-discipline undertaken in a peaceful and gentle way? Or is what passes as self-discipline merely an expression of a candidate's harshness and obstinacy?

Does the candidate persevere in praying, working, and studying, despite feelings of disinterest, repugnance, and distaste? Or do those feelings cause the candidate to neglect the daily practices and routines?

Is the candidate truly present to God in life as it is, however the candidate might feel in a particular moment? Or is the person trapped in a vortex wherein nothing seems to exist but feelings of abandonment, rejection, boredom, self-pity, nostalgia for the past, and pipe dreams about living anywhere but in this hermitage?

6. Evagrius Ponticus, *To Anatolos: On the Eight Thoughts*, 7. PG, 40, 1273, BC.

When assailed by acedia, does the candidate remain in the hermitage and undergo it peacefully? Or does the person feel compelled to leave the hermitage and go elsewhere for diversion?

Insatiability

Insatiability is another aspect of a hermit's participation in the paschal mystery of Jesus.

Every person experiences sooner or later an inability to be completely satisfied by anyone or anything but God in God's own self.[7] The eremitic life in no way removes that insatiability. On the contrary, the inability to be satisfied reaches astonishing pitch in the silence and solitude of a hermitage. However meaningful a hermit finds prayer, silence, solitude, relationships, and study, those values and practices leave a profound emptiness and a certain lack of satisfaction. Always the restless longing for more of God persists.

Its Positive Role

Confronted with the implacable void of insatiability, a hermit's first impulse might be to try to achieve relief by means of excessive indulgence in something created. The attempt ends inexorably in failure and frustration. However, that outcome does remind the hermit of the positive providential role of both human and nonhuman creatures in the spiritual journey. The role of the finite is to open human hearts to the Infinite and the purpose of the created is to point human beings toward the Uncreated.[8] With obedient submission to God's corrections, the hermit grows in peaceful acceptance of the insatiability and restlessness. Increasing capacity to love creation rightly and effective exercise of the ability to let go expectations for what creation cannot give constitute additional gains.

The inability to be totally satisfied is calibrated to make a significant contribution to a hermit's transforming union with God. Insatiability is an effect of the Spirit urging the hermit toward more wholehearted participation with Jesus in his Passover, until in death the hermit is filled with the utter fullness of God. It is a divinely implanted restlessness by which the Spirit moves the hermit into ever greater depths of God as Mystery.

---

7. See *Contemplation*, 62–65; *O Blessed Night*, 47–56.
8. See *O Blessed Night*, 57–68.

Certain Questions

A hermit's experience of continuing insatiability is paradoxically a sign of perseverance in living the paschal mystery in union with Jesus. Therefore, these questions present themselves in vocational discernment:

Does the candidate experience a lack of fulfillment?

Is the emptiness arising primarily from an inability to be totally satisfied by anyone or anything but God alone? Or does it spring mainly from a dissatisfaction and a discontentment that is probably indicative of the absence of an eremitic vocation?

Does the insatiability impel the candidate to continue searching for the Beloved? Or is the person settling into a complacent and mediocre existence, convinced that the goal of the spiritual journey has been attained and all life's questions are finally answered?

Aspects of both insatiability and dissatisfaction can coexist in a candidate. In that case, which tendency seems dominant? Even when insatiability is the more prevalent, for the sake of continuing spiritual growth the candidate must deal with the element of dissatisfaction.

CHAPTER 27

Concluding Pastoral Observations
on the Eremitic Life

THROUGHOUT THIS SECTION, WE have explored distinctive features of a vocation to the eremitic life. We discussed also principles for discerning that calling, especially as they pertain to maturing vocational consciousness. While the principles of discernment do not yield empirical proof of an eremitic vocation, they provide compelling positive signs of a possible calling. It is faith that enables recognition of the signs of an eremitic vocation. Paradoxically, although faith gives insight, faith persistently impels a hermit to go beyond the tangible and perceptive aspects of eremitic experience. Faith guides the hermit ever deeper into God as Mystery and into the mysteries of God revealed in Christ Jesus.

The contemplative life is marginal in relation to the usual flow of human activities and contemplatives abide on the fringes of society. The eremitic life is marginal vis-à-vis even the contemplative life, and hermits dwell on the fringes of the contemplative life itself. Hermits abide alone with Christ at the core of society and at the heart of the universe. There they participate in the Mystical Body of Christ in a real and effective manner. There, from within creation and for all creation, they become a leaven of the beatitudes.

The Transition to the Eremitic Life

Ordinarily, two vocations lay the foundation for an eremitic life: *first*, a calling to celibacy for the sake of Christ and the gospel; and *second*, passage through the apostolic life, followed by movement through the contemplative life.

Four consecutive phases unfold in the course of a person's transition from the contemplative life to the eremitic life.

Phase One: The contemplative uses constructively all the opportunities for silence and solitude readily at hand within the contemplative life.

Phase Two: While continuing in the contemplative life, the person secures further opportunities for silence and solitude, which are not usually available in communal living.

Phase Three: The contemplative moves into a hermitage and lives the eremitic life on an experimental basis for a period of one to three years.

Phase Four: The contemplative begins to live the eremitic life with an attitude of permanency toward the lifestyle and with a view to eventual permanent commitment to God through that lifestyle.

Summary of the Principles of Discernment

Phases One and Two above occur within the contemplative life itself. In fact, most maturing contemplatives find themselves situated somewhere within those two phases. As communion with God deepens, it is normal for a contemplative to desire an increase of aloneness with God. Yet most contemplatives find the means to fulfill their longing for more silence and solitude within their contemplative lifestyle. Vocational discernment during Phases One and Two pertains mainly to a person's capacity to persevere in the contemplative life and over time to integrate more silence and solitude into that mode of living.

A few contemplatives discover toward the end of Phase Two, however, that the contemplative life can no longer provide sufficient aloneness with God. These persons experience a calling to the eremitic life. During Phase Three and Phase Four of the vocational transition, a candidate for the eremitic life lives in a hermitage for a prolonged period on an experimental basis. Vocational discernment centers primarily upon the candidate's ability to persevere in living an eremitic lifestyle.

The following principles guide the discernment of perseverance in the eremitic life during Phase Three and Phase Four:

- Being-in-love with God is the sole purpose of the eremitic life. A hermit's love for God manifests itself in attentiveness to the Trinity and to the risen Christ.

- While the eremitic vocation remains essentially solitary, love of people is an integral aspect of a hermit's life.

- Love of the natural world is another essential component of an eremitic vocation. The context of a hermit's daily life is a natural environment:

a desert, a wilderness, or other green space. That locale constitutes the primary milieu for the hermit's transforming union with God.

- The hermit participates in the paschal mystery of Jesus.

Perseverance as Gift

Perseverance is indeed something that a hermit does. But, first and foremost, it is a grace bestowed by the Spirit and received by the hermit. A hermit abides alone in silence and solitude day after day, year after year, while undergoing God in dark faith, courageous hope, and unconditional love. Such perseverance can come only from an authentic sense of vocation. No human will of itself is tenacious enough to persist in that venture.

An Inability to Persevere

A candidate's ability to persevere in a hermitage is a significant sign of an eremitic calling. Conversely, a candidate's inability to remain in a hermitage despite sincerity, goodwill, and effort constitutes a convincing indication of the absence of an eremitic vocation. That kind of inability has its roots in something other than a momentary evasion of silence and solitude. That inability arises from the fact that God has not called the person to be a hermit and thus God has not given the person the grace of perseverance. Without the calling and the grace to persevere, the candidate finds it impossible to abide in silent aloneness with God.

A spiritual director or a person in a position of ecclesial authority may find it exceedingly difficult to help a candidate recognize an inability to persevere, especially if there exists a fixation on being a hermit. That candidate might claim to be living as a hermit. In reality, the person might be using the physical dwelling, the solitary location, and the means for daily sustenance in order to devise another quiet style of living that for this individual is more tolerable. Living in a hermitage does not a hermit make. God has indeed given the candidate a unique calling to a Christian lifestyle or combination of lifestyles, together with the grace to persevere in it; however, that vocation is to a lifestyle other than the eremitic life. It can take extensive time and prolonged discernment for a candidate to perceive that true vocational direction.

Two Examples

An inability to persevere in the eremitic life presents itself, for example, in this manner: A candidate makes frequent unnecessary trips from the hermitage to the community. Activities associated with those excursions might include seeking out one person or another for casual conversations, assuming responsibility for communal projects without sufficient reason, or participating in some of the recreational activities in the common life. The candidate may have elaborate rationalizations for those involvements. One recurring explanation is this: "They need me. They can't get along without me." The truth is otherwise. The candidate needs them, and cannot get along without them.

An inability to persevere is evident also when a person uses a hermitage as little more than a crash pad or a pit stop. In this case, the hermitage becomes a place to rest and to recuperate between travels, social events, work projects, and other activities.

The Mystery of a Divine Calling

Alone in a hermitage, a hermit engages daily in many activities: praying, working, studying, recreating, eating, sleeping, and so on. But an eremitic calling does not have a specific function as the basis of its existence. Nor are there personality profiles or sets of personality traits that constitute "eremitic types." In a sense, this way of life has no socially acceptable role or status. From a pragmatic stance, the eremitic life appears useless and nonproductive. It seems to be a waste of human talent and God-given resources. This lifestyle is an enigma to society and an utter mystery to hermits themselves.

More than any other factor, the experience of actual perseverance in the eremitic life instills in a hermit a profound sense of the mystery of this vocation. The hermit learns firsthand that perseverance in this solitary life is possible only because of God's calling. A contemplative becomes a hermit solely by God's choice, not by virtue of personal merits, creative initiatives, or special gifts. A contemplative receives an eremitic calling only by God's election, not because of greater worthiness or a higher degree of holiness than other people. A vocation to the eremitic life is a free gift, which God bestows upon a person out of God's own unique and unconditional love.

Eremitic Rapport with Society

From a certain perspective, an eremitic vocation places a person beyond the reaches of most social structures and institutions. It situates the hermit in a position of radical emancipation. By vocation the hermit embodies a unique quality of the "freedom of the children of God" (Rom 8:21). A saying that St. John of the Cross included in the upper area of his sketch of the spiritual ascent of Mount Carmel has application to the nature of that eremitic freedom: "No longer is there any way through here because there is no law for the just person. That person is a law unto him/herself."[1]

Eremitic freedom carries with it tremendous risk and bestows upon the hermit enormous responsibility. A vocation to an eremitic lifestyle is wholly uncharted. There exists within an eremitic life virtually none of the protections, safeguards, and supports found even in the contemplative life. A hermit strains forward daily with increasing dependence upon God alone. Thus, in relation to civil and ecclesial institutions, a hermit is probably the most emancipated of all citizens, the most liberated of all pilgrims, the most free of the children of God (Rom 8:21). Nonetheless, a hermit maintains rapport with both civil and ecclesial society.

A hermit remains a citizen, votes in elections, and serves on a jury, if impaneled. In certain situations, a hermit might deem it a matter of conscience to take a public position on an issue of justice, peace, or integrity of creation. Even so, the hermit lives outside the mainstream of society, and does not take a leading role in civic organizations and movements.

A hermit remains an integral member of the Christian community. Depending on circumstances, the person could be also a member of an institute or society of consecrated life, an individual with vows received by the bishop of a diocese, or one who lives privately as a hermit. In the Roman Catholic tradition, each canonically recognized hermit has a local bishop, a pastor, and a religious superior or a spiritual moderator. By virtue of living alone in silence and solitude for the purpose of contemplating God, a hermit does not participate ordinarily in the social activities or gatherings associated with the institutional aspect of the church.

Still, the following practices by a canonically recognized hermit express respectful relationships to civil and ecclesial authority: realistic attitudes toward structures; fidelity to a personal rule of life; and obedience to God's will as it is revealed through persons in positions of leadership.

---

1. To view a copy of the sketch, see Kavanaugh and Rodriguez, trans., *The Collected Works of St. John of the Cross*, 110–11.

A Realistic Attitude toward Structures

Some structure is integral to all biological and earthly existence—the eremitic life included. As a member of society, every hermit maintains a constructive attitude toward legitimate institutions. Like any other concerned citizen or spiritual pilgrim, the hermit affirms what is healthy and protests what is dysfunctional in those structures.

It would be unrealistic, however, for a hermit to expect from those institutions the kind or the extent of support, affirmation, and encouragement that other members, citizens, or pilgrims receive. A hermit is not only *sui juris* but also *sui generis*—in the sense, not of anarchy or rugged individualism, but of the freedom of the children of God. Every hermit is dependent on some elements of society for certain things. Nonetheless, a hermit has to maintain that dependence in a specific way; that is, as one who dwells on the fringes of society in terms of structure and institution and as one who lives at the core of that society in terms of spiritual and qualitative development.

Some hermits reach a relative emancipation from their expectations of civil and ecclesial structures, yet their self-imposed goals and schedules restrict their freedom. They become slaves of their agendas and of their times, places, and methods of doing things. They are rigid in their ways and fretful toward change. To whatever degree this behavior occurs, it is unfortunate and unhealthy. Those persons are not a law unto themselves in Christ, but rather their law is a law unto itself in spite of Christ.

A Personal Rule of Life

According to ancient eastern and western eremitic traditions, each hermit composes at some point a personal rule of life. A hermit submits this statement to an ecclesial authority, often through a spiritual director, a religious superior, or a spiritual moderator. A hermit first formulates that rule and seeks confirmation of it near the close of an initial prolonged time of living in a hermitage on an experimental basis (Phase 3). After further perseverance in the eremitic life and before making a permanent commitment (Phase 4), the hermit would be wise to reevaluate the rule and to re-present it to ecclesial authority for approval.

Obedience to God through Leadership Personnel

Each hermit needs in eremitic living an attitude of obedience, especially in the sense of action that follows upon intense listening.[2] In a spirit of mutual openness and dialogue, a candidate for the eremitic life, a spiritual director, and other significant persons listen together to discern God's calling as it unfolds throughout the candidate's experience of aloneness with God. In a spirit of obedience, the candidate then implements what can be discerned of God's desire.

With regard to the practice of obedience in the eremitic life, it is often hermits and not ecclesial authorities who create conflict. Most bishops, leaders of religious institutes, and spiritual moderators are rather freeing with their directives and guidelines toward hermits under their jurisdiction. But some persons pursuing an eremitic lifestyle do not want to cut the apron strings. These people have neither the independence nor the emancipation necessary for letting go their dependency. They want their relationship to ecclesial authority to remain parent-child, with many specific directives and meticulous instructions from those guiding them. They want to be told how to live and what to do. They want the authorities in their life to write their rule for them. They feel guilty, lost, and anxious if they cannot get permissions for the practical aspects of daily living. A candidate's inability to grow quickly out of this childish dependency could indicate lack of the maturity and strength of character necessary to continue an eremitic way of life.

Final Commitment

After living for a number of years in a hermitage and with sufficient signs to authenticate the presence of an eremitic vocation, a hermit makes a permanent commitment to God through the eremitic life.

Some hermits desire to make perpetual commitment with formal vows. Other hermits prefer no special rites or ceremonies. Some hermits desire a profession of vows or promises in the presence of the Christian community at large. Others want a profession of commitment with only a few significant persons present. Some hermits make the commitment within an ecclesial structure, while others do so privately before God alone. Whatever a person's chosen mode of commitment, the commitment is always *as a hermit for life.*

---

2. See *Spiritual Direction*, 175–77. In biblical Hebrew and Greek, the notion of obedience derives from verbs meaning "to listen." Obedience consists of putting into practice what one perceives with a listening heart in God's presence.

God does not bestow an eremitic vocation just for a while or for a few years. The calling is for the duration of the hermit's earthly sojourn. God is certainly free to call an authentic hermit out of a hermitage for some time, perhaps even for the rest of that person's life. At least one pope was a hermit prior to his election. Yet an authentic hermit remains a hermit at heart, no matter what the life situation or ministry. The hermitage does not make the hermit. Nor does taking the hermit out of the hermitage automatically terminate an eremitic vocation.

The presence of positive signs of an eremitic calling and the affirmation of that vocation by the other participants in the discernment process encourage a hermit to be faithful to God's calling. However, the hermit's permanent commitment is ultimately an act of self-abandonment to God in faith, hope, and love. Final commitment is a leap into the unknown, an entry upon an uncharted way, a plunge into mystery, a new beginning. Each day the hermit has to listen anew to the Spirit, discern God's way once more, and go forward on that path.

Permanent commitment is a celebration of God's love for the hermit and of the hermit's love for God in response. It witnesses to the hermit's awareness of Jesus's faithful presence and his free gift of this calling. It attests to the unique mission of the eremitic life within the Mystical Body of Christ:

You did not choose me.

No, I chose you,

and I appointed you to go out and to bear fruit,

fruit that will last.

(John 15:16)

A New Creation

IN REFLECTING UPON DEVELOPMENT in personal prayer, St. Teresa of Jesus made an observation that we believe applies especially well to our approach to vocation and to vocational discernment. Freely translated, this is what Teresa wrote:

> To receive a favor from God is a first grace.
> To understand the nature of that favor is a second grace.
> To be able to give an account of it and to explain it
> to another person is a third grace.[1]

At inception, a human being receives from God a vocation—*a first grace*. That calling is threefold: *who* one is, *how* one is to become, and *what* one is to do in becoming. Thus, God calls each human being to a unique self-identity, to a specific combination of vocational lifestyles, and to a distinct mission or constellation of missions.

Furthermore, throughout the spiritual journey, God offers each person some understanding of who one is, how one is becoming, and what one is doing—a *second grace*. God desires that a person cooperate knowingly and willingly in response to the divine initiative.

On many occasions, God wants a person to give an account to other people of a vocation—a *third grace*. This "giving an account" can be by means of sharing personal vocational experiences, by seeking spiritual direction in relation to vocational issues, or by helping other people discern their vocation in the context of spiritual direction.

The third grace pertains to the purpose of this book on vocation and vocational discernment, together with our previous two works, *Called by God: A Theology of Vocation and Lifelong Commitment* and *Discerning Vocations to Marriage, Celibacy and Singlehood.*

---

1. See Teresa of Jesus, *Complete Works*, 17, 6.

Our studies of vocation and vocational discernment have been directed toward these goals:

- to accentuate a contemplative approach toward vocational discernment;

- to heighten consciousness in relation to the mystery of a personal vocation;

- to raise awareness that all Christian vocational lifestyles complement each other and work in unison to build up the Body of Christ;

- to identify essential features of three basic and three general Christian vocational lifestyles;

- to elucidate principles of discernment for vocational authenticity in relation to each of those lifestyles.

Of the three dimensions of a personal vocation—the *who, how,* and *what*—we have concentrated in our studies primarily upon Christian lifestyles (the vocational *how*).

For all of us as Christians, the development of our calling from God, the evolution of our vocational consciousness, and the actualization of our response span most, if not all, of our earthly sojourn. When those three interrelated processes reach a certain critical intensity, a mature sense of vocation emerges within us. We experience then a spiritual imperative to commit to God through a specific vocation. We desire to follow that path freely and wholeheartedly so as to be true to the love of God.

Thus, we attain readiness to make a lifelong commitment to God through a specific lifestyle or combination thereof. Yet, instead of leaving us with certitude and security, that depth of vocational awareness and readiness for commitment thrusts us in the direction of the way that is no way— God as incomprehensible mystery, God as three persons, and the mysteries of God revealed in Christ Jesus.

For most of us, it takes extensive effort, time, and energy to attain basic self-identity and sufficient readiness for a permanent commitment. It is, therefore, indeed a paradox that making a lifelong commitment to God through a Christian vocational lifestyle begins immediately to move us beyond the lifestyle itself. As soon as we *attach* ourselves to the risen Christ through a certain Christian lifestyle, the Spirit begins *detaching* us from that lifestyle. No sooner do we commit ourselves to God through a way of life than we begin passing through and beyond that lifestyle to God in God's own self.

Whatever our vocational lifestyle—marriage, celibacy, or singlehood; the apostolic, the contemplative, or the eremitic life—that calling is not an end in itself. Its providential purpose is to nurture our love for God, to enable us to practice love for creation, and to point us beyond the lifestyle as such to the fullness of God. That vocation is an instrument through which God leads us to consummate transforming union in love with Father, Son, and Spirit and to communion with all creation in God as Trinity.

Thus, on our spiritual journey there comes an inevitable point where we begin to let go intentionally the specific combination of lifestyles to which we are called. This detachment does not mean necessarily ceasing to be married, celibate, or single. Neither does it imply necessarily desisting from our pursuit of the apostolic life, the contemplative life, or the eremitic life. Rather, as Christ increasingly becomes all within us, he himself becomes "the only One necessary" (Luke 10:41; Phil 3:10–15). Everything else pales by comparison, becoming more and more relative in its significance.

That intensity of interior detachment has a radical effect on our self-identity. All the labels we had previously used to describe ourselves—married, celibate, single; missionary, contemplative, hermit—become less and less important to us. We become ever more aware of ourselves as being primarily Christian pilgrims in the most pristine sense: "I have been crucified with Christ. I live now, no longer I, but Christ lives in me. The life I now live, I live by faith in the Son of God, who loved me and gave himself up for me" (Gal 2:20).

Finally, in the act of our personal death/resurrection, we pass from this earthly existence to the fullness of eternal life. We let go our vocational lifestyle not only in the sense of our desire and our will to sustain it, but also in the sense of our actual creative expression of this lifestyle as it exists in time and space. The Spirit brings to completion all that God desires to accomplish in us through our vocation. Thus, not only shall we ourselves be transformed in God, but also our way of life as we now know it will be transformed—whether we are married, celibate, or single; apostolic, contemplative, or eremitic. We will die to all, yet in the fullness of transforming union with God we will receive all in a new creation.

> *We, with unveiled face*
> *beholding in a mirror the glory of the Lord,*
> *are being transformed into the same image,*
> *going from glory to glory,*
> *by the work of the Spirit.*
>
> *(2 COR 3:18)*

Sic finis operis, non autem quaerendi, nequaquam mysterii.

Select Bibliography

Allchin, A. M., ed. *Solitude and Community: Papers on the Hermit Life Given at St. David's, Wales in the Autumn of 1975*. Oxford: SLG, 1977.

Anson, Peter. *The. Call of the Desert: The Solitary Life in the Christian Church*. London: SPCK, 1964.

Aquinas, Thomas. *Summa Theologiae*. Translated by Fathers of the English Dominican Province. New York: Benziger, 1947.

Athanasius. *The Life of Anthony*. In *Athanasius: The Life of Anthony and The Letter to Marcellinus*, Classics of Western Spirituality Series, translated by Robert C. Gregg, 29–99. Mahwah, NJ: Paulist, 1980. *PG* XXVI:835–976.

———. *On the Incarnation (De Incarnatione)* 54:3. In *St. Athanasius: Select Works and Letters*, The Nicene and Post-Nicene Fathers, vol. 4, edited by Philip Schaff and Henry Wace, 65. Grand Rapids: Eerdmans, 1975. *PG* 25:192B.

Augustine. "Commentary on 1 John 5:1–3," *Homilies on the First Epistle of John*. In *St. Augustin*, Nicene and Post-Nicene Fathers, vol. 7, edited by Philip Schaff, 520–526. Grand Rapids: Eerdmans, 1983. *PL* 35:2055.

———. "Commentary on Psalm 40." In *Saint Augustin: Expositions on the Book of Psalms*, The Nicene and Post-Nicene Fathers, vol. 8, edited by Philip Schaff, 119–128. Grand Rapids: Eerdmans, 1974. *PL* 36:437–38; *CCSL* 38:430.

———. *Letter X*. In *St. Augustine: Select Letters*, Loeb Classical Library Series, translated by J. H. Baxter, 9–12. Cambridge: Harvard University Press, 1980. *PL* 33:73–74.

The Book of the Elders: Sayings of the Desert Fathers. The Systematic Collection. Translated by John Wortley, 104 (*PG*, 65.424) and 114 (*SC*, 387.743). Collegeville, MN: Liturgical, 2012.

Bouyer, Louis. *The Spirituality of the New Testament and the Fathers*. New York: Seabury, 1963.

Butler, Cuthbert. *Western Mysticism*. London: Dutton, 1926.

Carthusian Monk [anon.]. *The Call of Silent Love: Carthusian Novice Conferences: Volume Two: Vocation and Discernment*. London: Darton, Longman and Todd, 1995.

Cashen, Richard Anthony. *Solitude in the Thought of Thomas Merton*. Kalamazoo, MI: Cistercian, 1981.

Chittister, Joan. *Following the Path: The Search for a Life of Passion, Purpose, and Joy*. New York: Image, 2012.

Clay, Rotha M. *The Hermits and Anchorites of England*. London: Methuen, 1914.

The Cloud of Unknowing. In Classics of Western Spirituality Series, edited by James Walsh, 156–66. Mahwah, NJ: Paulist, 1981.

"Contemplation." In *Dictionnaire de spiritualité*. Fascicules XIII–XV, mn1643–2193. Founded by Marcel Viller, et al. Paris: Beauchesne, 1950–52.

Coombs, Marie Theresa, and Francis Kelly Nemeck. *Called by God: A Theology of Vocation and Lifelong Commitment*. 1992. Reprint, Eugene, OR: Wipf and Stock, 2001.

————. *Contemplation*. 1982. Reprint, Eugene, OR: Wipf and Stock, 2001.

————. *Discerning Vocations to Marriage, Celibacy and Singlehood*. 1994. Reprint, Eugene, OR: Wipf and Stock, 2001.

————. *O Blessed Night: Recovering from Addiction, Codependency and Attachment, based on the insights of St. John of the Cross and Pierre Teilhard de Chardin*. New York: Alba House, 1991.

————. *The Spiritual Journey: Critical Thresholds and Stages of Adult Spiritual Genesis*. Collegeville, MN: Liturgical, 1990.

————. *The Way of Spiritual Direction*. Collegeville, MN: Liturgical, 1985.

Coriden, James A., et al., eds. *The Code of Canon Law: A Text and Commentary*. Mahwah, NJ: Paulist, 1985.

Cummings, Charles. *Monastic Practices* (Monastic Wisdom Series). Collegeville, MN: Liturgical, 2015.

Dardenne, Myriam. "The Christian Contemplative Community: Listening, Present, Welcoming." *Cistercian Studies* 3 (1968:4) 328–36.

Evagrius Ponticus, *To Anatolos: On the Eight Thoughts*, 7. In *Evagrius of Pontus: The Greek Ascetic Corpus*, translated by Robert E. Sinkewicz, 66–90. Oxford: Oxford University Press, 2003. *PG* 40, 1273, BC.

Fifth General Conference of the Latin American and Caribbean Bishops, 13–21 May 2007. *Aparecida Concluding Document*. 29 June 2007. https://store.usccb.org/concluding-document-aparecida-p/653-7.htm.

Francis. Apostolic Exhortation *Evangelii Gaudium* (The Joy of the Gospel). 24 November 2013. http://w2.vatican.va/content/francesco/en/apost_exhortations/documents/papa-francesco_esortazione-ap_20131124_evangelii-gaudium.html.

————. Encyclical Letter *Laudato Si* (On Care for Our Common Home). 18 July 2015. http://w2.vatican.va/content/francesco/en/encyclicals/documents/papa-francesco_20150524_enciclica-laudato-si.html.

Fredette, Paul A., and Karen Karper Fredette. *Consider the Ravens: On Contemporary Hermit Life*. Bloomington, IN: !Universe, 2008.

Fredette, Paul A., and Karen Karper Fredette, eds. *Raven's Bread: Food for Those in Solitude*. Quarterly Newsletter. Hot Springs, NC: Raven's Bread Ministries.

Gannon, Thomas M., and George W. Traub. *The Desert and the City: An Interpretation of the History of Christian Spirituality*. 152–172. London: Macmillan, 1969.

Gregory the Great. *The Homilies of Saint Gregory the Great on the Book of the Prophet Ezekiel*. Translated by Theodosia Gray, I, 3, 9–12; II, 2, 7–11. *PL*, 76:809–11; 76:952–55. Cambridge, MA: Center for Traditionalist Orthodox Studies, 1990.

Grimlaicus. *Rule for Solitaries*. Translated by Andrew Thornton. Collegeville, MN: Liturgical, 2011.

Guigo II: The Ladder of Monks and Twelve Meditations. Translated by Edmund Colledge and James Walsh. Kalamazoo, MI: Cistercian, 1981.

Haley, Joseph, ed. *Apostolic Sanctity in the World: A Symposium on Total Dedication in the World and Secular Institutes.* Notre Dame: University of Notre Dame Press, 1957.

Hamman, Adalbert. "'Mission' in Holy Scripture." In *Apostolic Life*, edited by Albert Plé, 3–30. Westminster, MA: Newman, 1958.

Heath, Elaine A. *The Mystic Way of Evangelism: Contemplative Vision for Christian Outreach.* Grand Rapids: Baker, 2008.

Holstein, Henri. "The History of the Development of the Word 'Apostolic.'" In *Apostolic Life*, edited by Albert Plé, 31–49. Westminster, MA: Newman, 1958.

Ignatius of Loyola. *The Spiritual Exercises.* In George E. Ganss, ed., *Ignatius of Loyola: Spiritual Exercises and Selected Works*, Classics of Western Spirituality Series, 9–63, 113–214. Mahwah, NJ: Paulist, 1991.

———. *The Spiritual Exercises.* In *The Spiritual Exercises of St. Ignatius: A Literal Translation and a Contemporary Reading*, David L. Fleming, trans., 20–143. St. Louis: Institute of Jesuit Sources, 1978.

Jasper, David. *The Sacred Desert: Religion, Literature, Art, and Culture.* Malden, MA: Blackwell, 2004.

Jerome. *The Life of Paul.* In *St. Jerome: Letters and Select Works*, Nicene and Post-Nicene Fathers, vol. 6, edited by Philip Schaff and translated by W. H. Fremantle, 299–303. Grand Rapids: Eerdmans, 1975. *PL* 23:18–30.

John of the Cross. *The Collected Works of St. John of the Cross*, translated by Kieran Kavanaugh and Otilio Rodriguez. Washington, DC: ICS, 1991.

———. *Vida y obras de San Juan de la Cruz.* Madrid: Biblioteca de Autores Cristianos, 1973.

John Paul II. Apostolic Exhortation *Christifideles Laici* (On the Vocation and Mission of the Lay Faithful) 30 December 1988. http://w2.vatican.va/content/john-paul-ii/en/apost_exhortations/documents/hf_jp-ii_exh_30121988_christifideles-laici.html.

———. Encyclical Letter *Redemptoris Missio* (Mission of the Redeemer) 7 December 1990. http://w2.vatican.va/content/john-paul-ii/en/encyclicals/documents/hf_jp-ii_enc_07121990_redemptoris-missio.html.

Johnson, Elizabeth A. *Ask the Beasts: Darwin and the God of Love.* London: Bloomsbury Continuum, 2014.

Keller, Timothy. *Every Good Endeavor: Connecting Your Work to God's Work.* New York: Penguin, 2012.

Louf, André. *In the School of Contemplation* (Monastic Wisdom Series). Collegeville, MN: Liturgical, 2015.

McDonough, Carol. "Christian Hermits and Solitaries: Tracing the Antonian Hermit Traditions." *The Way*, 54/1 (January 2015) 76–89.

———. "Hermits and the Roman Catholic Church: Recovering an Ancient Vocation." *The Way*, 54/2 (April 2015) 53–69.

McNary-Zak, Bernadette. *Seeking in Solitude: A Study of Select Forms of Eremitic Life and Practice.* Eugene, OR: Wipf and Stock, 2014.

Merton, Thomas. *The Asian Journal.* New York: New Directions, 1968.

———. *Conjectures of a Guilty Bystander.* Garden City: Doubleday, 1966.

———. *Contemplation in a World of Action.* Garden City: Doubleday, 1971.

———. *Contemplative Prayer.* New York: Herder and Herder, 1969.

———. "Epilogue: Meditatio Pauperis in Solitudine." In *Seven Storey Mountain,* 407–23. New York: Harcourt, Brace, 1948.

———. *The Journals of Thomas Merton.* 7 vols. Edited by Patrick Hart et al. San Francisco: HarperSanFrancisco, 1995–1998.

———. "A Life Free from Care." *Cistercian Studies* 5 (1970:3) 217–227.

———. *The Monastic Journey.* Kansas City, MO: Sheed Andrews McMeel, 1977.

———. *New Seeds of Contemplation.* New York: New Directions, 1961.

———. "Notes for a Philosophy of Solitude." In *Disputed Questions,* 177–207. New York: Farrar, Straus and Cudahy, 1960.

———. *Seeds of Contemplation.* New York: New Directions, 1949.

———. *Seven Storey Mountain.* New York: Harcourt, Brace, 1948.

———. *The Silent Life.* New York: Farrar, Straus and Cudahy, 1957.

———. *Thoughts in Solitude.* New York: Farrar, Straus and Cudahy, 1968.

———. *The Wisdom of the Desert: Sayings from the Desert Fathers.* New York: New Directions, 1960. 3–24.

Moses of Scete. In *The Sayings of the Desert Fathers: The Alphabetical Collection,* translated by Benedicta Ward, 118. Kalamazoo, MI: Cistercian, 1975. *PG,* 65:283–84.

Paul VI. Apostolic Exhortation *Evangelii Nuntiandi* (Evangelization in the Modern World) 8 December 1975. http://w2.vatican.va/content/paul-vi/en/apost_exhortations/documents/hf_p-vi_exh_19751208_evangelii-nuntiandi.html.

Pennington, Basil, ed. *Contemplative Community: An Interdisciplinary Symposium.* Washington: Cistercian, 1972.

Pomerius, Julianus. *The Contemplative Life.* Translated by M. J. Suelzer. New York: Newman, 1947.

Pseudo-Dionysius. *The Divine Names* and *Mystical Theology.* In *Pseudo-Dionysius: The Complete Works,* Classics of Western Spirituality Series, translated by Colm Luibheid, 47–141. Mahwah, NJ: Paulist, 1987. *PG,* 3, 586–1064.

RB 1980: The Rule of St. Benedict in Latin and English with Notes. Edited by Timothy Fry, 169–171. Collegeville, MN: Liturgical, 1981.

Rengstorf, Karl Heinrich. "*Apostellō.*" In *TDNT,* I, 398–447.

Rock, Michael. *St. Benedict's Guide to Improving Your Work Life: Workplace as Worthplace.* Toronto: Novalis, 2015.

The Rule of the Master. Edited by Luke Eberle. Kalamazoo, MI: Cistercian, 1977.

Savage, Anne, and Nichola Watson, trans. *Anchoritic Spirituality: Ancrene Wisse and Associated Works.* Classics of Western Spirituality Series. Mahwah, NJ: Paulist, 1991.

Schiller, Verena. *A Simplified Life: A Contemporary Hermit's Experience of Solitude and Silence.* London: Canterbury, 2010.

Schneider, Johannes. "*Erchomai.*" In *TDNT,* II, 666–84.

Second Vatican Ecumenical Council. *Ad Gentes* (Decree on the Church's Missionary Activity). 7 December 1965. In *Vatican Council II: The Conciliar and Post Conciliar Documents,* edited by Austin Flannery, 813–856. Northport, NY: Costello, 1980.

———. *Apostolicam Actuositatem* (Decree on the Apostolate of Lay People). 18 November 1965. In *Vatican Council II: The Conciliar and Post Conciliar Documents,* edited by Austin Flannery, 766–798. Northport, NY: Costello, 1980.

———. *Gaudium et Spes* (Pastoral Constitution on The Church in the Modern World). 7 December 1965. In *Vatican Council II: The Conciliar and Post Conciliar Documents*, edited by Austin Flannery, 903–1001. Northport, NY: Costello, 1980.

———. *Lumen Gentium* (Dogmatic Constitution on the Church). 21 November 1964. In *Vatican Council II: The Conciliar and Post Conciliar Documents*, edited by Austin Flannery, 350–426. Northport, NY: Costello, 1980.

———. *Presbyterorum Ordinis* (Decree on the Ministry and Life of Priests). 7 December 1965. In *Vatican Council II: The Conciliar and Post Conciliar Documents*, edited by Austin Flannery, 863–902. Northport, NY: Costello, 1980.

Sheils, W. J., ed. *Monks, Hermits and the Ascetic Tradition: Papers Read at the 1984 Summer Meeting and the 1985 Winter Meeting of the Ecclesiastical History Society.* Oxford: Blackwell, 1985.

Steele, Francesca. *Anchoresses of the West.* London: Sands, 1903.

Steindl-Rast, David. *A Listening Heart: The Art of Contemplative Living.* New York: Crossroad, 1983.

Swan, Laura. *The Forgotten Desert Mothers: Sayings, Lives, and Stories of Early Christian Women.* Mahwah, NJ: Paulist, 2001.

Teilhard de Chardin, Pierre. *Building the Earth.* Wilkes-Barre, PA: Dimension, 1965.

———. "Christ the Evolver." In *Christianity and Evolution*, translated by René Hague, 138–50. New York: Harcourt Brace Jovanovich, 1969.

———. "Christianity and Evolution." In *Christianity and Evolution*, translated by René Hague, 76–95. New York: Harcourt Brace Jovanovich, 1969.

———. "The Christic." In *The Heart of the Matter,* translated by René Hague, 80–102. New York: Harcourt Brace Jovanovich, 1979.

———. *The Divine Milieu.* New York: Harper and Row, 1960.

———. "The Heart of the Matter." In *The Heart of the Matter,* translated by René Hague, 14–79. New York: Harcourt Brace Jovanovich, 1979.

———. "My Universe," in *Science and Christ*, translated by René Hague. 37–85. New York: Harper & Row, 1968.

———. "The Spiritual Energy of Suffering." In *Activation of Energy*, translated by René Hague. 247–49. New York: Harcourt Brace Jovanovich, 1971.

———. "The Zest for Living." In *Activation of Energy*, translated by René Hague. 229–43. New York: Harcourt Brace Jovanovich, 1971.

Teresa of Jesus. *The Complete Works of Saint Teresa of Jesus.* Translated and edited by E. Allison Peers. 3 vols. New York: Sheed and Ward, 1946.

Thérèse of Lisieux. *Story of a Soul: The Autobiography of St. Therese of Lisieux.* Translated by John Clarke, 222–223, 225, 237. Washington, DC: I.C.S., 1975.

Torkington, Rayner. *Peter Calvay, Hermit (A personal rediscovery of prayer).* New York: Alba House, 1980.

Vicaire, M. H. *The Apostolic Life.* Chicago: Priory, 1966.

Villeux, Armand, trans. *Pachomian Koinonia.* vols 1–3. Kalamazoo, MI: Cistercian, 1980, 1981, 1989.

Weisenbeck, Marlene. *The Vocation to Eremitic Life: A Guidebook on the Formation Process for the Eremitic Life.* LaCrosse, WI: Office of Consecrated Life, 1997.

Zagano, Phyllis. *Twentieth-Century Apostles: Contemporary Spirituality in Action.* Collegeville, MN: Liturgical, 1999.